PRAISE FO

"A lucid exposition of the Bayesian approach to statistics, accessible to those new to this approach."

—David Greenberg, *New York University*

"The book's presentation of the logic of the Bayesian approach is one of the better illustrations that I've encountered. The level of mathematical precision used here is technical, but the layout makes it approachable."

—Matthew Phillips, *University of North Carolina at Charlotte*

Applied Bayesian Statistics

QUANTITATIVE APPLICATIONS IN THE SOCIAL SCIENCES

Applied Bayesian Statistics

Scott M. Lynch
Duke University

Los Angeles | London | New Delhi
Singapore | Washington DC

Los Angeles | London | New Delhi
Singapore | Washington DC

FOR INFORMATION:

SAGE Publications, Inc.
2455 Teller Road
Thousand Oaks, California 91320
E-mail: order@sagepub.com

SAGE Publications Ltd.
1 Oliver's Yard
55 City Road
London EC1Y 1SP
United Kingdom

SAGE Publications India Pvt. Ltd.
B 1/I 1 Mohan Cooperative Industrial Area
Mathura Road, New Delhi 110 044
India

SAGE Publications Asia-Pacific Pte. Ltd.
33 Pekin Street # 02-01
Far East Square
Singapore 048763

Copyright ©2023 by SAGE Publications, Inc.

Printed in the United States of America

ISBN: 978-1-5443-3463-9

Associate Editor: Helen Salmon
Editorial Assistant: Yumna Samie
Production Editor: Astha Jaiswal
Copy Editor: Gillian Dickens
Typesetter: Integra
Indexer: Integra
Cover Designer: Candice Harman
Marketing Manager: Victoria Velasquez

This book is printed on acid-free paper.

22 23 24 25 26 10 9 8 7 6 5 4 3 2 1

CONTENTS

LIST OF TABLES

LIST OF FIGURES

ABOUT THE AUTHOR

Scott M. Lynch is a professor in the departments of Sociology and Family Medicine and Community Health at Duke University. He is a demographer, statistician, and social epidemiologist and is currently the director of the Center for Population Health and Aging in Duke's Population Research Institute, where he is the associate director. His main substantive interests are in life course and cohort patterns in socioeconomic, racial, and regional disparities in health and mortality in the United States. His main statistical interests are in the use of Bayesian statistics in social science and demographic research, especially in survival and life table methods. He has published more than 60 articles and chapters in these areas in top demography, gerontology, methodology, sociology, and other journals, as well as two prior statistics texts on Bayesian methods and introductory statistics. He has taught undergraduate- and graduate-level statistics courses on a variety of statistical methods at Princeton University and Duke University, as well as a number of seminars on Bayesian statistics in academic, business, and other venues.

SERIES EDITOR'S INTRODUCTION

Although most social scientists are trained in the classical frequentist tradition, many of us are curious about Bayesian statistics and what this approach has to offer. Barriers to entry can be high, however. Learning Bayesian statistics requires substantial mathematical knowledge and facility and can be particularly daunting when the focus of the pedagogy is theory, the presentation of material is abstract, and the examples come from other disciplines. Applied Bayesian Statistics is an introduction geared toward social scientists. In it, Professor Lynch makes the material accessible by emphasizing application more than theory, explaining the math in a step-by-step fashion, and demonstrating the Bayesian approach in analyses of U.S. political trends drawing on data from the General Social Survey (GSS).

The best way to describe Applied Bayesian Statistics is as a short course. This self-contained "little green cover" has everything you need to understand basic concepts and procedures and could serve as a supplement in a graduate-level statistics course or an introductory text for self-study. Chapter 1 covers necessary preliminaries such as the contrast between Bayesian and classical statistics, the questions to be addressed in the examples, the data and measures that will be used to answer them, and the mathematical knowledge needed. Chapter 2 reviews foundational material needed for the chapters that follow, with particular attention to aspects of probability and distribution theory commonly used in Bayesian statistics. Chapter 3 develops Bayes' theorem, shows how it applies in the case of a univariate normal distribution with two parameters, and illustrates with an analysis of trends in political identification and positions based on responses in the GSS. Chapter 4 takes up the Markov chain Monte Carlo (MCMC) methods that make possible sophisticated analyses of more meaningful social science questions. The development of MCMC methods and their incorporation into data analysis software packages such as R helped make Bayesian analysis broadly accessible to social scientists. Chapter 5 is the capstone. It demonstrates the application of a Bayesian approach to three classes of models—the linear model, the dichotomous probit model, and latent class models—showing how to build and evaluate models using GSS data to answer meaningful research questions. Chapter 6 concludes with reflections about the advantages of a Bayesian over the classical approach.

Professor Lynch's passion for Bayesian statistics and his experience teaching social scientists is evident throughout the volume. As Professor Lynch says, "The goal of this volume is to illustrate the use of Bayesian methods to answer realistic social science questions using realistic social science methods." It is easy to imagine him at the front of a class and following along as he presents the material in a careful and methodical way, describing procedures both at a high level and also in detail. He carefully leads the reader through the thicket of notation so that it all flows and makes sense. He comments on practical matters of relevance to social scientists, especially related to the nature of our data, and shares tips based on his own experience. Understanding is built one step at a time, with many references back to material that has already been covered so that the reader can see how it is done. Professor Lynch makes a strong and convincing case for the value of Bayesian statistics in the social sciences. Not everyone who reads this book will become a Bayesian, but for sure, they will develop an understanding and respect for this approach.

—Barbara Entwisle
Series Editor

ACKNOWLEDGMENTS

This volume was written slowly over a 2+-year period and finished well beyond the anticipated deadline. I thank the editors for their patience. I also thank my colleagues and friends, Steve Vaisey and Kieran Healy, for their suggestions on the examples, although they're not to blame for any shortcomings in my analyses. This volume is dedicated to the memory of Glenn Bruden (1965–2019), who died during the writing of this monograph. His tombstone says he was a great son and brother. He was far more than that. He was an avid and superb fisherman; he was the front-man for a cutting-edge punk rock band on the East Coast in the 1980s; he was an amazing baker of Christmas and birthday cookies; he was a great friend to many; and he was an all-around good guy. He left this world far, far too soon. We can all only hope to be remembered as fondly after we're gone.

SAGE and the author would like to thank the following reviewers for their input into the development of this volume:

- Salem Boumediene, *University of Illinois Springfield*

- Kenneth A. Bollen, *University of North Carolina at Chapel Hill*

- Cody Ding, *University of Missouri–St. Louis*

- Jennifer Hayes Clark, *University of Houston*

- David Greenberg, *New York University*

- Mike Helford, *Roosevelt University*

- Matthew Phillips, *University of North Carolina at Charlotte*

- Steven Venette, *The University of Southern Mississippi*

- Joshua N. Zingher, *Old Dominion University*

CHAPTER 1. INTRODUCTION

The main goal of statistical analysis is to estimate unknown quantities and quantify our uncertainty about them. The unknown quantities are often population parameters, such as a population mean or variance, and the data are usually obtained from a (quasi)random sample. Suppose, for example, someone asserts that the United States is a center-right country politically, based on how individuals define themselves on a liberal ("left") to conservative ("right") political spectrum. Evaluating whether that statement is true requires (1) obtaining a sample of size n of data in which such an item is asked $(y_1 \ldots y_n)$; (2) estimating some quantity such as the population mean, μ, using a sample statistic such as the sample mean, $\bar{y}$, that can be used to represent leftness, centrality, or rightness; (3) quantifying our uncertainty about μ based on the use of $\bar{y}$ as our estimate; and (4) following some strategy for deciding whether our uncertainty about μ is low enough that we can draw a solid conclusion regarding the truth of the original claim. The "classical" and Bayesian approaches to statistics offer two different approaches to Steps 2 to 4 of this process.

In general, under both statistical paradigms, the data, y, are considered to be random realizations of a data generation process governed by unknown parameters, (generically) θ, of probability distributions, $f(y|\theta)$. Classical estimation of θ generally involves construction of a "likelihood function," the application of some differential calculus to it, and some programming to obtain estimates of θ—$\hat{\theta}$—and estimates of the variance of $\hat{\theta}$ in potential repeated samples. Under the classical paradigm, θ is considered a fixed quantity (i.e., a constant), while y is considered random, and so testing hypotheses about θ relies on theory regarding the sampling distribution for statistics like the sample mean obtained under repeated sampling from the population. For example, the central limit theorem states that the distribution of sample means, $\bar{y}$, that can be obtained via random sampling of n-sized samples of y from the population is asymptotically normal with a mean equal to the true population mean of y (μ) and a variance equal to the true population variance of y (σ^2) divided by the sample size (n). In this context, both μ and σ^2 are both considered constants, and only the data, y—and therefore functions of it, such as $\bar{y}$—are random. Thus, probabilistic statements are constrained to reference the probability of obtaining $\bar{y}$ from a population with a hypothesized value of μ. The process of evaluating hypotheses is therefore fundamentally a deductive one that fits well within the Popperian view of theory falsification (Popper, 2002): If the probability of observing $\bar{y}$

is small under our hypothesized value for μ (or generically, the probability of observing $\hat{\theta}$ is small under a hypothesized value for θ), we reject the hypothesis.

In contrast, the Bayesian paradigm argues that probabilistic language and concepts may be used to refer to any quantity about which we are uncertain, even if that quantity is a constant. As a classic example, whether it will rain tomorrow is a fixed, but currently unknown, fact. Yet, the fact that tomorrow's weather is unknown today naturally encourages us to use probabilistic language when discussing it. Thus, from a Bayesian perspective, both data and parameters can be viewed as random quantities to which probability rules apply, so we can use mathematical representations in which they share the same sample space as random variables, such as in a joint probability density function: $f(\theta, y)$. As we will discuss, whereas the classical paradigm relies entirely on the conditional expression $f(y|\theta)$, the Bayesian paradigm reverses this conditional using the joint density for θ and y to obtain the "posterior" distribution $f(\theta|y)$. The goal of the Bayesian approach is to obtain this posterior distribution in order to produce probabilistic summaries regarding the state of knowledge (and lack thereof—i.e., uncertainty) about θ after observing the data.

Bayesian statistical analyses have become increasingly common over the past two decades not only in statistics but also in social science research. The development of Markov chain Monte Carlo (MCMC) methods in the early 1990s and the rapid increase in computing power that facilitated their implementation no doubt contributed to the increase in Bayesian applications. However, the ability to conduct Bayesian analyses by itself is not a sufficient explanation for the paradigm's rise as an alternative to the classical paradigm. Instead, these developments in computational ability have coincided with major changes in the research interests of, and data availability for, social scientists. Specifically, the past two decades have seen a tremendous increase in the availability of panel data sets and other hierarchically structured data sets including spatially organized data, along with interests in life course processes and the influence of context on individual behavior and outcomes. The Bayesian approach to statistics is well suited for these types of data and research questions.

In addition, at the same time that computational abilities have increased and research interests have shifted, there has been growing recognition over at least the past decade that the classical statistical approach involving the computation of p-values and the rejection of null hypotheses that we learn as undergraduates and graduate students is significantly flawed. First, the classical approach to hypothesis testing guarantees that false-positive results occur 5% of the time. Indeed, the very definition of the p-value is that we are willing to reject true null hypotheses at a rate of α. The growth in the number of researchers and in the publication rate under the publish-or-perish paradigm of contemporary academia, coupled with the bias against publishing null findings, implies that there is no shortage of potential to publish false findings (Ioannidis, 2005). Indeed, it is increasingly apparent that published social science findings are often not replicable, posing a credibility crisis for social science (Freese & Peterson, 2017; S. M. Lynch & Bartlett, 2019). This is not a criticism of any particular scholars who have published papers under the classical paradigm (including the author of this volume); it is a general indictment of the way the social sciences approach statistical analyses and select papers for publication.

Second, it is well known that large sample sizes—which have become increasingly common—almost always assure small p-values so that we can reject "null" hypotheses and claim support for our pet "alternative" hypotheses (a fundamentally *inductive* conclusion), no matter how weak or meaningless such support may be. As a result, interest in effect sizes, and not simply statistical significance, is growing. The Bayesian approach offers several ways to construct interval estimates that are easily interpreted. Importantly, although the Bayesian approach to statistics is not generally focused on testing point hypotheses—such as the null hypothesis that a regression coefficient is 0—the Bayesian approach can be used to directly assess the probability that a substantive hypothesis is true. It therefore aligns much more clearly with the direct scientific questions we are generally asking.

In this volume, I introduce the Bayesian approach to statistical thinking and contemporary estimation. In this process, I illustrate the Bayesian approach using several models that are commonly used in social science research. Although the models are commonly estimated using classical methods, I show how a Bayesian may approach these models and interprets the results of them. Further, I show how the Bayesian approach offers more than the classical approach in flexibility in modeling, model evaluation and comparison, and secondary analysis, that is, computation and analysis of quantities not directly estimated in the main analysis that are useful for evaluating additional hypotheses.

This volume necessarily contains a large number of equations. My experience (both teaching and learning) suggests that a key impediment to learning mathematically based concepts is the lack of explication in many texts, in terms of showing how one gets from Equation 1 to, say, Equation 10. Most texts skip Equations 2 to 9 and simply say something like "obviously, Equation 1 implies Equation 10." Sometimes, however, it is not so obvious. In this volume, I either explicitly show the steps for getting from an initial equation to the final one or I refer to a previous example to which the current derivation is similar. I have tried to present equations throughout the volume so that those who understand the ideas and underlying mathematics can jump from the first to the last equation in a block of equations without reading the intervening equations, while simultaneously presenting the step-by-step derivations for those who would like to see them to get a more complete understanding of the process involved in Bayesian math.

Data and Topics Explored in Examples

Throughout this volume, in addition to using toy examples to illustrate basic ideas, I use real data from one source: the General Social Survey (GSS). I use these data so that my analyses are easily replicable. The GSS data are publicly available, and the programming code used to extract and recode the data is available on this volume's website, as is the code used to conduct the analyses and report the results of it. For access to the data, as well as access to the programming code used for all analyses discussed in the volume, go to *link*.

The GSS is a nationally representative, repeated cross-sectional study that has been conducted at least biennially since 1972 (Smith et al., 2018). In early years of the study, data were collected annually, but since 1994, the data have been collected only in even years. Although the survey now includes some data from rotating panels, I use only the cross-sectional data.

The GSS collects a variety of information, including demographic and attitudinal data, and is well known for its use in evaluating trends in social and political attitudes. In examples in this volume, I focus on measures of political views and attitudes in exploring political trends and potential polarization in the United States. Political trends and interest in polarization have been of interest in social science for decades. In 1996, DiMaggio and colleagues argued that, although the media and scholars often claim the United States is becoming increasingly politically polarized, little research had actually investigated the truth of that claim. Instead, DiMaggio et al. note that most prior research had simply investigated trends in means—measures of central tendency—of political attitudes and policy positions. They defined polarization as both a condition and a process, reflecting the extent to which members of society vary in their identification and positions, and investigated polarization by examining variance and kurtosis in the distributions of measures using data from the first two decades of the GSS. They conclude that, as of the early 1990s, there was little evidence of polarization.

Over the past few decades, and especially in recent years, the popular media and some social scientists have continued to claim the United States is becoming increasingly polarized. The fundamental questions addressed in the examples in this volume include the following: (1) What do trends in political identification and positions look like over the past half century? (2) Has the United States become increasingly politically polarized over the past five decades? (3) Are there differences in trends in identification and positions, and do conclusions regarding the extent of polarization depend on what is measured? My fundamental hypothesis is that American society has almost surely become more politically liberal and homogeneous in cultural and economic positions over time, but rhetoric among politicians and the media has become sharper over time so that we may be more polarized in how we identify ourselves despite the lack of large differences in positions. These questions, and my hypothesis, are not particularly novel (e.g., see Hopkins & Sides, 2015; McCarty, 2019), but the goal of this volume is to illustrate the use of Bayesian methods to answer realistic social science questions using realistic statistical methods.

To address these questions, I use of a number of consistently measured political items, including items asking respondents to identify their political party (GSS mnemonic: PARTYID) and political ideology (POLVIEWS), as well as a collection of items measuring respondents' views on social issues and government spending. PARTYID and POLVIEWS are seven category ordinal variables with outcomes ranging from strong Democrat (0) to strong Republican (6) and from extremely liberal (0) to extremely conservative (6), respectively. For the examples, I have recoded "don't know" and "other" responses to the midpoint of the range. There are relatively few such missing values on these items ($< 5\%$). Throughout the text, I refer to these items as "Republican" and "conservative," respectively, and I refer to an index of their sum as "political claims" or "political identification." It is worth noting that some of those who are coded at the midpoint of either measure may, in fact, be extremists who would be better placed at one or the other end of the spectrum, but I suspect that there are relatively few such cases, and errors in placement probably average/cancel out.

The items measuring social attitudes include 12 questions asking whether respondents agree with capital punishment (CAPPUN*), abortion for any reason (ABANY), gun registration laws (GUNLAW), marijuana legalization (GRASS), provision of birth control to teenagers (PILLOK), sex education in schools (SEXEDUC), lenient divorce laws (DIVLAW), premarital sex (PREMARSX), homosexual sex (HOMOSEX), spanking of children (SPANKING*), euthanasia for those with terminal illnesses (LETDIE1), and whether courts are too lenient with criminals (COURTS*). These items were all coded to take values of 0, .5, or 1, with 0 representing the liberal position on the item and 1 representing the conservative position on the item, based on traditional conceptions of "liberal" and "conservative" positions on these issues in the United States. All items listed above except those with an asterisk were reverse coded to follow this patterning. Those with a middle value on the item or a don't know or no answer/refused response were coded as .5. An index of these items was constructed by creating an average of the responses to the items each respondent was asked and multiplying by 6 to yield a range similar to the Republican and conservative items discussed above. Throughout the text, I refer to this index as "cultural conservatism." The Cronbach's alpha for the index for the entire GSS sample was .64. Exploration of change in this value over time is certainly worth further study.

The items measuring economic views include 11 questions asking whether respondents think the government spends too much money on the space program (NATSPAC*), the environment (NATENVIR), the problems of the cities (NATCITY), fighting crime (NATCRIME*), the national drug problem (NATDRUG), education (NATEDUC), the military (NATARMS*), foreign aid (NATAID), and welfare programs (NATFARE). These items were coded so that higher scores reflect the more traditionally conservative view: 1 indicated disagreement and 3 indicated agreement, with 2 indicating that we spend about the right amount. Three items (those with asterisks) were reverse coded, given that conservatives in the United States tend to support greater spending on the military and fighting crime, and given that examination of raw correlations showed that views on spending on the space program were negatively correlated with all other measures (less the crime and military measures). An index of the items was constructed in a fashion similar to that for the social attitude items and rescaled so that its range was also 0 to 6. Throughout the text, I call this index "economic conservatism." The Cronbach's alpha for the index across the GSS sample was .52. Finally, I create an index of these two subindexes. This index has a theoretical range from 0 to 12, mirroring the range of the claims index. I call this index "political positions" throughout the text.

It is important to note that no GSS participants were asked all questions in any year. Only about half of all GSS respondents were asked the spending items, but those who were asked one of them were asked all of them. Of the social issues items, not all individuals were asked all items in each year, and some items were not asked in every year. However, almost all items were asked throughout the entire span of the study. The two exceptions were that the items regarding birth control and spanking were not asked prior to 1985. On average, in most years, individuals were missing on just over three items. From 1974 to 1987, individuals averaged missing five to six items in several years. In general, despite these inconsistencies in measurement from year to year, I believe the index for cultural conservatism is comparable across years, given (1) that assignment to question subsets is random; (2) almost all items are measured across the time period, even if they are missing in some years; and (3) the index is "standardized" to have the same range in all years. Nonetheless, these measurement issues suggest one should be cautious when interpreting trends. Ultimately, however, the goal in this volume is not to make a major substantive contribution but to illustrate the Bayesian approach with real social science data and analyses.

In addition to these items, some of the examples in this volume also include survey year or decade, age, sex, race, region of the country, and educational attainment as covariates. Table 1.1 shows how these variables are coded in the examples and displays basic descriptive statistics for them.

Several notes are in order regarding the GSS data. First, the GSS sample is not a simple random sample. The survey design has changed a few times over its history, and Blacks were oversampled in 2 years. I removed the Black oversamples from the data to be used in this volume. Further, throughout most of the volume, although the GSS provides sample weights, I ignore them and treat the data as if it were obtained via simple random sampling. This seems to be of little consequence with these data: Classical analyses with and without the weights produce almost identical results—to two decimal places in many cases. In the concluding chapter, I provide some recent references on sampling design in a Bayesian context.

Second, for the purposes of most of the examples, I have simply deleted cases with missing data. In general, there were very little missing data, however. A key question (POLVIEWS) was not asked prior to 1974, so the 1972 sample was excluded. Most respondents were not asked all questions; they were retained if they were not missing on all measures in the two indexes. As stated above, the indexes were constructed by averaging respondents answers across those items to which they responded. Nonetheless, missing data can be handled quite easily in the Bayesian context. Indeed, multiple imputation—the most common contemporary method for handling missing data in social science apart from listwise deletion—is fundamentally a Bayesian approach (Allison, 2002; Little & Rubin, 2002; S. M. Lynch & Bartlett, 2019). Although I do not discuss missing data directly in this volume, I discuss the incorporation of latent data into probit and latent class models via "data augmentation," and the latent data can be viewed as missing data (Chapter 5). Thus, it is straightforward to see how handling missing data can be handled in Bayesian analyses.

Third, whether it is reasonable to code "don't know" and "refuse" responses to the midpoint of an item is questionable. However, there were few such responses to any of the items. Further, the goal of the examples

Variable	Mean (*SD*)[range] or %	Comments
Republican	2.7 (2.0) [0, 6]	
Conservative	3.1 (1.3) [0, 6]	
Identification	5.8 (2.7) [0, 12]	Republican + Conservative
Cultural conservative	3.5 (1.3) [0, 6]	Rescaled index of 12 items
Economic conservative	2.6 (.83) [0, 6]	Rescaled index of 11 items
Positions	6.1 (1.7) [.3, 12]	Culture + Economic
Year	92.2 (13.2) [74, 116]	Includes 74–78, 80, 82, 83–91, 93, 94, biennially from 96–116
Decade		
1970s	22.9%	
1980s	24.2%	
1990s	21.0%	
2000s	16.7%	
2010s	15.3%	
Age	48.7 (16.4) [25, 89]	Ages < 25 excluded
Male	44.5%	
Nonwhite	16.7%	Excluding 1982 & 1987 Black oversamples
South	34.7%	
Education	12.7 (3.3) [0, 20]	

Table 1.1 Descriptive statistics for GSS data used in examples ($n = 28,273$). Data are unweighted; weighted results are nearly identical.

in this volume is to illustrate Bayesian methods and not to make definitive claims regarding political change and polarization. All code and data are available from the author for alternative, follow-up analyses.

Mathematical Knowledge Required for this Volume

There is, invariably, a fair amount of mathematics involved in understanding statistics in general and Bayesian statistics in particular. Unlike classical statistical analysis, which can be conducted using canned statistical software commands, much of Bayesian analysis involves some hands-on derivations and programming by the analyst. To be sure, in recent years, a number of user-friendly programs have been developed to facilitate Bayesian analysis, and even larger statistical packages such as Stata have begun to incorporate procedures that conduct Bayesian analysis. Nonetheless, Bayesian analyses simply cannot be fully automated for a number of reasons, as we will discuss throughout the volume.

I assume all readers have strong basic algebra skills. A working knowledge of calculus is important, but as long as one understands the concepts of limits, derivatives, and integrals, the text should be readable. Specifically, one needs to know that a limit is the value a function tends toward as some quantity in the function approaches a specified value. For example, the limit of $f(x) = \frac{1}{x}$, as x approaches infinity, is 0. We express this as

$$\lim_{x \to \infty} \frac{1}{x} = 0. \tag{1.1}$$

For some functions, limits are easy to determine, while other functions may require substantial algebraic manipulation to find the limit.

A derivative is the slope of a tangent line to a curve, where a tangent line is a line that touches a curve at a single point. It takes two points to determine a line, not one, however. Thus, the slope of a tangent line is determined by taking the limit of the formula for the slope of a line as two points on a curve converge to the one point on the tangent line. Formally, we define the derivative as

$$\frac{\Delta y}{\Delta x} = \lim_{\Delta x \to 0} \frac{f(x + \Delta x) - f(x)}{\Delta x}. \tag{1.2}$$

This is simply the algebraic formula for the slope of a line, where the numerator is the difference in y values and the denominator is the difference in x values at two points, x and $x + \Delta x$. However, as Δx approaches 0, we are left with a division by 0 problem, thus necessitating some algebraic manipulation in most functions before evaluating the limit. Formulas for computing derivatives for many functions are well known and readily available, and we usually denote derivatives as $\frac{dy}{dx}$. In functions of more than one variable, we may take a derivative in only one dimension. Such derivatives are called "partial derivatives," and they are represented as $\frac{\partial y}{\partial x}$. The process of taking derivatives is called differentiation, and so the branch of calculus concerned with slopes is called "differential calculus."

Differential calculus is used extensively in classical statistics, including especially in maximum likelihood (ML) analysis. In ML analysis, a key goal is to find the values of parameters that maximize the likelihood function, and finding maxima (and minima) of curves involves taking derivatives of the likelihood function, setting the derivative to 0—representing a horizontal tangent line and thus a maximum or minimum of a curve—and solving for the unknown parameters at that location.

The Bayesian approach to statistics, in contrast to the classical statistical approach, involves more integral calculus than differential calculus. The integral of a curve provides the area under the curve—between the curve and the x axis—over a given domain. Although the areas of some figures, such as triangles, rectangles, and circles, are easy to compute, areas under most curves are not easy to compute. However, we can imagine computing and summing the areas of rectangles of different heights under a curve to approximate the area under the curve. The narrower the rectangles, the closer the approximation will be, and so once again, we invoke the concept of limits: The (Riemann) integral is simply the sum of the areas of rectangles under a curve as the width of the rectangles approaches 0. If we wish to find the area, A, under a curve $f(x)$ from a to b, then

$$A = \lim_{\Delta x \to 0} \sum_{i=0}^{k} f(a + i\Delta x)\Delta x, \tag{1.3}$$

where k is the value such that $a + (k+1)\Delta x = b$. In this equation, $a + i\Delta x$ represents the x location of the left side of each rectangle, so $f(a + i\Delta x)$ is its height, which, when multiplied by the width—Δx—yields the area of the rectangle. The upper bound on the sum, k, is simply the location of the left side of the last rectangle. k necessarily increases as Δx gets smaller and smaller.

We represent integrals with an elongated S to represent continuous summation as

$$A = \int_{a}^{b} f(x)dx. \tag{1.4}$$

In this equation, A is the area of interest; a and b are called the "limits of integration," meaning they reflect the domain over which we wish to compute the area; $f(x)$ is the function height; and dx is the width of the rectangles we sum. When limits of integration are specified, the integral is called a "definite integral." Conversely, when limits are not specified, the integral is called "indefinite." I will occasionally use indefinite integrals when the limits of integration are either implicit or unimportant in understanding a concept.

The fundamental theorem of calculus relates derivatives and integrals. The theorem shows that integrals and derivatives are inverse functions, so that $\int d[f(x)]/dx = f(x)$. In words, the integral of the derivative of a function is the function itself. Thus, many integral formulas can be obtained from derivative formulas. This theorem is important in some derivations shown in the volume.

Bayesian statistics involves a lot of integral calculus because a probability distribution for a random variable y can be represented via an algebraic curve, and quantiles such as the proportion of the population with values of $y < a$ involve integrating the curve from $-\infty$ to a. We will discuss this in greater detail in the next chapter.

In addition to understanding these basic calculus concepts, the reader should be familiar with basic matrix algebra, including the manipulation of matrices and functions such as the transpose, determinant, and inverse. Early examples will not involve matrix algebra, but it is impossible to avoid matrix representations entirely in realistic social science models because of their multivariate nature. Understanding these basic concepts should enable a reader to follow most of the text.

Layout of the Book

The remainder of this book is organized into five chapters. In Chapter 2, I cover key concepts of probability and distribution theory required for understanding Bayesian statistics, and I review the classical statistical approach using ML estimation. Although both topics may be a review for some, I emphasize key ideas and terminology of probability theory that are commonly used in Bayesian statistics and may be unfamiliar to many. Further, I emphasize the key ideas underlying classical statistics based on ML estimation so as to contrast them with the Bayesian approach in subsequent chapters.

In Chapter 3, I introduce the Bayesian paradigm. I begin by developing Bayes' theorem and providing a contrived example involving a point probability, but I then show how the theorem can be extended to probability distributions. I pay particular attention to the concept of prior distributions and to the interpretation of results of a Bayesian analysis in simple examples involving the political identification and positions variables. It will become clear in that chapter that a key difficulty with conducting Bayesian analyses is performing the computations necessary to obtain parameter estimates and interval estimates, especially when analyses become more complicated. Thus, in Chapter 4, I develop and illustrate MCMC methods, which are the workhorse computational method used in contemporary Bayesian analysis.

In Chapter 5, I present realistic examples involving the linear model, the dichotomous probit model, and latent class (finite mixture) models for trends in political identification and positions. In this process, I demonstrate features of Bayesian analyses that make it a useful alternative to the classical approach, including constructing and evaluating hypotheses regarding parameters that are not directly modeled but are functions of modeled parameters (i.e., secondary analyses). In the last section of the chapter, I discuss the evaluation and comparison of models using posterior predictive distributions. I also define the Bayes factor and Bayesian information criterion.

Given inherent page constraints for a volume such as this one, there is a limit to how much material can be covered. A key topic not covered in examples in this volume is hierarchical modeling. Nearly every exposition of Bayesian analysis focuses on hierarchical modeling, primarily because the Bayesian approach is naturally suited for such analyses, as will become clear. Nonetheless, realistic regression-based hierarchical analyses require substantial development and discussion. Thus, in Chapter 6, I conclude by pointing readers to some key, extended volumes in the field, including ones focused on hierarchical modeling. Still, this volume should provide a sufficient introduction to the Bayesian approach to allow readers to begin conducting their own Bayesian analyses.

CHAPTER 2. PROBABILITY DISTRIBUTIONS AND REVIEW OF CLASSICAL ANALYSIS

Probability theory is the foundation of statistical analysis. Regardless of statistical paradigm and underlying definition or interpretation of probability, several basic probability axioms form the foundation of statistics and are important for a solid understanding of Bayesian statistics. Thus, I review some of the key terminology and ideas here. An excellent and complete introduction to probability theory and mathematical statistics can be found in DeGroot & Schervish (2011).

Let x represent an event that might occur in a given trial (i.e., a realization of a random variable), and let S be the sample space, representing all events that can possibly occur in a trial. For example, consider the toss of a single six-sided die. The sample space is the set $S = \{1, 2, 3, 4, 5, 6\}$, and an event would be a specific realization from a roll (e.g., $x = 3$). We use $p(x)$ to represent the probability of obtaining a value, x, drawn from S in a trial. Given these basic terms, the key axioms include the following:

1. Probabilities range from 0 to 1 (i.e., $0 \leq p(x) \leq 1$). Events that cannot occur have probability 0; events that must occur have probability 1.

2. The sum of the probabilities of all disjoint (i.e., nonoverlapping) events in a sample space is 1, or, if the sample space is continuous, the integral of all probabilities in sample space is 1 (i.e., $\sum_S p(x) = 1$ or $\int_S f(x)dx = 1$).

3. If two events, x_1 and x_2, are independent, meaning that the occurrence of one event has no bearing on the occurrence of the other, their joint probability is the product of their respective probabilities: $p(x_1, x_2) = p(x_1)p(x_2)$. "Joint" in this context means the probability that both events occur. For example, the probabilities that I obtain a value of $x_1 = 3$ on one die roll AND a value of $x_2 = 6$ on a second roll are independent, because rolling a 3 on the first roll does not influence what I may obtain on the second roll.

4. If two events are not independent, their joint probability is $p(x_1, x_2) = p(x_1|x_2)p(x_2)$, where $p(x_1|x_2)$ is called the conditional probability of x_1 given knowledge of x_2. For example, suppose I will first flip a coin to determine whether I will then roll a regular six-sided die (if heads) or an eight-sided die (if tails). The probability that I will roll

a value of 5 on the die roll is conditional on the coin toss: the conditional probability $p(5|H) = 1/6$, while $p(5|T) = 1/8$. Thus, $p(5,H) = (1/6)(1/2) = 1/12$ and $p(5,T) = (1/8)(1/2) = 1/16$.

5. The probability of two nondisjoint (i.e., overlapping) events is $p(x_1 \cup x_2) = p(x_1) + p(x_2) - p(x_1,x_2)$. For example, suppose I am to flip a coin and then roll a six-sided die. Obtaining a head on the coin flip or a 5 on the die roll are not disjoint events, because both may occur. Importantly, the word "or" in mathematics generally means "and/or," and so the joint probability must be included in the probability calculation. However, we must subtract the joint probability once, because it is counted twice when we add the respective probabilities of each event. In the example, $p(H) = 1/2$, and $p(5) = 1/6$. Unlike the example above, here the coin toss and the die roll are independent, so $p(H,5) = (1/2)(1/6) = 1/12$. Thus, $p(H \cup 5) = 1/2 + 1/6 - 1/12 = 7/12$.

All other probability rules can be derived from these axioms and are generally straightforward extensions of them. For example, the joint probability rule for nonindependent events extends to three events as

$$p(x_1,x_2,x_3) = p(x_1|x_2,x_3)p(x_2|x_3)p(x_3). \tag{2.1}$$

This is sometimes called a "chain" rule, because the joint distribution of the three events can be constructed as a chain of products of conditional probabilities. Consider the latter two terms: $p(x_2|x_3)p(x_3)$. By Rule 4 above, this is $p(x_2,x_3)$. Then, it is clear that this term and the leftmost term—$p(x_1|x_2,x_3)p(x_2,x_3)$—follow the same structure as shown in Rule 4. This chain rule is of considerable use in Bayesian analysis, including in developing hierarchical models.

The law of total probability is another important rule that can be derived from these axioms and is frequently used in Bayesian statistics. Suppose we partition a sample space, S, into a set of disjoint and exhaustive components $B_1, B_2, \ldots, B_k$. If A is an event contained within S, then the total probability of A can be computed as the sum of the probability of A under the different components of the partition, weighted by the size of the components. For discrete sample spaces:

$$p(A) = \sum_{i=1}^{k} p(A|B_i)p(B_i), \tag{2.2}$$

with $\sum_{i=1}^{k} p(B_i) = 1$. This rule follows from combining Rule 4 and Rule 5: Each term in the sum is a joint probability for A and B_i, and the B_i are disjoint. For continuous partitions:

$$p(A) = \int_S f(A|B)f(B)dB, \qquad (2.3)$$

where we use $f(.)$ rather than $p(.)$ to reflect the continuousness of the partition.

Probability Distributions

Most sample spaces of interest in statistics are large or infinite, and so we commonly use algebraic, transcendental, or other mathematical functions to map probabilities (or relative frequencies) onto events in a sample space, rather than set notation as we might for the roll of a single die. When the sample space of interest is discrete, we call such functions "probability mass functions" (pmfs); when the space is continuous, we call them "probability density functions" (pdfs).

A key distinction between pmfs and pdfs is the value the function returns. In discrete sample spaces, the number of possible events is finite, and probabilities for events can be directly computed from the pmf. In continuous sample spaces, probabilities for single events are 0. Recall that one way to define a probability is as the number of successes out of the number of equally likely events. For example, for a fair coin, there are two possible events—heads and tails. The probability of obtaining a head on a coin flip is 1/2, because there is one event defined as a success out of two equally likely events possible in the sample space. In a continuous sample space, such as real numbers over the $[0, 1]$ interval, there are an infinite number of possible events. Thus, the probability for any specific event (number) is $1/\infty$, which is, in the limit, 0 as shown in the last chapter. Thus, we generally distinguish pmfs and pdfs in notation. Specifically, we use $p(x) = \ldots$ to represent pmfs and $f(x) = \ldots$ to represent pdfs. The letter "p" indicates that the function returns a probability, whereas the letter "f" indicates that the function returns the density height—or, loosely, a relative frequency—but not a probability. Technically, f should be subscripted to differentiate its use for different variables. For example, it is common to use $f_x(x)$ to indicate that this particular pdf is for the random variable x. However, it is common to drop the subscript in applied work, and I will do so throughout the text. Further, I will generally use lowercase letters to refer to scalar quantities and uppercase letters to refer to vectors or matrices.

Probabilities in continuous distributions are found by integrating the density function between two values in the sample space: The probability that an event falls in the interval $[a, b]$ is $\int_a^b f(x)dx$. Note that, because there is 0 probability associated with any given value, it does not generally matter whether we define the interval as noninclusive (i.e., (a, b) rather than $[a, b]$). One common probability of interest is $p(x < z)$, the probability that an event that occurs is less than some value, z. We define the cumulative distribution function (cdf), $F(x)$, to be the sum or area under the curve from the smallest value possible in the sample space (often $-\infty$) up to the point z. For continuous sample spaces, $F(z) = \int_{-\infty}^z f(x)dx$. For discrete sample spaces, the integral is replaced with a sum.

Nearly any mathematical function can be treated as a density function so long as it follows the key axioms listed above. In particular, the function must return nonnegative values (because probabilities must be between 0 and 1), and the function must sum or integrate to 1 over the sample space for the random variable. A pmf or pdf that follows these two key rules is said to be a "proper" distribution.

Many functions that may be useful as pdfs or pmfs may not sum or integrate to 1, but they may do so with the incorporation of a "normalizing constant" that rescales the function so that it does integrate to 1. For example, suppose x is distributed on the interval $[a, b]$, with all values of x in that range being equally likely, meaning $f(x) = c$ over the interval. In order for this function to be a "proper" distribution, c must be set to the value that ensures the distribution integrates to 1. Given that the distribution is bounded vertically by the x-axis and c, and horizontally by a and b, the distribution is rectangular. The value c can be computed using the well-known formula for the area of a rectangle: $A = width \times height = (b-a)c = 1$, so $c = 1/(b-a)$.

This distribution is the most basic of continuous distributions and is called the "uniform distribution" because of the uniformity of height over the domain for x. Because of its shape, it is often called a "flat" or "rectangular" distribution. The standard uniform distribution has bounds of $[0, 1]$ and is the distribution from which computers generate (quasi)random numbers: Random generation of values from all other distributions originates from draws from the $U(0, 1)$.

Below, I detail a number of distributions that are important in Bayesian statistics. Most will be used in examples in this volume, but all are common in the Bayesian literature and therefore require familiarization. In each case, the random variable is x, we use "$\sim$" to represent "is distributed as," and I provide either the name of the distribution or a recognizable/common abbreviation along with the parameters of the distribution in parentheses. For example, if x is uniformly distributed on the $[a, b]$ interval, we say $x \sim U(a, b)$. The density function is specified with parentheses indicating both the random variable and its conditioning on the parameters. Further, I specify the domain (sample space) for x. In order to save space, I do not spell out that $f(x|.) = 0$ if x is outside its domain, where the "." after the conditioning bar is used in various places in this volume as a shorthand for variables and parameters (when the conditioning is clear) to save space.

For each pmf or pdf, I bracket the normalizing constant that ensures the distribution sums or integrates to 1. Importantly, this integral is taken *over the domain for the random variable*. In Bayesian statistics, a density function generally contains more than one quantity that can be considered a random variable versus a constant, depending on context. Thus, what is considered a normalizing constant in a density function may vary from one setting to another.

Finally, I show the "kernel" of the density with the normalizing constant removed. Thus, in the second line of each density function equation, I substitute the proportionality symbol, $\propto$. Proportionality is an important concept in Bayesian statistics. If k is a multiplicative constant so that $x = ky$, then $x \propto y$, and k is called a proportionality constant. It can be removed with the substitution of the proportionality symbol for the equality symbol, because what matters for a density function is its fundamental shape, in terms of relative heights of the density function at different values across its domain. A normalizing constant ensures a density integrates to 1, but it does not change its fundamental shape. So, in Bayesian statistics, we routinely ignore or discard such constants, as we will discover in subsequent chapters. What is important is that the density *can* integrate to 1 with the inclusion of a constant. Again, it is important to note that what constitutes a normalizing constant varies depending on what quantities are considered fixed (versus random) in a given density function.

Important Distributions in Bayesian Statistics

Uniform Distribution

If $x \sim U(a,b)$, the density function for x is

$$f(x|a,b) = \left[\frac{1}{b-a} \right] (1), \quad x \in [a,b] \tag{2.4}$$

$$\propto 1. \tag{2.5}$$

The uniform distribution was described briefly above. It is flat over the $[a,b]$ interval, meaning that all values of x in that interval are equally likely. The values of a and b can be any real number. The distribution is improper if either boundary is infinite. The distribution is proportional to 1; the explanation for the normalizing constant was shown above. The mean of x is $(b+a)/2$, and the variance is $(b-a)^2/12$. These values can be found by computing $\mu = \int_a^b x f(x)\, dx$ and $\sigma^2 = \int_a^b (x-\mu)^2 f(x)\, dx$, respectively, for any continuous density (DeGroot & Schervish, 2011).

Uniform distributions, while relatively unfamiliar to most social scientists, are commonly used in Bayesian statistics as prior distributions for parameters for which we have little prior information. Because the distribution is flat over its domain, as a prior distribution, the uniform density implies that all values of a parameter are equally likely a priori: No value of the parameter is favored prior to observing data. Although the distribution is typically considered continuous, we can also have a uniform distribution on integers, which is a discrete distribution. We will use uniform distributions in many of the examples.

The $U(0,1)$ distribution is called the standard uniform distribution and is the basis for nearly all random number generators. Statistical packages generally produce draws from the standard uniform distribution via a deterministic algorithm that starts from a "seed" and uses a specified function involving the modulus (remainder) operator to produce a new number (the new "random" number) that replaces the seed, and the process is iterated. The function used and the modulus divisor, M, are fixed and determine the sequence of "random" numbers that are generated. Thus, any specific seed will always produce the same sequence of numbers, so that random number generators produce quasi-random and not truly random values. However, the mark of a good random number generator is that it produces sequences of values that behave like random numbers. These quasi-random uniform numbers are then transformed via an appropriate function to produce a sequence of samples from a desired distribution. Ripley (1987) provides a solid, classic introduction to random number generation.

Seeds in software packages can be set by the programmer or generated by the software using—commonly—a numeric representation of the time of day when the programming code is implemented. In the examples in this volume, I set the seeds using the set.seed() function in R so that numeric results and figures can be replicated exactly.

Binomial Distribution

If $x \sim Bin(n,p)$, the mass function for x is

$$p(x|n,p) = \binom{n}{x} p^x (1-p)^{n-x}, \quad x \in [0,n] \tag{2.6}$$

$$\propto \frac{1}{x!(n-x)!} p^x (1-p)^{n-x}. \tag{2.7}$$

The binomial distribution is a distribution for counts of successes, x, in n trials in which p is the success probability for each trial. The parameters are n and p. n must be an integer greater than or equal to 1, and $0 \le p \le 1$. For example, the number of heads obtained in a series of coin flips follows a binomial distribution. If the coin is fair, $p = .5$. n is the number of flips, and x is the number of heads obtained, which can range from 0 to n. The mean of x is np, and the variance is $np(1-p)$. The normalizing constant is contained in the combinatorial expression, which represents the number of ways x successes can occur in n trials. For example, if a coin is tossed five times, there are five ways a single head could be obtained (i.e., on the first flip, the second flip, etc.). It is computed as $n!/(x!(n-x)!)$. The denominator of this combinatorial contains the random variable, and so only the numerator, $n!$, can be removed as the normalizing constant (*when this functional form is considered a distribution for x, rather than p, as in the beta distribution below!*).

When n is 1, the binomial distribution is called the Bernoulli distribution. The binomial or Bernoulli distribution is commonly used for modeling binary outcomes such as agreement or disagreement with an attitudinal item, a vote for a Republican versus a Democrat, or the experience of an event, such as death. In many cases, such as in the logit, probit, and other generalized linear models, the p parameter of the Bernoulli/binomial distribution is treated as a function of covariates.

Beta Distribution

If $x \sim Beta(\alpha, \beta)$, the density function for x is

$$f(x|\alpha,\beta) = \left[\frac{\Gamma(\alpha+\beta)}{\Gamma(\alpha)\Gamma(\beta)} \right] x^{\alpha-1}(1-x)^{\beta-1}, \quad x \in [0,1] \tag{2.8}$$

$$\propto x^{\alpha-1}(1-x)^{\beta-1}. \tag{2.9}$$

The beta distribution is the distribution for a proportion or any quantity that can take only values in the $[0, 1]$ interval. In some definitions, 0 and 1 are included in the domain; in others, the boundaries may not be. The parameters of the distribution are α and β, respectively, both of which must be nonnegative. They can be considered counts of successes and failures in a total of $\alpha + \beta$ trials; however, the parameters need not be integers. The mean of x is $\alpha/(\alpha+\beta)$, and the variance is $(\alpha\beta)/((\alpha+\beta)^2(\alpha+\beta+1))$. The normalizing constant contains gamma functions, where the gamma function is the generalization of the factorial function to nonnegative real numbers, with $\Gamma(n) = (n-1)!$ when n is an integer. The kernel of the beta distribution looks very much like that for the binomial distribution. However, in the binomial distribution, the *exponent* is the random variable, whereas in the beta distribution, the *base* is the random variable. In Bayesian statistics, this similarity in the functional form of the binomial and beta distributions is useful: The beta distribution is commonly used as a prior distribution for the p parameter from the binomial distribution, as we will see in the next chapter.

Poisson Distribution

If $x \sim Poi(\lambda)$, the mass function for x is

$$p(x|\lambda) = \left[e^{-\lambda}\right] \frac{\lambda^x}{x!}, \quad x \in [0, \infty) \tag{2.10}$$

$$\propto \frac{\lambda^x}{x!}. \tag{2.11}$$

The Poisson distribution is a distribution for counts, where λ—which must be nonnegative—is the only parameter and is both the mean and variance of the distribution. Whereas the binomial distribution is also a distribution for counts (of successes) out of a fixed number of trials, the Poisson distribution is a distribution for counts of events usually in a given time interval. Thus, λ can be considered a rate parameter. The Poisson distribution is commonly used to model count outcomes such as numbers of arrests, numbers of symptoms of disease, and other variables that are bounded at 0 and may have a significant righthand skew. As λ becomes larger, the skew of the distribution decreases, so that the distribution converges toward the normal distribution (see below). Because the distribution's mean and variance are a single parameter, the distribution is often considered too restrictive for most social science applications. It can be extended to the negative binomial distribution, which includes an overdispersion parameter. It can also be the basis for a "zero-inflated Poisson model," which is a mixture model in which values of $x = 0$ can be seen to arise from two sources: as part of the underlying Poisson data generation process or as part of a secondary population that is not part of the Poisson process or is otherwise not at risk of experiencing an event.

Gamma Distribution

If $x \sim Gamma(\alpha, \beta)$, the density function for x is

$$f(x|\alpha, \beta) = \left[\frac{\beta^{\alpha}}{\Gamma(\alpha)}\right] x^{\alpha-1} e^{-\beta x}, \quad x \in (0, \infty) \tag{2.12}$$

$$\propto x^{\alpha-1} e^{-\beta x}. \tag{2.13}$$

The gamma distribution is a distribution for positive real numbers. The parameters α and β can take any value greater than 0. As written, the distribution is parameterized with α and β, which are "shape" and "rate" parameters, respectively, where a shape parameter affects the fundamental shape of a distribution, while the inverse of the rate parameter (called a scale parameter) stretches a distribution horizontally. Under this parameterization, the mean is α/β, and the variance is α/β^2. However, the distribution can be parameterized differently, depending on the application. In Bayesian statistics, the distribution is often used as a prior distribution for the λ parameter of the Poisson distribution. When used as such, the parameterization is commonly specified as shown. In other settings, the gamma distribution is used to model waiting times (times to events). In that case, the distribution is often parameterized with a scale, rather than rate, parameter by setting $k = \alpha$ and $\theta = 1/\beta$. In some cases, such as frailty modeling, the distribution may be parameterized so that the mean is set to 1. In that case, $k = 1/\theta$ and the variance is θ. In each case, the normalizing constant changes slightly.

Normal Distribution

If $x \sim N(\mu, \sigma^2)$, the density function for x is

$$f(x|\mu, \sigma^2) = \left[\frac{1}{\sqrt{2\pi\sigma^2}}\right] \exp\left\{-\frac{(x-\mu)^2}{2\sigma^2}\right\}, \quad x \in \mathbb{R} \tag{2.14}$$

$$\propto \exp\left\{-\frac{(x-\mu)^2}{2\sigma^2}\right\} \tag{2.15}$$

The normal distribution is the most commonly used distribution in statistics. The distribution has a bell shape, with a mean of μ at the center of the distribution and a variance σ^2 that determines its spread. The bell shape indicates that values close to the mean occur with greater frequency than extreme values, which mirrors many variables in the social and natural world. It is commonly used to model not only variables of interest but also error terms in statistics. Error terms frequently follow a normal distribution, because they represent a combination of numerous factors that average out to produce a bell shape. The $N(0,1)$ distribution is called the "standard normal" distribution or the "z" distribution.

Inverse Gamma Distribution

If $x \sim IG(\alpha, \beta)$, the density function for x is

$$f(x|\alpha, \beta) = \left[\frac{\beta^{\alpha}}{\Gamma(\alpha)} \right] x^{-(\alpha+1)} e^{-\beta/x}, \quad x \in (0, \infty) \tag{2.16}$$

$$\propto x^{-(\alpha+1)} e^{-\beta/x}. \tag{2.17}$$

The inverse gamma distribution, like the gamma distribution, is a continuous distribution for positive real numbers. The distribution is derived from the gamma distribution via a change of variables: If $1/x$ follows a gamma distribution with parameters α and β, then x is inverse gamma distributed with those parameters. The inverse gamma distribution is primarily used in Bayesian statistics as a prior distribution for the variance parameter, σ^2 in a normal distribution, as we will see in the next chapter.

Multinomial Distribution

If $X_{K \times 1} \sim MN(n, P_{K \times 1})$, the mass function for X is

$$f(X|n, P) = \frac{[n!]}{\prod_{k=1}^{K} x_k!} \prod_{k=1}^{K} p_k^{x_k}, \quad x_k \in [0, n], \ \sum_{k=1}^{K} x_k = n \tag{2.18}$$

$$\propto \frac{1}{\prod_{k=1}^{K} x_k!} \prod_{k=1}^{K} p_k^{x_k}. \tag{2.19}$$

The multinomial distribution is a generalization of the binomial distribution to more than two types of events (i.e., more than successes vs. failures). For example, the multinomial distribution may be used to model votes for multiple candidates in an election, values on n rolls of a $K-$sided die, or other outcomes for which two or more events are possible. The multinomial distribution of dimension K is a discrete distribution for x_k counts of events in each of K distinct categories, where n is the total number of trials. The probability of an event occurring in each category, k, is p_k, so $\sum_{k=1}^{K} p_k = 1$. The mean of x_k is np_k, and the variance of x_k is $np_k(1 - p_k)$, for all k. In social science research, the p parameters are often modeled as a function of covariates, as in the multinomial logit regression model.

Dirichlet Distribution

If $X \sim Dirich(\alpha)$, the density function for X is

$$f(X|\alpha) = \left[\frac{\Gamma(\sum_{k=1}^{K}\alpha_k)}{\prod_{k=1}^{K}\Gamma(\alpha_k)}\right] \prod_{k=1}^{K} x_k^{\alpha_k-1}, \quad x_k \in [0,1], \sum_{k=1}^{K} x_k = 1 \quad (2.20)$$

$$\propto \prod_{k=1}^{K} x_k^{\alpha_k-1}. \quad (2.21)$$

The Dirichlet distribution is a generalization of the beta distribution to multiple proportions, x_k, that total 1. The parameters, α, can be considered counts of events in each of the K categories, so that $\alpha_k > 0$, for all α. Just as the beta distribution is used in Bayesian statistics as a prior distribution for the p parameter in the binomial distribution, the Dirichlet distribution is commonly used as a prior distribution for the p parameters of the multinomial distribution.

Multivariate Normal Distribution

If a d-dimensional vector $X_{d \times 1} \sim MVN(\mu, \Sigma)$, the density function for X is

$$f(X|\mu,\Sigma) = \left[(2\pi)^{-\frac{d}{2}}|\Sigma|^{-\frac{1}{2}}\right] \exp\left\{\left(-\frac{1}{2}\right)[X-\mu]^T\Sigma^{-1}[X-\mu]\right\} \quad (2.22)$$

$$\propto \exp\left\{\left(-\frac{1}{2}\right)[X-\mu]^T\Sigma^{-1}[X-\mu]\right\}. \quad (2.23)$$

The multivariate normal distribution is a generalization of the normal distribution to more than one random variable, x. As shown above, X is a $d \times 1$ (column) vector, the means of X are contained in the vector μ, and Σ is the $d \times d$ covariance matrix of X. As a covariance matrix, Σ must be positive definite. The diagonal elements of Σ are the variances of each x, and the off-diagonal elements are the covariances between variables. Each member of X has a univariate normal distribution, and if Σ is a diagonal matrix (with 0 for all off-diagonal elements), the distribution is equivalent to d independent univariate normal distributions. When d is 2, the distribution is called the "bivariate normal distribution," and its density function is sometimes shown in scalar form as

$$f(X|\mu,\Sigma) = C \times \exp\left\{\left(-\frac{1}{2}\right)\left(\frac{(x_1-\mu_1)^2}{\sigma_1^2(1-\rho^2)}\right) - \left(\frac{2\rho(x_1-\mu_1)(x_2-\mu_2)}{\sigma_1\sigma_2(1-\rho^2)}\right) + \left(\frac{(x_2-\mu_2)^2}{\sigma_2^2(1-\rho^2)}\right)\right\}$$
$$(2.24)$$

$$\propto \exp\left\{\left(-\frac{1}{2}\right)\left(\frac{(x_1-\mu_1)^2}{\sigma_1^2(1-\rho^2)}\right) - \left(\frac{2\rho(x_1-\mu_1)(x_2-\mu_2)}{\sigma_1\sigma_2(1-\rho^2)}\right) + \left(\frac{(x_2-\mu_2)^2}{\sigma_2^2(1-\rho^2)}\right)\right\},$$
$$(2.25)$$

where the normalizing constant is $C = \left(2\pi\sigma_1\sigma_2\sqrt{1-\rho^2}\right)^{-1}$. In this distribution, ρ is the correlation between x_1 and x_2. If $\rho = 0$, the center term in the exponential expression is 0, and the density function can be rewritten as

$$f(X|\mu,\Sigma) = (2\pi\sigma_1\sigma_2)^{-1}\exp\left\{\left(-\frac{1}{2}\right)\left[\left(\frac{(x_1-\mu_1)^2}{\sigma_1^2(1-\rho^2)}\right) + \left(\frac{(x_2-\mu_2)^2}{\sigma_2^2(1-\rho^2)}\right)\right]\right\} \qquad (2.26)$$

$$= (2\pi\sigma_1\sigma_2)^{-1}\exp\left\{-\left(\frac{(x_1-\mu_1)^2}{2\sigma_1^2}\right)\right\}\exp\left\{-\left(\frac{(x_2-\mu_2)^2}{2\sigma_2^2}\right)\right\} \qquad (2.27)$$

$$= \left[\frac{1}{\sqrt{2\pi\sigma_1^2}}\exp\left\{-\frac{(x_1-\mu_1)^2}{2\sigma_1^2}\right\}\right]\left[\frac{1}{\sqrt{2\pi\sigma_2^2}}\exp\left\{-\frac{(x_2-\mu_2)^2}{2\sigma_2^2}\right\}\right]. \qquad (2.28)$$

This result illustrates that, when $\rho = 0$, the bivariate normal density reduces to the product of two independent normal densities, a result that extends to the full multivariate normal distribution as stated above.

The multivariate normal distribution is used extensively in Bayesian statistics. In particular, for linear regression modeling, the outcome y conditional on x (i.e., the error term) is assumed to be univariately normally distributed, but the regression coefficients, β, turn out to be multivariately normally distributed (conditional on σ^2), as we will see in Chapter 5.

Inverse Wishart Distribution

If $X_{d\times d} \sim IW(S,v)$ the density function for X is

$$f(X|S,v) = \left[\frac{|S|^{\frac{v}{2}}}{2^{\frac{vd}{2}}\Gamma_d\left(\frac{v}{2}\right)}\right]\exp\left\{\left(-\frac{1}{2}\right)tr(SX^{-1})\right\} \qquad (2.29)$$

$$\propto \exp\left\{\left(-\frac{1}{2}\right)tr(SX^{-1})\right\}. \qquad (2.30)$$

The inverse Wishart distribution is a generalization of the inverse gamma distribution to $d \times d$ matrices. It has two parameters, including a degrees of freedom parameter, v, and a scale matrix parameter S. v must be greater than $d - 1$, and S must be positive definite. The distribution is used in Bayesian statistics as a prior distribution for the covariance matrix, Σ, in the multivariate normal distribution. Although the kernel of the inverse Wishart distribution looks very different, as written, from the kernel of the multivariate normal distribution, a useful identity in matrix algebra shows that they are similar. Specifically, $X^T A X = tr(XX^T A)$. So, if we let $S = [X - \mu][X - \mu]^T$, the kernel of the multivariate normal density becomes $\exp\left\{-(1/2)tr(S\Sigma^{-1})\right\}$, which indeed looks much like the kernel of the inverse Wishart.

Marginal and Conditional Distributions

Multivariate distributions (or joint distributions of multiple random variables) are used frequently in both classical and Bayesian statistics. In the Bayesian setting, model parameters are considered random variables, and interest often centers only on one or two key parameters in multiparameter models. The remaining parameters may be an important part of the model in that they cannot be ignored, but they are merely "nuisance" parameters. For example, in a normal distribution problem, the mean, μ, is generally of primary interest, but the variance, σ^2, cannot simply be ignored, because uncertainty about σ^2 affects our degree of uncertainty about μ. As another example, the threshold parameters in an ordinal regression model are an important part of the model, but they are usually of little direct interest. In these cases, we may wish to make inference about one parameter while "marginalizing" across all possible values of the nuisance parameters, or we may wish to "condition" on particular values of them. Thus, deriving marginal and conditional distributions is an important part of Bayesian statistics.

Formally, if $p(x,y)$ is the joint pmf for two discrete variables, x and y, the marginal distribution for x is

$$p(x) = \sum_y p(x,y). \qquad (2.31)$$

That is, the marginal distribution for x is the sum of the joint distribution taken over values of y. If the variables are continuous, then the marginal distribution for x involves an integral rather than a sum:

$$f(x) = \int_y f(x,y)\,dy. \qquad (2.32)$$

As an illustration, consider the bivariate normal distribution shown earlier, with $x = x_1$ and $y = x_2$. For simplicity, assume the distribution is the standard bivariate normal distribution so that $\mu_x = \mu_y = 0$ and $\sigma_x^2 = \sigma_y^2 = 1$. Then, if we are interested in the marginal distribution for x, we must compute:

$$f(x) = \int_{-\infty}^{\infty} f(x,y)\,dy \qquad (2.33)$$

$$= \int_{-\infty}^{\infty} \frac{1}{2\pi\sqrt{1-\rho^2}} \exp\left\{ -\left(\frac{x^2 - 2\rho xy + y^2}{2(1-\rho^2)} \right) \right\} dy. \qquad (2.34)$$

This integration is not as difficult as it may seem. First, we can rearrange terms and complete the square in y to obtain the following inside the exponential function:

$$f(x) = \int_{-\infty}^{\infty} \frac{1}{2\pi\sqrt{1-\rho^2}} \exp\left\{-\left(\frac{x^2 - \rho^2 x^2 + y^2 - 2\rho xy + \rho^2 x^2}{2(1-\rho^2)}\right)\right\} dy.$$

(2.35)

$$= \int_{-\infty}^{\infty} \frac{1}{2\pi\sqrt{1-\rho^2}} \exp\left\{-\left(\frac{x^2(1-\rho^2) + (y-\rho x)^2}{2(1-\rho^2)}\right)\right\} dy. \quad (2.36)$$

Next, we can break up the exponential, extract terms that are constant over y outside the integral, and rearrange terms to obtain

$$f(x) = \frac{1}{\sqrt{2\pi}} \exp\left\{-\frac{x^2}{2}\right\} \times \int_{-\infty}^{\infty} \frac{1}{\sqrt{2\pi}\sqrt{1-\rho^2}} \exp\left\{-\frac{(y-\rho x)^2}{2(1-\rho^2)}\right\} dy.$$

(2.37)

The integral on the righthand side of the multiplication sign is simply the integral of a normal random variable, y, with mean $\mu = \rho x$ and variance $\sigma^2 = (1-\rho^2)$. Thus, its integral, by the definition of a probability density function described earlier, is 1. What remains, then, is the term on the lefthand side of the multiplication sign. This is the density function for a normally distributed random variable, x, with mean $\mu = 0$ and variance $\sigma^2 = 1$. Thus, the marginal distribution for x is $N(0,1)$.

Whereas the marginal distribution for a variable, x, in a joint distribution for x and y is the distribution of x integrated across all values for y, the conditional distribution for x, denoted $f(x|y)$, is the distribution for x given a specified value for y. It can be represented using the probability rule for nonindependent joint events as

$$f(x|y) = \frac{f(x,y)}{f(y)} = \frac{f(x,y)}{\int_x f(x,y)dx},$$

(2.38)

where $f(y)$ is the marginal distribution for y, obtainable as described immediately above. Considering the bivariate normal distribution again, and recognizing the symmetry of x and y, the conditional distribution for x is

$$f(x|y) = \frac{\frac{1}{2\pi\sqrt{1-\rho^2}} \exp\left\{-\left(\frac{x^2 - 2\rho xy + y^2}{2(1-\rho^2)}\right)\right\}}{\frac{1}{\sqrt{2\pi}} \exp\left\{-\frac{y^2}{2}\right\}}$$

(2.39)

$$= \frac{1}{\sqrt{2\pi(1-\rho^2)}} \exp\left\{-\left(\frac{x^2 - 2\rho xy + y^2}{2(1-\rho^2)}\right)\right\} \exp\left\{\frac{y^2}{2}\right\} \quad (2.40)$$

$$= \frac{1}{\sqrt{2\pi(1-\rho^2)}} \exp\left\{-\left(\frac{x^2 - 2\rho xy + y^2 - y^2 + \rho^2 y^2}{2(1-\rho^2)}\right)\right\} \quad (2.41)$$

$$= \frac{1}{\sqrt{2\pi(1-\rho^2)}} \exp\left\{-\frac{(x-\rho y)^2}{2(1-\rho^2)}\right\}. \quad (2.42)$$

Thus, the conditional distribution $f(x|y)$ is a normal distribution with a mean of ρy and a variance of $1 - \rho^2$.

Conditional distributions play an extremely important role in Bayesian statistics and contemporary Bayesian computation and can be simple to derive by recognizing and discarding proportionality constants, rather than using integration to first obtain a marginal distribution, which may be difficult or impossible. Reconsider the standard bivariate normal density in the numerator of Equation 2.39 and note the following steps for finding the conditional distribution for x using proportionality:

Step	Equation	Explanation
1.	$f(x,y) = \frac{1}{2\pi\sqrt{1-\rho^2}} \exp\left\{-\left(\frac{x^2-2\rho xy+y^2}{2(1-\rho^2)}\right)\right\}$	Bivariate Normal
2.	$f(x|y) \propto \exp\left\{-\left(\frac{x^2-2\rho xy+y^2}{2(1-\rho^2)}\right)\right\}$	Dropped leading constant
3.	$f(x|y) \propto \exp\left\{-\left(\frac{x^2-2\rho xy}{2(1-\rho^2)}\right)\right\}$	Extracted & dropped y^2 as constant
4.	$f(x|y) \propto \exp\left\{-\left(\frac{x^2-2\rho xy+\rho^2 y^2-\rho y^2}{2(1-\rho^2)}\right)\right\}$	Completing the square Step 1
5.	$f(x|y) \propto \exp\left\{-\left(\frac{(x-\rho y)^2-\rho y^2}{2(1-\rho^2)}\right)\right\}$	Completing the square Step 2
6.	$f(x|y) \propto \exp\left\{-\left(\frac{(x-\rho y)^2}{2(1-\rho^2)}\right)\right\}$	Dropped $-\rho y^2$ as a constant

Step 1 shows the standard bivariate normal distribution. In Step 2, the leading term outside the exponential is removed under proportionality. In Step 3, the y^2 term inside the exponential is removed as a constant, also under proportionality (recall that $e^{a+b} = e^a e^b$). In Step 4, ρy^2 is added and subtracted in the first step of completing the square in x. In Step 5, the square is completed and a quadratic term constructed in the numerator of the exponential. Finally, in Step 6, $-\rho y^2$ is removed under proportionality (technically, the exponential term involving ρy^2 is removed). What remains is the kernel of the normal distribution we obtained previously. Thus, $x|y \sim N(\rho y, 1 - \rho^2)$, and we obtained this result without performing any integral calculus.

I show these steps in detail, because this process of dropping constants, rearranging terms, and completing the square is repeated often in Bayesian statistics. We will see this in many of the examples throughout the volume.

Review of Maximum Likelihood Analysis

In classical statistics, observed data are viewed as a random realization of a data generation process governed by fixed, but unknown, parameters. Maximum likelihood (ML) estimation is the workhorse method for estimating parameters (and standard errors), given the data, in classical statistical modeling. The basic principle of the maximum likelihood approach is that the best estimate for a parameter is the value of it that makes the data we have observed most likely to have occurred. Put a different way, the best guess for a parameter's value is that which maximizes the probability of observing the data.

For example, if I flip a coin 10 times and observe no heads, we might immediately understand that the binomial parameter p, for the probability of a head on a given toss, cannot be 1, because if $p = 1$, the probability of observing no heads would be 0. Instead, $p = 0$ might seem like a reasonable guess. The probability of observing no heads in 10 coin flips if $p = 0$ is 1, so $p = 0$ is clearly a better guess for p than $p = 1$. The randomness in the process of coin flipping, however, implies that different possible values of the parameter could also produce the observed data. Here, .1 is also a reasonable value for p, because it is quite possible that we would see no heads in 10 tosses when p is that small. In fact, the probability of observing no heads if $p = .1$ is .35, which is much less than 1—making $p = 0$ appear to be a better guess. To extend this simple example, suppose in one experiment, I flip a coin twice and obtain no heads, while in another experiment, I flip a coin 100 times and obtain no heads. In both cases, my best guess for p is 0. However, the second experiment provides much more convincing evidence than the first that $p = 0$, rather than, say, $p = .1$, because the data are much less probable to be observed if $p = .1$ than if $p = 0$. The probability of observing no heads in two coin tosses is 1 if $p = 0$, but the probability is .81 if $p = .1$, which is still quite high. In 100 tosses, however, the probability of observing no heads is still 1, but the probability is .00003 if $p = .1$. The goal of ML estimation is both to obtain a "best guess" for a parameter's value and to quantify our uncertainty about that guess, given how much information we have.

These goals—estimation of parameters and quantification of uncertainty about them—are achieved first by constructing a "likelihood function" that represents the data generation process and contains both the data and the parameter(s). The likelihood function is a (usually unnormalized) joint distribution for the observed data. As a simple but contrived example we can extend in introducing the Bayesian approach in the next chapter, suppose we observe 3 rolls of 6 in 10 rolls of a standard six-sided die, and we question whether the die is weighted to come up 6 more often than the other numbers. Answering this question requires that we estimate the parameter associated with producing 6s on the dice rolls, which, in turn, requires that we decide upon a model for the process of dice-rolling. One approach would be to assume each die roll comes from a Bernoulli distribution, where success is defined as a roll of 6 and a failure is any other value. Under that model, the density function for a single die roll is $f(y|p) = p^y(1-p)^{1-y}$, where p is the parameter, and y is the observed roll of either 6 ($y = 1$) or some other number ($y = 0$).

To construct a likelihood function for all 10 rolls, it is common to assume the observations (rolls in this case) are independent, so that the joint distribution of all rolls is the product of their individual probabilities:

$$L(p|y) = \prod_{i=1}^{n} p^{y_i}(1-p)^{1-y_i} \tag{2.43}$$

$$= \prod_{i=1}^{10} p^{I(y_i=6)}(1-p)^{I(y_i \neq 6)}. \tag{2.44}$$

In this equation, $L(p|y)$ is the notation representing the likelihood function, and $I(.)$ is an indicator function, which takes the value of 1 if the argument to it is true and the value of 0 otherwise. Note that the likelihood function is proportional to a joint density for all the data, but it is not normalized. Thus, it is not a proper joint distribution for y. Further, it is not a distribution for the parameter, p, even though it is seemingly written as a conditional distribution for p given y; it is conventionally understood that "$L(\theta|y)$" means that the term on the right-hand side is a likelihood function and not a conditional density for θ.

The original question was whether the die was weighted. If it were not weighted, then the p parameter in this model should be $1/6$, with $1 - p = 5/6$.

The question can then be restated in terms of whether p could reasonably be 1/6, given the three observed 6s in 10 rolls. The likelihood function tells us something about this, because it tells us how probable it is to obtain our observed data under any value of p. The "most likely" value for p, then, is the value of p that maximizes this function. Recalling from calculus that the derivative represents the slope of a curve at a given point, a slope of 0 reflects the location of a maximum (for a concave-downward curve). Thus, maximizing the likelihood function involves the following steps:

1. Simplify the likelihood: $L(p|y) = p^{\sum y}(1 - p)^{n-\sum y}$. Here I have replaced the indicator functions to simplify the presentation; $\sum y$ is the count of 6s rolled.

2. Take the logarithm to further simplify (this has no consequence for the maximum):
   $LL(p|y) = (\sum y) \ln p + (n - \sum y) \ln(1 - p)$

3. Take the derivative with respect to the parameter: $\frac{dL}{dp} = \frac{\sum y}{p} - \frac{n - \sum y}{1 - p}$

4. Set $\frac{dLL}{dp} = 0$ and solve for p: $p = \frac{\sum y}{n}$

In Step 4, we see that our estimate is simply the sample proportion of rolled 6s. We generally denote this estimate as $\hat{p}_{MLE}$, or often just $\hat{p}$.

In our example, our estimate for p would be .3, which is considerably larger than $1/6 \approx .17$. However, it is certainly possible, of course, to obtain three 6s in 10 rolls of a fair die, so how can we assess whether the hypothesis that $p = 1/6$ is reasonable?

The second part of ML estimation is to quantify uncertainty in our estimate of the parameter of interest. This process involves the following steps:

1. Take the second derivative of the log-likelihood function with respect to the parameters. This is called the "Hessian matrix" and is generically denoted $\frac{\partial^2 LL}{\partial \theta \partial \theta^T}$; θ may be a vector or scalar so that the Hessian matrix may be a matrix or a scalar.

2. Take the negative expected value of this result to obtain the "Information matrix," $I(\theta)$.

3. Replace the parameters in $I(\theta)$ with the ML estimates of them, and invert the matrix to obtain the covariance matrix of the estimates.

It may not be intuitive why these steps give us estimates of uncertainty in our parameter estimates, so some description is warranted. The likelihood function is a product of probability densities and is usually a concave-down function with a single maximum. The second derivative tells us the extent of curvature in the function and therefore gives us a sense of how narrow or wide the likelihood function is. With more data, the likelihood function tends to be narrower and therefore steeper around the maximum, so that the second derivative is larger. Inverting a larger number yields a smaller number and therefore a smaller standard error, indicating less uncertainty about our parameter estimate.

The matrix obtained in Step 3 is often called the asymptotic covariance matrix of the estimates and is usually denoted acov or vcov in popular software. Most software packages will provide these matrices if requested; otherwise, procedures typically report only the standard errors, which are the square roots of the diagonal elements of this matrix.

In our die-rolling example, there is only one parameter, so that the Hessian matrix is a scalar. Following Step 3 in parameter estimation, we can rewrite the first derivative as

$$\frac{dLL}{dp} = \left(\sum y\right) p^{-1} - \left(n - \sum y\right) (1-p)^{-1}. \tag{2.45}$$

Next, take the second derivative:

$$\frac{d^2 LL}{dp^2} = -\left(\sum y\right) p^{-2} - \left(n - \sum y\right) (1-p)^{-2}. \tag{2.46}$$

Then, we can take the negative expected value of this result to obtain

$$I(p) = \frac{n}{p} + \frac{n}{(1-p)} = \frac{n}{p(1-p)}. \tag{2.47}$$

This equation follows, because $E(\sum y) = np$, and $E(n - \sum y) = n(1-p)$. Finally, replacing p with $\hat{p}$, inverting and square-rooting yields

$$\widehat{se(\hat{p})} = \sqrt{\frac{\hat{p}(1-\hat{p})}{n}}. \tag{2.48}$$

Note that the wide "hat" over the standard error is there because the standard error is a measure of the standard deviation of the sampling distribution for sample values of $\hat{p}$ in repeated samples. The true standard error is a function of p, rather than $\hat{p}$. Since we are using $\hat{p}$ in the computation, it is, in fact, an estimate itself. To avoid overcomplicating equations, however, I will not generally put a hat over standard errors.

In our die-rolling example, $se(\hat{p}) = \sqrt{(.3)(.7)/10} = .145$. We can now answer the question posed earlier: Is the die weighted to favor the value of

6? In the classical statistical paradigm, we would commonly assume the die were fair, so that our (null) hypothesis were $H_0 : p = 1/6$, and we could construct a normal theory interval estimate for p using $\hat{p} \pm t_{\alpha/2} se(\hat{p})$, where $t_{\alpha/2}$ is the t required to obtain a (two-tailed) confidence level of $100(1 - \alpha)\%$. Here, the degrees of freedom are $n - 1 = 9$, so $t = 2.26$, and a 95% interval estimate would be $[-.028, .628]$. Since 1/6 is contained in that interval, we would conclude that there is insufficient evidence to reject our null hypothesis that the die is fair. Put another way, it is reasonable that p could be 1/6 and produce the data we observed.

An alternative approach to addressing the question would be to conduct a z test. In that case:

$$z = \frac{\hat{p} - H_0}{se(\hat{p})} = \frac{.3 - .167}{\sqrt{(.167)(.833)/10}} = 1.13, \qquad (2.49)$$

where $se(\hat{p})$ is the *known* standard deviation of the sampling distribution for $\hat{p}$ under the population value for p implied by the null hypothesis, as shown in the denominator. This z statistic is well below 1.96, and so we could not reject the null hypothesis. Again, we have insufficient evidence to reject the null hypothesis that the die is fair. The result would not change if we used a directional test: The p-value in that case would be .13, rather than .26, which is still well above the usual cutoff of .05.

There are at least two reasons why this classical approach is unsatisfying. First, the confidence interval we constructed included values for p that were below 0. This is impossible for a proportion but is a consequence of our implicit assumption that the sampling distribution for $\hat{p}$ is t-distributed. It clearly cannot be in this sample, but this is a common assumption used in classical statistics involving ML estimation. In large samples, this assumption is usually not problematic—sampling distributions of ML estimates are asymptotically normal—but in small samples, it can be.

Second, our inability to reject the null hypothesis that the die is fair is not a direct answer to the original question. Our question was whether the die is weighted, not whether it is reasonable to assume it isn't. This conclusion ultimately does not tell us the extent to which it may be reasonable to think the die is weighted versus unweighted: We would not be able to reject a null hypothesis that suggested the die were only slightly weighted either, using the classical logic. As we will see beginning in the next chapter, the Bayesian approach helps ameliorate both of these problems.

Three final notes are in order regarding the likelihood approach we developed in this chapter. First, I presented only a single, one-parameter example illustrating maximum likelihood methods. The key reason is that the differential calculus involved in that approach and the logic of classical inference are not necessary for understanding the Bayesian approach. Other sources, including a volume in this series, offer extensive coverage of ML estimation and the classical approach (Eliason, 1993).

Second, we developed the likelihood function in this example using the Bernoulli distribution for individual die rolls. We could also have developed the likelihood function using the binomial distribution. The only difference between the product of Bernoulli distributions and the binomial distribution with $n = 10$ and $x = 3$ is the combinatorial function as shown earlier in this chapter. This combinatorial simply tells us how many different ways x successes could be arranged in n trials. It does not contain the parameter p, and so this term drops when taking the derivative of the log likelihood with respect to p. Thus, the Bernoulli and binomial approaches are equivalent.

Third, although a six-sided die has six possible outcomes, we treated the outcome as dichotomous: Either a 6 came up on each roll or it didn't. An alternative model might involve the multinomial distribution, which can handle multiple outcomes. We will explore this model in the next chapter.

CHAPTER 3. THE BAYESIAN APPROACH TO PROBABILITY AND STATISTICS

Suppose I know the probability of testing positive for a disease if I have a disease—$p(\text{test} + \mid \text{have disease})$—and I tested positive for the disease. What I really want to know is the probability I have the disease, given that I tested positive: $p(\text{have disease} \mid \text{test} +)$. Or, suppose we know the probability that an owner of an assault weapon is involved when a mass shooting occurs: $p(\text{AW owner} \mid \text{shooting})$. What we may really want to know, before developing new gun control policy, is the probability that an assault weapon owner will engage in a mass shooting: $p(\text{shooting} \mid \text{AW owner})$. These conditional expressions may seem alike at first, but they are not interchangeable. Tests for diseases often produce false-positive results, so that testing positive does not automatically imply one has a disease. Although assault weapon owners may be involved in almost every mass shooting in the United States, very few assault weapon owners engage in mass shootings. Or, as an even more apparent example, the probability of being attacked by a great white shark if one is swimming in the ocean is almost 0, but the probability that one was swimming in the ocean if one were attacked by a great white shark is almost certainly 1 (despite some sci-fi movie suggestions otherwise).

Although these reverse conditionals are not interchangeable, Bayes' theorem provides a recipe for relating them using the basic rule for joint probabilities of nonindependent events. The theorem is straightforward to derive:

$$p(B,A) = p(A,B) \tag{3.1}$$

$$p(B|A)p(A) = p(A|B)p(B) \tag{3.2}$$

$$p(B|A) = \frac{p(A|B)p(B)}{p(A)}. \tag{3.3}$$

In words, the last equation says that the "posterior" probability of B given A is equal to the conditional probability of A given B, multiplied by the "prior" probability of B (a total—or marginal—probability) divided by the total probability of A, where the total probability of A is computed using the law of total probability. Returning to our die-rolling example from the last chapter, the total probability for A would be the probability of obtaining a roll of 6 in one roll of the die and is the sum of the probabilities of obtaining a 6 given that the die is fair, weighted (i.e., multiplied) by the probability that the die is fair, and the probability of obtaining a 6 if the die is unfair, weighted by the probability that the die is unfair. The prior probability comes from prior knowledge or possibly speculation, as we will discuss throughout the remainder of this volume.

As a first illustration of the theorem, let's consider a modified version of our die-rolling example. Suppose that I am told that the die is either fair (F) or is weighted so that 6 comes up twice as often as it should (W). In that case, there are two beliefs about the state of the world (i.e., hypotheses about the binomial parameter p): $p = 1/6$ or $p = 1/3$. Before observing any rolls of the die, there may be no reason to prefer one hypothesis over the other, so my prior probabilities for the hypotheses about p might be $p(F) \equiv pr(p = 1/6) = 1/2$ and $p(W) \equiv pr(p = 2/6) = 1/2$. Suppose I roll the die once, and it is a 6. How does this change—or "update"—my belief about p? Applying Bayes' theorem yields

$$p(W|6) = \frac{p(6|W)p(W)}{p(6|W)p(W) + p(6|F)p(F)} \tag{3.4}$$

$$= \frac{(1/3)(1/2)}{(1/3)(1/2) + (1/6)(1/2)} \tag{3.5}$$

$$= 2/3. \tag{3.6}$$

Thus, after observing a 6 on the very first roll, we now favor the hypothesis that the die is weighted. That is, our prior probability that the die was weighted was 1/2, but our posterior probability for that hypothesis is 2/3 after observing a 6 on the very first roll.

In the previous chapter, we rolled the die another nine times and observed two more 6s. Bayes' theorem can handle this additional information in two, equivalent ways. First, we could update our belief about the hypothesis that the die is weighted each time we roll the die. Suppose that the ordered sequence of all 10 rolls was $Y = \{6, 4, 1, 3, 6, 2, 6, 5, 4, 3\}$. Then, we could take our posterior probability of 2/3 derived above as the prior probability, $p(W)$, in a second application (where we do not observe a 6—the symbol "¬" means "not"). In that case:

$$p(W|\neg 6) = \frac{p(\neg 6|W)p(W)}{p(\neg 6|W)p(W) + p(\neg 6|F)p(F)} \tag{3.7}$$

$$= \frac{(4/6)(2/3)}{(4/6)(2/3) + (5/6)(1/3)} \tag{3.8}$$

$$= 8/13. \tag{3.9}$$

Thus, after two rolls of the die, our posterior probability for the hypothesis that the die is weighted is $8/13 \approx .62$. This posterior probability is not as great as it was after the first roll, but it is still greater than the original prior probability of $1/2$. This is because, although the second roll was not a 6, observing one of them in two rolls is not particularly likely with a fair die; it is much more likely with a die weighted as hypothesized.

If we were to continue this sequential updating approach, after all 10 rolls, the posterior probability the die is weighted would be about .63. The sequence of posterior probabilities after each trial is

$$[.67, .62, .56, .51, .67, .62, .77, .72, .68, .63].$$

Notice that, after each roll of a 6, the posterior probability favoring the hypothesis that the die is weighted increases, while after each roll of another number, the posterior probability for the hypothesis is reduced. Also notice, however, that each additional roll of the die leads to a slightly smaller change in the posterior probability for the hypothesis. This is because each new roll of the die provides proportionately less additional information relative to the total prior information we have.

Second, as an alternative to sequential updating, we could incorporate all of the data simultaneously via either a normalized joint probability distribution for all the data or an unnormalized likelihood function as developed in the previous chapter. That likelihood function was constructed as the product of 10 Bernoulli distributions, one for each die roll. Inserting this product into Bayes' theorem, we obtain

$$p(W|Y) = \frac{p(Y|W)p(W)}{p(Y|W)p(W) + p(Y|F)p(F)} \tag{3.10}$$

$$= \frac{[(1/3)^3(2/3)^7](1/2)}{[(1/3)^3(2/3)^7](1/2) + [(1/6)^3(5/6)^7](1/2)} \tag{3.11}$$

$$= .63, \tag{3.12}$$

which is identical to the result obtained via sequential updating. After observing three 6s in 10 rolls of the die, the hypothesis that the die is weighted is favored over the hypothesis that the die is fair.

We could have specified a normalized probability distribution for the data (likelihood/sampling distribution) by using a binomial distribution for the collection of rolls, as mentioned at the end of the previous chapter, with

$$p(Y = 3 \mid n = 10, p = P) = \binom{10}{3} P^3 (1 - P)^7, \tag{3.13}$$

where P is the probability of rolling a 6 under the hypothesized (or possible) values for p. Had we done so, our results would be no different than under the Bernoulli setting. Although p varies across the two hypotheses in the denominator, the leading combinatorial that normalizes the collection of Bernoulli data is the same in all three terms in the numerator and denominator and therefore cancels.

Including a Prior Distribution and Summarizing the Posterior

We usually do not have a discrete pair of hypotheses as in this example, in which the die is either fair or weighted to produce a 6 twice as often as a fair die would. Instead, more often we have multiple discrete hypotheses or even continuous hypotheses about a parameter. Alternatively, if one prefers not to think in terms of hypotheses, we commonly have general uncertainty about the value of a parameter assumed to generate the data, so we may be interested in determining a reasonable range for its value, rather than assessing the probability it takes a precise value. For example, in the die-rolling example as originally described in the last chapter, the question was simply whether the die was weighted to favor a roll of 6 without specifying a particular extent of the weighting. If the parameter p is thought of as a continuous quantity that can take any real value between 0 and 1, then this question is simply whether $p > (1/6)$ rather than whether $p = 1/3$ versus $p = 1/6$. Bayes' theorem can be easily extended to handle such cases by replacing the discrete point prior probabilities associated with a few possible parameter values with a prior *distribution* representing the relative probabilities of all (perhaps an infinite number of) values a parameter might take over a given domain.

The beta distribution described in Chapter 2 is an appropriate prior distribution for the parameter p in the example. The beta distribution is flexible in shape over the domain [0,1], as Figure 3.1 illustrates. Recall from the previous chapter that the beta distribution has two parameters, α and β. When the beta distribution is used as a prior for a parameter (e.g., p), these "hyperparameters" can be considered prior successes and prior failures, respectively, from a collection of previous trials and can take any positive value (including fractional/decimal values). Values that are closer to zero indicate that we have little prior information regarding the parameter p, while large values indicate that we have considerable information. The relative magnitudes of the two parameters indicate whether we believe p is closer to 0 versus 1 as well as the degree to which we believe so: Recall that the mean and variance of the beta distribution is a function of the size of α and β. If the mean is held constant, larger values of these parameters serve to produce smaller prior variance.

The figure shows four beta distributions with some different values for the α and β parameters chosen to reflect the flexibility of the distribution.

38

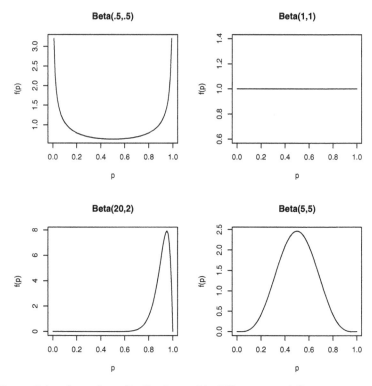

Figure 3.1 Some beta distributions with different α and β parameter values.

In the upper-left plot, the parameters are small and equal at .5. This parameterization yields a U-shaped distribution in which extreme values of p are weighted more heavily than central values, but both extremes are equally weighted. The upper-right figure shows the Beta(1, 1) distribution. This distribution is uniform over the [0,1] interval, indicating that, when used as a prior for p, all values of p are considered equally likely prior to observing data. The lower-left figure shows a Beta(20, 2) distribution. This density clearly favors large values of p, with values of p less than about .6 receiving little or no prior support. Finally, the lower-right plot shows a Beta(5, 5) distribution. This distribution favors values of p close to .5 but gives some (diminishing) prior support to values toward the extremes. Thus, we may choose values of α and β to reflect our a priori knowledge or belief regarding the true value of p when using this distribution as a prior distribution.

If we combine a Bernoulli/binomial likelihood function (or, the joint sampling distribution for the data) with a beta prior distribution for p, we obtain a posterior *distribution* for p rather than a posterior probability for a single hypothetical value of p. Here, the generic posterior distribution for a parameter p from a Bernoulli or binomial likelihood for a collection of data consisting of y successes out of n trials with a beta prior distribution is

$$f(p|y) = \frac{f(y|p)f(p)}{f(y)} \tag{3.14}$$

$$f(p|y,n,\alpha,\beta) = \frac{\binom{n}{y}p^y(1-p)^{n-y}\left[\frac{\Gamma(\alpha+\beta)}{\Gamma(\alpha)\Gamma(\beta)}\right]p^{\alpha-1}(1-p)^{\beta-1}}{\int_0^1 \binom{n}{y}p^y(1-p)^{n-y}\left[\frac{\Gamma(\alpha+\beta)}{\Gamma(\alpha)\Gamma(\beta)}\right]p^{\alpha-1}(1-p)^{\beta-1}dp}. \tag{3.15}$$

This posterior distribution looks complicated, but it can be simplified substantially. First, the posterior distribution is a distribution for p. After integration, the denominator of the posterior distribution does not contain p, is therefore a constant with respect to p, and can be removed under proportionality. Second, the binomial coefficient, $\binom{n}{y}$, is a constant with respect to p and can also be removed under proportionality (and, if we used the Bernoulli specification as before, the combinatorial would not be included in the first place). Third, the gamma functions in brackets are also constants with respect to p and can be removed. Thus, the posterior can be rewritten much more cleanly as

$$f(p|y,n,\alpha,\beta) \propto p^y(1-p)^{n-y}p^{\alpha-1}(1-p)^{\beta-1} \tag{3.16}$$

$$\propto p^{y+\alpha-1}(1-p)^{n-y+\beta-1}. \tag{3.17}$$

In general (beyond the beta/binomial model), the denominator of a posterior always constitutes a constant with respect to the quantities of interest and can be removed under proportionality. This term—called the "integrated likelihood"—is used in computing Bayes factors but is simply a normalizing constant and is not relevant for direct inference about the quantities of interest. Further, the likelihood function is typically a product of density functions for data conditional on the parameter of interest and is not usually expressed as a normalized distribution for either the data or the parameter. Thus, Bayes' theorem for probability distributions is often presented as

$$posterior \propto Likelihood \times prior. \tag{3.18}$$

Equivalently, we can say *posterior* $\propto$ *prior* $\times$ *Likelihood*, which simply emphasizes that the prior comes before data.

In our example, the simplified, unnormalized posterior in Equation 3.17 is recognizable as an unnormalized Beta distribution with parameters $A = y + \alpha$ and $B = n - y + \beta$. Thus, our posterior distribution is of the same distributional form as our prior. In Bayesian terminology, a prior and likelihood that combine to yield a posterior that is of the same distributional form as the prior are called a conjugate pair. Put another way, the beta distribution is a conjugate prior for a binomial likelihood.

The use of conjugate priors often simplifies inference because, if the prior is a known distribution, the posterior distribution will also be a known distribution. This fact was most useful historically, prior to the development of the sampling methods discussed in the next chapter, because it usually enabled straightforward summarization of the posterior distribution rather than the use of complicated and costly numerical methods. The use of conjugate priors is less important now given today's methods of Bayesian computation, but conjugate priors are still commonly used and will be in most of the examples in this volume. The key reason is that many conjugate priors are flexible in representing prior uncertainty (so why *not* use them?), and their use generally leads to more elegant solutions than the use of nonconjugate priors.

What remains to complete the derivation of the posterior distribution for p in this example is to specify values for the α and β hyperparameters in the beta prior distribution. As we discussed earlier, we have no reason to prefer the weighted or unweighted hypothesis at the outset. So, we perhaps should choose values of α and β that reflect this ignorance. A reasonable choice might be $\alpha = \beta = 1$, as shown in Figure 3.1, indicating that we have the equivalent prior information of two dice rolls in which one toss was a 6 and the other was not. Although that choice for the hyperparameters suggests a prior mean for p of .5 (which we will discuss below), this prior is uniform over the interval as shown in the figure, thus representing prior ignorance about p:

$$f(p) \propto p^0 (1-p)^0 = 1, \tag{3.19}$$

Thus, no particular value of p is favored a priori. Our posterior mean under that prior would be $A/(A+B) = 4/12 \approx .33$, and our posterior variance would be $(AB)/((A+B)^2(A+B+1)) = 32/((12)^2(13)) \approx .017$, so that our posterior standard deviation is .131.

We can summarize our posterior for p in a number of ways in the Bayesian context. The posterior mean (PM) and posterior standard deviation (PSD) are two summary measures, but we can also construct several types of interval estimates as well. One such interval estimate would be a 95% "credible interval" obtained under normal theory, much like we constructed a confidence interval in classical statistics in the previous chapter. That interval would be

$PM \pm t_{\alpha/2} PSD = [.034, .626]$. This interval is similar to that obtained under maximum likelihood ([-.028, .628]) but not identical. A key reason is that the posterior mean is larger than our ML estimate (.33 vs. .3), and our posterior standard deviation is smaller than the ML estimate of the standard error (.131 vs. .145). These differences reflect the influence of the prior on the results.

Figure 3.2 displays the posterior distribution. As the figure shows, the posterior distribution is not symmetric: The distribution is bounded on the left at 0 and has a long right tail that stretches to 1, but it is centered over roughly $p = .3$. Thus, a normal theory interval estimate does not provide a good summary of where the bulk of the distribution lies. An alternative to the normal theory interval is an empirical interval based on quantiles of the posterior. For example, a 95% "central interval" can be obtained by finding the values of p at the 2.5th and 97.5th percentiles of the beta distribution. We

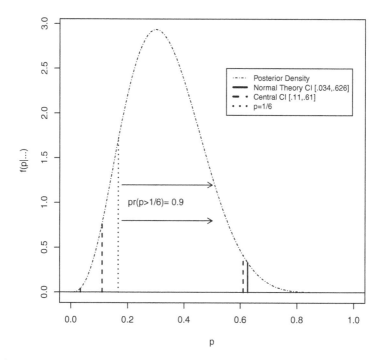

Figure 3.2 Beta posterior distribution in die-rolling example, with interval estimates (normal = solid; central = dashed) and value of 1/6 (dotted) displayed.

can find those values using the qbeta() function in R or an equivalent function in another package. Those values give us an interval of [.11, .61]. The figure displays both the normal theory interval and the central interval. As the figure shows, the central interval is considerably narrower than the normal theory interval. The reason is that the beta density is more peaked than the normal, thus having more mass concentrated around the mean. Throughout the remainder of this volume, I will show central intervals, rather than normal theory intervals, because there is no inherent need to make assumptions about the shape of the posterior distribution when using Markov chain Monte Carlo methods.

More important, even if the classical and Bayesian interval estimates were identical, *they do not have the same interpretation*. In the Bayesian paradigm, the posterior distribution summarizes our knowledge about the parameter, and we can make probabilistic statements about it that represents that uncertainty. Here, we would interpret the 95% central credible interval as containing p with probability .95. This interpretation is commonly used by laypersons to describe classical confidence intervals, but that interpretation is wrong. The correct interpretation for a classical confidence interval is as follows: The given interval either does or does not contain p, but 95% of intervals that would be produced in repeated samples following the recipe for interval construction would contain p, and this one is therefore very likely to be one of them. Arguably, an advantage of the Bayesian paradigm is the ease of interpretation of interval estimates.

Addressing specific hypotheses regarding parameter values is also straightforward in the Bayesian paradigm. Here, our original question was whether the die is weighted to favor rolling a 6: Mathematically, is $p > 1/6$? The figure displays a dotted vertical line at $p = 1/6$. Assessing the hypothesis regarding whether the die is weighted simply requires us to compute the probability that $p > 1/6$ under the posterior distribution and use our judgment regarding whether that probability is sufficiently large so as to merit believing the hypothesis. The probability that $p > 1/6$ is the area under the curve to the right of the dotted line, which can be found using a cumulative distribution function, such as pbeta() in R. This probability is .9, so we would mostly likely conclude that there is sufficient evidence, based on 10 rolls of the die, to believe that the die is weighted. Importantly, while it may be debatable whether this probability is high enough to warrant believing the hypothesis to be true, our posterior probability provides at least a clear statement of the amount of support we have for the hypothesis given the prior assumptions and the observed data. It is not an indirect statement regarding the probability of observing the data under a hypothesis that is not of interest but is simply set up to be rejected (or not).

More on Priors

As the foregoing simple example illustrates, the posterior distribution is a compromise between the prior and likelihood. In a Bayesian analysis, we start with a prior and let the data reweight it in producing a posterior that has updated our prior based on the new information contained in the likelihood. Our Beta(1, 1) prior in the die-rolling example implied a prior mean of 1/2 for p, while the data yielded a maximum likelihood estimate (the sample mean) of 3/10 for p. The prior was equivalent to having two prior data points (a single "success" and a single "failure"), while our data contained 10 data points, three of which were "successes." Thus, the posterior mean was a weighted average of the prior mean and the data mean: $PM = (2/12)(.5) + (10/12)(.3) = 4/12$. Given the difference between the data mean and the posterior mean, it is clear that the choice for a prior may possibly have significant consequences for inference. But must it?

Priors are commonly differentiated into two classes—noninformative and informative—based on how much effect the prior has on posterior inference. A noninformative prior is one that contributes little to inference about a quantity of interest over what the data contribute. That is, the prior is weak so that data drive the results. In contrast, an informative prior is one that, when combined with the likelihood function, has a potentially substantial effect on inference.

In our example, our choice of 1 for the values of both α and β produced a uniform prior that gave no prior preference for any value of p. Uniform priors are generally considered to be noninformative, because they explicitly place equal weight on all values of a parameter. In our example, the result was that the posterior mean of .33 was not far from the maximum likelihood value of $3/10 = .3$, which was only determined by the data. In contrast, if we selected $\alpha = \beta = 1000$, the posterior mean would have been $1003/2010 \approx .5$, which is roughly equal to the prior mean. That is, under that prior, the data would have contributed almost nothing to inference about p. That would have been an incredibly informative prior.

So what type of prior should one use? On the one hand, the Bayesian paradigm offers a coherent approach to incorporating the current state of scientific knowledge into analyses of new data to update our knowledge about a parameter of interest. In contrast, the classical approach has no formal method for incorporating prior knowledge into analyses. Instead, prior knowledge is merely discussed in the literature review. That approach may help researchers determine what type of model to use for a given research question and guide them to focus on a specific model parameter, but it generally leads to testing, retesting, and retesting the same—and often uninteresting—null hypotheses that a regression parameter is 0, or that the difference between two groups is 0, without moving the field toward determining true effect sizes or differences between groups. One might ask, "How many times do we need to reject the null hypothesis that those with a high school diploma have the same risk of premature mortality as those without a diploma?" when the more interesting question is, "Exactly how large is the effect of having a high school education on the risk of premature mortality?"

Repeated testing of null hypotheses cannot definitively and precisely answer that question, because every study treats its data as a unique source of information, ignoring all previous studies' estimates. Formalizing prior knowledge in a prior distribution, in contrast, allows us to systematically and increasingly refine our estimates of effect sizes or group differences. Thus, it may be reasonable or even ideal to use informative priors in well-developed areas of study, although there are very few such instances so far of doing so in the social sciences. A side benefit of such an approach, nonetheless, would be that it would rarefy fluke findings that occur under the classical statistical testing paradigm that guarantees rejections of true null hypotheses 5% of the time.

On the other hand, a common historical criticism of the Bayesian paradigm has been that incorporating informative priors into analyses risks introducing too much subjectivity (bias) into results, overturning what the data show in favor of support for the pet hypotheses of researchers. Of course, it could be argued that, so long as a researcher is transparent in presenting his or her priors, any biases can be easily discerned. Furthermore, a good Bayesian analysis should involve evaluating the sensitivity of results to different choices of priors. Nonetheless, throughout the history of Bayesian statistics, Bayesians have expended considerable effort to develop, obtain, and use noninformative priors. As it turns out, however, it is quite difficult to obtain noninformative priors because true ignorance is hard to quantify.

Uniform ("flat") priors are commonly used as noninformative priors—and will be in some of the examples in this volume—but they can be problematic for a few reasons. First, uniform priors on parameters that span the real line are not proper distributions: They cannot integrate to 1 with any normalizing constant, because in the limit, the domain is infinite and the density height is 0 across the domain (and $c \times \infty \times 0 \neq 1$, for any value of c). The consequence is that a posterior distribution derived under uniform priors may not be proper either, making summarizing it impossible or meaningless. To be sure, there are many cases in which improper priors can be combined with proper sampling distributions/likelihoods to yield proper posteriors, but there is no general guarantee. In contrast, proper priors ensure proper posterior distributions.

Second, even uniform priors may introduce *some* information into a model and therefore may not be truly noninformative in a given analysis. For example, in the above example in which a Beta(1,1) prior was used, the posterior mean was pulled away from the ML estimate of .3 and toward the prior mean of .5. Thus, even the flat prior for p pulled the posterior mean 10% higher than the ML estimate, and so it may be considered somewhat informative. Suppose we had used a Beta(1,5) prior rather than the Beta(1,1) prior. This prior has a mean of 1/6, which may seem more reasonable than a prior mean of 1/2, given that we have no reason upfront to dispute the claim that the die is fair and certainly no reason to believe the value of p is close to 1/2. If that prior were chosen, the posterior mean would be .25 rather than .33. Furthermore, the posterior probability for the hypothesis that the die is weighted would be .77 under that prior rather than .9 (found using 1-pbeta(1/6, 4, 12) and 1-pbeta(1/6, 4, 8) in R, respectively), because the posterior variance would be reduced, given that that prior indicates that we have six pieces of prior information. Although the hypothesis that the die is weighted is still preferred over the hypothesis that the die is fair, the probability is meaningfully smaller: A chance of 1 out of 4 that the die is fair is a much less compelling argument for the weighted die hypothesis than a chance of 1 out of 10. In short, it is often the case that even seemingly innocuous priors can affect posterior inference.

Third, priors that are noninformative in one metric may be informative if the parameterization of a model were changed to another metric, a fact that seems unreasonable. If we have no prior information for a coefficient in a linear probability model, for example, why should we have prior information for the same coefficient in a logit model specification? Yet, parameter transformations often lead to converting noninformative priors to informative ones.

As a simple example, consider the variance, σ^2, from a normal distribution. The variance is constrained to be nonnegative. Thus, we might consider a uniform prior distribution over the real line for $\ln(\sigma^2)$ (i.e., $\ln(\sigma^2) \sim U(-\infty, \infty)$), but suppose we wish to work with σ^2 rather than $\ln(\sigma^2)$. Then, it seems that it would be equivalent to (1) use a $U(0, \infty)$ prior for σ^2 or (2) transform the improper uniform prior in the $\ln(\sigma^2)$ metric to the σ^2 metric using a change of variables. Let $x = \ln \sigma^2$, and let $y = e^x$ be the transformation, so that $y = \sigma^2$. If $x \sim U(-\infty, \infty)$, then $f(x) \propto c$, a constant. So:

$$e^x = y \tag{3.20}$$

$$x = \ln y \tag{3.21}$$

$$\frac{dx}{dy} = 1/y \tag{3.22}$$

$$= 1/\sigma^2 \tag{3.23}$$

$$f(y) = f_x(y^{-1})\frac{dx}{dy} \tag{3.24}$$

$$= c(1/\sigma^2) \tag{3.25}$$

$$\propto 1/\sigma^2. \tag{3.26}$$

Thus, the uniform prior over the real line in the $\ln(\sigma^2)$ metric translates to $1/\sigma^2$ in the σ^2 metric. This is the positive portion of a hyperbola (the part in the first quadrant) and not a $U(0, \infty)$ distribution! How can $1/\sigma^2$ be noninformative when it clearly favors smaller values of σ^2? In fact, this noninformative prior can also be obtained from the inverse gamma distribution. Recall from Chapter 2 that the inverse gamma distribution has density $f(x) \propto x^{-(\alpha+1)}e^{-\beta/x}$, with $x \in (0, \infty)$. If we substitute $\sigma^2 = x$, letting the α and β parameters tend toward 0 stretches and flattens the right tail of the distribution, seemingly indicating having less prior information than when α and β are large. Then we obtain

$$f(\sigma^2) \propto \lim_{\alpha, \beta \to 0} (\sigma^2)^{-(\alpha+1)} e^{-\beta/\sigma^2} \tag{3.27}$$

$$\propto (\sigma^2)^{-1} e^{-0/\sigma^2} \tag{3.28}$$

$$\propto 1/\sigma^2. \tag{3.29}$$

Thus, both approaches yield a prior that purports to be noninformative but appears to favor smaller values of σ^2. However, if we had simply used a uniform prior for σ^2 restricted to the positive numbers—that is, $\sigma^2 \sim U(0, \infty)$—no value of σ^2 greater than 0 would be favored a priori. These are clearly different priors, even though they both stem from the assumption that we have no prior information.

The "Jeffreys prior" also turns out to be $1/\sigma^2$ for the normal distribution problem. Jeffreys—one of the biggest historical proponents of noninformative priors—developed "reference priors" ("Jeffreys priors"), which are priors that remain noninformative when parameterizations of models are transformed, seemingly resolving this third problem (see Robert et al., 2009). The Jeffreys prior is defined as the square root of the determinant of the information matrix, which we defined in Chapter 2 to be the negative expectation of the Hessian matrix. For the binomial distribution, the information matrix was shown in Equation 2.47 to be $n/[p(1-p)]$. (Note that when referring to the Jeffreys prior, the information matrix refers to the value of this matrix for $n = 1$ observation, but this is immaterial because n is ultimately a proportionality constant.) If we square root the determinant of this matrix—a scalar in this case—we obtain

$$f(p) \propto p^{-1/2}(1-p)^{-1/2}, \qquad (3.30)$$

which corresponds to a Beta(.5, .5) distribution, as shown in the upper-left plot in Figure 3.1. Without showing the steps involved in order to save space, for the normal distribution, $1/\sigma^2$ is the Jeffreys prior. We will use this prior in subsequent examples.

In this volume, I will not spend much time focusing on priors for both theoretical and practical reasons. From a theoretical perspective, although one may argue that priors inject subjectivity into statistical analyses, all statistical analyses involve subjectivity. Choosing a model is a subjective decision. In the classical paradigm, the choice of null hypothesis is a subjective decision. Specifying α, the value below which to declare a p-value "significant" is a subjective decision, even if it is agreed upon within a discipline. Finally, and importantly, whether a parameter is a fixed quantity so that probabilistic language does not apply to it versus an unknown quantity to which one can ascribe probabilities is a philosophical issue that one must resolve at the point at which one engages in an analysis.

From a practical perspective, the choice of prior usually does not matter much in contemporary social science research because our data sets tend to be large enough that most priors are overwhelmed by the data even if they are seemingly informative. Thus, the choice of prior is often of little consequence. To be sure, there are certain priors that will not be overwhelmed by data, no matter how large a data set may be. For example, a prior distribution that places all prior probability for a parameter on a given value (and 0 everywhere else; a "point mass" prior) will not be changed by data. This prior, however, is akin to specifying a priori that we are certain about the parameter's value. If that is the case, then we should probably not spend our time considering new data! It should be noted that, although placing a point prior on a parameter may seem unreasonable, doing so is also akin to simply placing a restriction on the parameter that forces it to be a specific value. In many cases, unidentified parameters can be identified by such priors. Often, a prior that is not a point mass but rather a very narrow, bounded prior may be used for a parameter about which we have some uncertainty but not enough uncertainty to otherwise make the parameter unidentifiable (e.g., see Cheng et al., 2008).

In subsequent examples, I will generally use noninformative priors that are of a form that makes computation easier than an alternative prior might. Given the size of the data sets involved, the choice of prior will not have much impact on the results, but this highlights a key concern of Bayesian analysts: Sensitivity testing to determine the extent to which changing priors affects inference. Thus, in most examples, I will show or mention results obtained under different priors. In some cases, I will also use highly restrictive priors in order to demonstrate their utility for model identification.

Extending the Beta/Binomial Model to the Dirichlet/Multinomial

The contrived die-rolling example that we have used to illustrate the concepts underlying Bayes' theorem, as well as its extension from point probabilities to distributions using the beta prior and binomial likelihood, can also be used to illustrate the Dirichlet prior and multinomial likelihood. Although we have investigated whether a die is weighted to come up 6 more often than it should using the beta and binomial distributions, a standard die has six sides, not two. A more natural distribution for modeling die rolls may therefore be the multinomial distribution. The multinomial distribution extends the binomial distribution to more than two possible outcomes (e.g., success vs. failure). A multinomial distribution likelihood function for our die-rolling data would be

$$L(P|Y) \propto \prod_{i=1}^{10} p_1^{I(y_i=1)} p_2^{I(y_i=2)} p_3^{I(y_i=3)} p_4^{I(y_i=4)} p_5^{I(y_i=5)} p_6^{I(y_i=6)} \tag{3.31}$$

$$\propto p_1^1 \cdot p_2^1 \cdot p_3^2 \cdot p_4^2 \cdot p_5^1 \cdot p_6^3. \tag{3.32}$$

Just as the beta distribution is the conjugate prior distribution for the binomial likelihood, the Dirichlet distribution—a multivariate generalization of the beta distribution—is the conjugate prior distribution for the multinomial likelihood. The Dirichlet distribution was shown in Chapter 2, so here I only show the posterior distribution that results when a Dirichlet prior with parameters $\alpha_1 \dots \alpha_6$ is combined with the likelihood:

$$f(P|Y, \alpha) \propto p_1^{1+\alpha_1-1} p_2^{1+\alpha_2-1} p_3^{2+\alpha_3-1} p_4^{2+\alpha_4-1} p_5^{1+\alpha_5-1} p_6^{3+\alpha_6-1} \tag{3.33}$$

$$\propto p_1^{\alpha_1} p_2^{\alpha_2} p_3^{1+\alpha_3} p_4^{1+\alpha_4} p_5^{\alpha_5} p_6^{2+\alpha_6}. \tag{3.34}$$

A relatively noninformative prior can be obtained by setting each α parameter to 1, just as we set $\alpha = \beta = 1$ in the beta distribution to obtain a uniform prior. However, note that the Dirichlet(1,1,1,1,1,1) prior implies a prior mean of 1/6 for each face of the die, while the Beta(1,1) prior implies a prior mean of 1/2 for rolling a 6. Thus, this Dirichlet prior is more akin to the Beta(1,5) we discussed in terms of assuming fairness of the die a priori. Under this Dirichlet prior, the posterior distribution for P is Dirichlet with parameters $\alpha = [2, 2, 3, 3, 2, 4]$. The posterior means for the P vector are

$\left[\frac{1}{8}, \frac{1}{8}, \frac{3}{16}, \frac{3}{16}, \frac{1}{8}, \frac{1}{4}\right]$, and the posterior variances are computed as $Var(p_i) = \bar{p}_i(1 - \bar{p}_i)/(1 + \sum \alpha)$. Thus, the posterior standard deviations of p are $PSD(p) = [.080, .080, .095, .095, .080, .105]$.

Summarizing this posterior may seem more difficult than summarizing the beta distribution posterior, because it is multivariate. That is one reason, potentially, to prefer the simpler beta/binomial model, given our substantive question. Still, under the Dirichlet/multinomial model, one approach to summarizing the posterior is to obtain the marginal distribution for p_6, the key parameter of interest. The marginal distributions for each p parameter from a Dirichlet distribution are beta distributions and can be obtained as

$$f(p_i|P, \alpha, Y) \propto p_i^{\alpha_i - 1}(1 - p_i)^{(\sum \alpha - \alpha_i) - 1}, \qquad (3.35)$$

where $\sum \alpha$ is just the sum of all α parameters in the posterior (here, 16). The marginal posterior distribution for p_6 is thus a Beta(4,12) distribution just as it was previously when the beta distribution prior had parameters $\alpha = 1$ and $\beta = 5$. This leads to the same options for summarization discussed above. Furthermore, the variances of the p parameters in the Dirichlet are equivalent to those of the marginal beta distributions.

The Dirichlet posterior offers additional possibilities for summarizing what we know about P. The initial question was whether the die was weighted to come up 6 more often than it should if the die were fair. Other questions might be whether the die is weighted to come up 6 more often than any other number and whether the other sides of the die are underweighted. Figure 3.3 shows the marginal posterior beta distributions for each p. The density plots shown in the figure were obtained by sampling directly from the Dirichlet distribution with the appropriate parameters, a process we will discuss in detail in the next chapters. There are only three densities shown in the figure, but this is because several are equivalent.

The vertical reference line in the figure is at 1/6, the value expected for each p if the die were fair. The posteriors for p_3 and p_4 appear to be close to being centered over 1/6, while the posteriors for p_1, p_2, and p_5 appear to be centered at a lower value. p_6 is, as before, centered above 1/6. The probability that the die is weighted is .77, as it was above under the Beta(1,5) prior. The probabilities that the other values of the die—from 1 to 5—are underweighted are .74, .74, .47, .47, and .74, respectively (obtained as the proportion of each density to the left of 1/6). These results suggest that 3 and 4 are just about as likely to be overweighted as underweighted, while 1, 2, and 5 are most likely underweighted. All in all, the results suggest that the die is probably not fair but instead favors rolling a 6.

A final summary measure that may be useful to consider is the probability that each die face is weighted relative to the others. That is, what is the

50

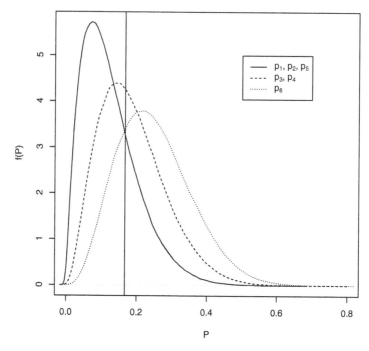

Figure 3.3 Dirichlet posterior distribution for *P* vector in the die-rolling example (or, equivalently, corresponding marginal beta distributions). Several marginal posterior are identical.

probability that Side 1 has a greater chance of occurring than 2, 3, 4, 5, and 6; Side 2 has a greater chance of occurring than 1, 3, 4, 5, and 6; and so on. These probabilities are difficult to compute analytically but are very easy to compute from samples from the posterior distribution—and we will perform such calculations throughout subsequent examples. Those probabilities are .07, .07, .19, .19, .07, and .40 for the six sides in order. This result suggests that, if any side is weighted, it is most likely 6, given it has a probability more than twice as large as any other side of being the most probable side to come up. This probability may seem low, but even if one side is twice as likely to come up as it should (implying a probability of 4/30 for each of the other sides), the probability of obtaining something other than a 6 on a given roll is $1 - (2/6) = .67$.

Normal Distribution Examples

The beta distribution is a useful starting point for learning about the Bayesian approach and the use of prior distributions because of its univariate form, and the Dirichlet distribution is useful because, although it is multivariate, the outcome in each dimension is binary. However, one-parameter models are rare in social science: Most of our models involve many continuous parameters (e.g., regression models). Although the Dirichlet distribution is multivariate, it does not exhibit some of the complexities of other multivariate distributions, because the marginal distributions are all beta distributions. Most common multiparameter models contain a mix of parameters that have differing forms for their marginal distributions and also may involve differing forms for their priors. In this section, I highlight the use of priors in a common two-parameter model—the normal distribution. The normal distribution has two parameters, a mean (μ) and a variance (σ^2). Interest generally centers on the mean, with the variance being a nuisance parameter. We will consider subsequent examples in this volume in which this usual case is true but also cases in which the variance itself is also of interest.

Most introductory-level Bayesian texts offer several normal distribution examples, including one in which μ is unknown but σ^2 is known or fixed, one in which μ is known or fixed while σ^2 is unknown, and one in which both parameters are considered to be unknown (e.g., Gelman et al., 2013). The latter is the most realistic case in social science research: We rarely know either parameter. Although all three types of examples are useful for thinking about priors in multiparameter models, we will only consider cases in which σ^2 is known versus unknown; we will assume μ is always unknown. We will start with examples in which σ^2 is assumed to be known.

Returning to the question posed at the beginning of the volume, is the United States a "center-right" country politically? If so, has this always been the case? Does the answer depend on exactly what is measured? For example, the word "liberal" is argued to have developed a negative connotation over the Reagan years, so people may be less inclined to call themselves "liberal" now than in previous decades. At the same time, however, actual political positions on issues such as government spending and cultural issues may have trended toward the liberal end of the political spectrum, leading to increased acceptance of the term "liberal" (Massey, 2005).

As described in Chapter 1, the GSS asks a number of questions about political views in each year of the survey, which I have combined into four measures with ranges from 0 to 6: a measure of ideological leaning (liberal = 0 to conservative = 6), a measure of party affiliation (strong Democrat = 0 to strong Republican = 6), an index of cultural views, and an index of economic views (both measured from liberal = 0 to conservative = 6). I have summed the former two measures to create an index of political identification and the latter two measures to create an index of actual political positions, each with a range from 0 to 12. Histograms of the measures suggest that the collection of responses across all years appears to be approximately normal. Thus, let's assume the data in each survey year arise from a normal distribution with a mean μ and variance σ^2. The likelihood function (sampling density) for a sample of size n of normally distributed measures is

$$L(Y|\mu, \sigma^2) = \prod_{i=1}^{n} \frac{1}{\sqrt{2\pi\sigma^2}} \exp\left\{ -\frac{(y_i - \mu)^2}{2\sigma^2} \right\} \tag{3.36}$$

$$f(Y|\mu, \sigma^2) \propto (\sigma^2)^{-n/2} \exp\left\{ -\frac{\sum_{i=1}^{n}(y_i - \mu)^2}{2\sigma^2} \right\}, \tag{3.37}$$

where Y is a vector representing all the data, $y_1 \dots y_n$, and $f(.)$ is used in place of $L(.)$ in the second equation to indicate that, while $L(.)$ is a function and not a density, it can be renormalized as a joint distribution for the data.

We can use this likelihood to model the identification and position measures at multiple points in time. Here, we will consider five decades: the 1970s, the 1980s, the 1990s, the 2000s, and the 2010s. What remains for us to model the means and variances in each decade is to specify a prior for μ and σ^2. We will consider two priors in the case in which σ^2 is assumed to be known. If σ^2 is known, we only need a prior for μ. If we have no prior information, we may use a uniform prior over the real line: $f(\mu) \propto c$. This is an improper prior but will produce a proper posterior when combined with the normal likelihood. Under that prior, we obtain a posterior that is proportional to the likelihood. In order to determine the form of the posterior distribution for μ, it is necessary to expand the quadratic within the exponential (Equation 3.40), rearrange terms and complete the square in μ (Equation 3.41), and group terms and discard proportionality constants (Equation 3.42):

$$f(\mu|Y, \sigma^2) \propto f(\mu)f(Y|\mu, \sigma^2) \tag{3.38}$$

$$\propto c \times (\sigma^2)^{-n/2} \exp\left\{ -\frac{\sum_{i=1}^{n}(y_i - \mu)^2}{2\sigma^2} \right\} \tag{3.39}$$

$$\propto \exp\left\{ -\frac{\sum y^2 - 2\mu \sum y + \sum \mu^2}{2\sigma^2} \right\} \tag{3.40}$$

$$\propto \exp\left\{ -\frac{n\mu^2 - 2n\bar{y}\mu - n\bar{y}^2 + n\bar{y}^2}{2\sigma^2} \right\} \tag{3.41}$$

$$\propto \exp\left\{ -\frac{(\mu - \bar{y})^2}{\frac{\sigma^2}{n}} \right\}. \tag{3.42}$$

The result shows that the posterior distribution for μ is normal with a mean equal to the sample mean for y and a variance equal to σ^2/n. This result is reminiscent of the classical central limit theorem, which states that means from repeated samples of size n are distributed normally around the population mean with a variance of σ^2/n. However, in the Bayesian paradigm, μ is considered to be the random variable, while the observed data are considered fixed once observed. A posterior summary can be easily obtained by reporting the sample mean and the quantity σ^2/n and/or by constructing an interval estimate using the quantiles of the normal distribution.

A second, common alternative prior for μ is a normal distribution with a mean of M and a variance of τ:

$$f(\mu|M,\tau) \propto \frac{1}{\sqrt{\tau}}\exp\left\{-\frac{(\mu-M)^2}{2\tau}\right\}. \tag{3.43}$$

This prior says that μ is most likely M, but we have enough uncertainty about it that it could differ from M within a reasonable range reflected by τ. If we are confident that μ is close to M, then τ should be chosen to be small. In contrast, if we are not confident about μ, then τ should be chosen to be large. In the limit, as $\tau \to \infty$, this prior is equivalent to the uniform prior above, because the distribution flattens and widens as τ increases. If we combine this prior with the normal likelihood function, we obtain

$$f(\mu|Y,\sigma^2) \propto f(\mu)f(Y|\mu,\sigma^2) \tag{3.44}$$

$$\propto \tau^{-1/2}\exp\left\{-\frac{(\mu-M)^2}{2\tau}\right\}(\sigma^2)^{-n/2}\exp\left\{-\frac{\sum_{i=1}^{n}(y_i-\mu)^2}{2\sigma^2}\right\} \tag{3.45}$$

$$\propto \exp\left\{-\frac{1}{2}\left[\frac{(\mu-M)^2}{\tau}+\frac{\sum(y-\mu)^2}{\sigma^2}\right]\right\} \tag{3.46}$$

$$\propto \exp\left\{-\frac{1}{2}\left[\frac{\mu^2-2M\mu}{\tau}+\frac{-2n\bar{y}\mu+n\mu^2}{\sigma^2}\right]\right\} \tag{3.47}$$

$$\propto \exp\left\{-\frac{1}{2}\left[\frac{\sigma^2\mu^2-2\sigma^2M\mu-2\tau n\bar{y}\mu+\tau n\mu^2}{\tau\sigma^2}\right]\right\} \tag{3.48}$$

$$\propto \exp\left\{-\frac{1}{2}\left[\frac{(\sigma^2+n\tau)\mu^2-2(\sigma^2M+\tau n\bar{y})\mu}{\tau\sigma^2}\right]\right\} \tag{3.49}$$

$$\propto \exp\left\{-\frac{1}{2}\left[\frac{\left(\mu-\frac{\sigma^2M+\tau n\bar{y}}{\sigma^2+n\tau}\right)^2}{\frac{\tau\sigma^2}{\sigma^2+n\tau}}\right]\right\}, \tag{3.50}$$

where, as before, we must perform some algebraic gymnastics to put the posterior distribution into a recognizable form. In order to conserve space, I eliminated the hyperparameters M and τ from the conditional expression on the left in the first equation above. In Equation 3.46, I combined terms under the exponential. In Equation 3.47, I expanded the quadratic terms and dropped proportionality constants (i.e., terms that do not involve μ). In Equation 3.48, I obtained a common denominator and summed the terms within the exponential. In Equation 3.49, I grouped terms involving μ by their exponent, completed the square in μ, and dropped proportionality constants. Finally, in Equation 3.50, I divided the numerator and denominator through by the term preceding μ^2 and rewrote the numerator as a quadratic form. Thus, under this prior, the posterior for μ is shown to be normal with a mean of $M_{new} = (\sigma^2 M + \tau n\bar{y})/(\sigma^2 + n\tau)$ and a variance of $\tau_{new} = \tau\sigma^2/(\sigma^2 + n\tau)$. Thus, the hyperparameters M and τ have been updated and can be used in a future prior.

Some inspection of this mean and variance reveals that the posterior mean is a weighted compromise between the prior mean and data mean, where the weighting is determined by the relative magnitude of the known data variance, σ^2, and the prior variance for μ, τ. In the extreme case in which $\tau = 0$, the posterior mean reduces to M and the posterior variance reduces to 0. That is, the value of μ is known exactly to be M, which is implied by a prior variance of 0 around the prior mean.

In the case in which τ is infinite, the posterior mean reduces to $\bar{y}$ and the posterior variance is σ^2/n. This can be found by taking the limit of the term within the exponential (ignoring the $-1/2$):

$$\lim_{\tau \to \infty} \frac{\left(\mu - \frac{\sigma^2 M + \tau n\bar{y}}{\sigma^2 + n\tau}\right)^2}{\frac{\tau\sigma^2}{\sigma^2 + n\tau}} = \lim_{\tau \to \infty} \frac{\left(\mu - \frac{\sigma^2 M/\tau + \tau n\bar{y}/\tau}{\sigma^2/\tau + n\tau/\tau}\right)^2}{\tau\sigma^2/\tau} \tag{3.51}$$

$$= \frac{\left(\mu - \frac{0 + n\bar{y}}{0 + n}\right)^2}{\sigma^2/(0 + n)} \tag{3.52}$$

$$= \frac{(\mu - \bar{y})^2}{\sigma^2/n}. \tag{3.53}$$

Thus, as mentioned above, if we have no prior information, using this prior with a large τ is equivalent to using the uniform prior. Importantly, we can also take limits to see what happens as $n \to \infty$. Following the same strategy as used in Equation 3.51, we can divide every fractional term's numerators and denominators by n and take the limit to obtain $(\mu - \bar{y})^2/0$. This result is undefined, but it is clear that the posterior variance shrinks toward 0 as

n increases, implying that μ is exactly $\bar{y}$. This contextualizes my claim earlier in the chapter that the data tend to dominate the prior in social science research with large samples—in this case, regardless of the prior mean and (nonzero) prior variance, a large sample size will overwhelm the prior distribution.

We rarely, if ever, know σ^2 if we do not know μ in social science. A more realistic scenario is one in which we need a joint prior for both parameters: $f(\mu, \sigma^2)$. There are many ways one can construct such a prior. One approach is to assume μ and σ^2 are independent in their priors so that $f(\mu, \sigma^2) = f(\mu)f(\sigma^2)$. Then, assuming we have little or no prior knowledge about these parameters, we may choose an improper uniform prior as before for μ along with the prior we derived for σ^2 previously by assuming a uniform prior on $\ln(\sigma^2)$ and transforming back to σ^2, so that $f(\sigma^2) \propto 1/\sigma^2$. In that case, the posterior distribution is

$$f(\mu, \sigma^2 | Y) \propto f(\mu)f(\sigma^2)f(Y | \mu, \sigma^2) \tag{3.54}$$

$$\propto c \times (1/\sigma^2) \times (\sigma^2)^{-n/2} \exp\left\{ -\frac{\sum_{i=1}^{n}(y_i - \mu)^2}{2\sigma^2} \right\} \tag{3.55}$$

$$\propto (\sigma^2)^{-(n/2+1)} \exp\left\{ -\frac{\sum y^2 - 2n\mu\bar{y} + n\mu^2}{2\sigma^2} \right\} \tag{3.56}$$

$$\propto (\sigma^2)^{-(n/2+1)} \exp\left\{ -\frac{n\mu^2 - 2n\mu\bar{y} + n\bar{y}^2 + \sum y^2 - n\bar{y}^2}{2\sigma^2} \right\} \tag{3.57}$$

$$\propto (\sigma^2)^{-(n/2+1)} \exp\left\{ -\frac{n(\mu - \bar{y})^2 + (n-1)s^2}{2\sigma^2} \right\}, \tag{3.58}$$

where the last lines follow from completing the square as we did above (by adding and subtracting $n\bar{y}^2$) and recognizing that $\sum y^2 - n\bar{y}^2$ is the numerator of the "computational form" of the sample variance, s^2. If σ^2 were assumed to be known, then the latter term in the numerator could be extracted as a proportionality constant, and we would have the same result as earlier, in Equation 3.42.

An alternative to assuming that μ and σ^2 are independent in their priors is to assume that μ depends on σ^2 in some way and use the joint probability rule for nonindependent events to establish a joint prior: $f(\mu, \sigma^2) = f(\mu | \sigma^2)f(\sigma^2)$. In this case, we might assume a normal distribution prior for μ: $\mu | \sigma^2 \sim N(M, \sigma^2/n_0)$. Next, we might assume an inverse gamma prior for σ^2: $\sigma^2 \sim IG(\alpha, \beta)$, so that

$$f(\sigma^2) \propto (\sigma^2)^{-(\alpha+1)} \exp\left\{ -\frac{\beta}{\sigma^2} \right\}. \tag{3.59}$$

The joint prior is then the product of the normal prior for μ and this prior for σ^2. This prior recognizes the implicit dependence between τ and σ^2, which the normal prior that treated σ^2 as known ignored. That τ and σ^2 are related is suggested by the central limit theorem: because the variance of sample means is σ^2/n, our uncertainty about the value of μ should be related to σ^2. If we therefore use σ^2/n_0 as our value for τ, n_0 effectively represents how much our prior information about μ's value (i.e., M) is "worth" in terms of prior observations (i.e., a previous sample or collection of samples).

Under this prior, the posterior is

$$f(\mu, \sigma^2|Y) \propto f(\sigma^2)f(\mu|\sigma^2)f(Y|\mu, \sigma^2) \tag{3.60}$$

$$\propto (\sigma^2)^{-(\alpha+1)} \exp\left\{-\frac{\beta}{\sigma^2}\right\} \times (\sigma^2/n_0)^{-1/2} \exp\left\{-\frac{(\mu-M)^2}{2\sigma^2/n_0}\right\}$$

$$\times (\sigma^2)^{-n/2} \exp\left\{-\frac{\sum_{i=1}^{n}(y_i-\mu)^2}{2\sigma^2}\right\}$$

$$\tag{3.61}$$

$$\propto \frac{1}{(\sigma^2)^{\alpha+3/2+n/2}} \exp\left\{-\frac{2\beta + n_0(\mu-M)^2 + \sum_{i=1}^{n}(y_i-\mu)^2}{2\sigma^2}\right\}. \tag{3.62}$$

This posterior can be simplified somewhat, but it is ultimately a bivariate density for μ and σ^2. If we were to complete the square in μ, we would find that the updated (posterior) mean for μ is again a weighted average of the prior mean and the data mean. Indeed, the posterior mean is

$$\bar{\mu} = \frac{n_0 M + n\bar{y}}{n_0 + n}. \tag{3.63}$$

However, the distribution for μ is no longer normal, because σ^2 is not fixed. The *conditional* distributions for μ are normal (i.e., for fixed values of σ^2), but the *marginal* distribution for μ is not. Instead, we must integrate the bivariate posterior distribution over σ^2 to obtain the marginal distribution for μ: that is, $f(\mu|y) = \int f(\mu, \sigma^2|y)d\sigma^2$. If we do so, we will find that the marginal distribution for μ is a t-distribution (Gelman et al., 2013). Performing this integration analytically, while neither simple nor terribly difficult, is not necessary, however, if one uses the sampling methods discussed in the next chapter, as we will see. The nonnecessity of performing this integration, in fact, is a *key reason* for the explosion in the use of Bayesian statistics over the past few decades.

Table 3.1 displays the posterior means and standard deviations for the political identification and positions variables described earlier, based on the

Priors/Models

	(1)	(2)	(3)	(4)
$\mu \sim$	$U(-\infty,\infty)$	$N(M=6, \tau=.5^2)$	$U(-\infty,\infty)$	$N(M=6, \frac{\sigma^2}{n_0=100})$
$\sigma^2 \sim$	known	known	$1/\sigma^2$	$IG(\alpha=1, \beta=1)$
See Equation:	3.42	3.50	3.58	3.62
Identification				
1970s	5.5 (.031)	5.5 (.031)	5.5 (.031)	5.5 (.031)
1980s	5.8 (.032)	5.8 (.032)	5.8 (.032)	5.8 (.032)
1990s	6.0 (.036)	6.0 (.036)	6.0 (.037)	6.0 (.036)
2000s	5.9 (.042)	5.9 (.042)	5.9 (.042)	5.9 (.041)
2010s	5.8 (.044)	5.8 (.044)	5.8 (.044)	5.8 (.044)
Positions				
1970s	6.5 (.021)	6.5 (.021)	6.5 (.021)	6.5 (.021)
1980s	6.4 (.019)	6.4 (.019)	6.4 (.020)	6.4 (.020)
1990s	6.1 (.021)	6.1 (.021)	6.1 (.021)	6.1 (.021)
2000s	5.8 (.024)	5.8 (.024)	5.8 (.025)	5.8 (.024)
2010s	5.6 (.028)	5.6 (.028)	5.6 (.028)	5.6 (.028)

Table 3.1 Results of normal distribution models for political identification and positions. 1974–2016 GSS data. The results in the table are the posterior mean and its standard deviation. Posterior summaries for σ^2 are not shown in the table.

four models above. In Models 1 and 2 in which σ^2 is assumed to be known, I treated the sample variance in each era as the "known" value. In Model 1, I assumed a flat, improper uniform prior for μ. In Model 2, I assumed a normal distribution prior for μ and set the hyperparameters M and τ to 6 and .25 (.5^2), respectively, reflecting my prior belief that the country is (and always has been) centrist on average but may lean slightly left or right at any given point in time. Specifically, 6 is the midpoint of both the identification and positions variables, but I am willing to assume that the mean of the country may be reasonably within $\pm$ 1 point of this value. Model 3 uses a uniform prior for μ and the reference prior for the variance, thus requiring no set values for any hyperparameters. Finally, in Model 4, I set $M = 6$, $\alpha = 1$, $\beta = 1$, and $n_0 = 100$. These values indicate that I have little prior information regarding the value of σ^2 and that my prior value for μ is worth about 100 prior cases. The results for Models 1 and 2 were obtained via direct calculation based on the equations for the posterior mean and variance shown above. The results for Models 3 and 4 were obtained via Gibbs sampling, rather than by direct computation performed on the appropriate marginal t-distributions. Gibbs sampling, and its advantages, will be discussed in the next chapter.

The table shows that, regardless of the chosen prior, the posterior means for μ are equal in all cases to the first decimal place (within decades). Furthermore, the posterior standard deviations for μ are also nearly equal in all cases to the third decimal place. At most, the posterior standard deviations differ in the thousandths place in a couple of models. Other alternative prior specifications were tried, but so long as the priors are relatively uninformative, the sample sizes are large enough to drown out their influence so that results did not vary from those presented.

Substantively, the results show two very different trends for identification and positions across the five decades. The mean for political identification was below the index's midpoint of 6 in the 1970s, increased to the midpoint in the 1990s, and fell after but has not returned to its 1970s level (5.8 in the 2010s vs. 5.5 in the 1970s). In contrast, the mean for political positions began to the right of the midpoint of the index in the 1970s (6.5) but has fallen every decade since, to 5.6 in the most recent decade. It should be noted that, although there is a true midpoint for the identification index, there is no true midpoint for the positions index. That is, the identification variable has symmetric response categories with neither conservative nor liberal and neither Republican nor Democrat as the middle values. In contrast, the positions variables ask about views on cultural issues and government spending priorities. The index of these items has no meaningful midpoint. However, values in each decade can be compared with those of earlier decades, and the results show clear trending toward more "liberal" positions over the span of the GSS.

The results suggest that there may be a discrepancy between what people claim their political views are and what their actual policy positions are, although it is not possible to determine that by examining these macro-level trends. This issue will be explored in more depth in Chapter 5. At the macro level, we can assess whether changes in the means of identification and positions are "significant" or meaningful in some way. A classical approach to addressing this question might involve conducting t-tests to compare means across decades. A Bayesian approach may involve simply computing the probability that the means of each index in decades subsequent to the 1970s are larger or smaller than their means in 1970. This computation can be performed by drawing N values of μ from its marginal posterior distribution in each decade and comparing them across decades. For example, if we wish to compute the probability that the mean value of political identification in the 1980s is more conservative than the mean of identification in the 1970s, we can draw a value for the mean in the 1970s from its posterior and likewise for the 1980s and assess which is larger. The proportion of draws in which $\mu_{80s} > \mu_{70s}$ is the probability that the mean of identification is more conservative in the 1980s than in the 1970s. Alternatively, we may compare the probabilities that the mean in each decade is above or below some meaningful value, such as the midpoint of an index.

Table 3.2 shows three sets of probabilities, based on the Gibbs sampling results for Model 4. The first column shows the probability that the mean of political identification and positions in each era is below the midpoint of these indexes (6). The probability that the mean of identification is below the midpoint of the index is 1 or nearly so in all decades but the 1990s, when the probability is .48. This indicates that the country's mean political identity has almost certainly leaned to the left in all decades except the 1990s. In contrast, the probability that the mean political position is below the midpoint of the index was 0 for the first three decades but then 1 for the latter two decades, suggesting a change in mean political position at least after the 1990s.

As we discussed above, the political positions index has no clear center point, because whether a set of positions regarding cultural and economic policies is considered liberal or conservative depends to some extent on historical context. For example, support for interracial marriage (not measured in the index) might be considered the "liberal" view historically but is surely considered the mainstream view today. Thus, determining whether the United States has moved toward the left or right requires that we compare positions across time with some decade as an anchor/reference point. The second column of the table shows the probability that the mean in each subsequent decade is less than it was in the 1970s. This probability is 0 for all decades for the identification index, indicating that the mean identification is more conservative now than it was in the 1970s, even if, as the pattern in the posterior means shows, there was an inflection in the 1990s. In contrast, the probability that political positions are to the left of what they were in the 1970s is .91 for the 1980s and 1 for the subsequent decades. Together, these results suggest significant and opposite trends for political identification and positions over the past five decades. While the average political identity is

Posterior Probabilities

Era	$p(\mu < 6)$	$p(\mu_t < \mu_{1970})$	$p(\sigma_t^2 > \sigma_{1970}^2)$
Identification			
1970s	1	NA	NA
1980s	1	0	1
1990s	.48	0	1
2000s	.99	0	1
2010s	1	0	1
Position			
1970s	0	NA	NA
1980s	0	.91	0
1990s	0	1	0
2000s	1	1	.41
2010s	1	1	1

Table 3.2 Probabilities that (column 1) the mean of the identification/position indexes is below the midpoint of each index in each decade, (column 2) the mean of the identification/position variables is below the mean in 1970s, and (column 3) the variance of the indexes is larger than their counterparts in the 1970s.

more conservative now than in the earliest decade, actual political positions are more liberal than they were in the earliest decade.

The third column of Table 3.2 shows probabilities that the variance parameter, σ^2, is larger in each decade subsequent to the 1970s. As we discussed earlier in this chapter, the variance parameter is often not of interest in normal distribution problems. However, change in σ^2 over time indicates something about whether political identities and positions are becoming more or less diverse over time. As we will discuss in Chapter 5, political polarization could be modeled as a bifurcation in a normal distribution evolving over time as two-component distributions emerge and separate from an original, single distribution. We might first find some evidence of this process by seeing a growing variance in a single distribution. As the table shows, the probabilities that the variances in political identification are larger in decades subsequent to the 1970s are 1 in each decade. For positions, the probabilities that the variances are larger than that in the 1970s are 0 for the 1980s and 1990s, .41 for the 2000s, and 1 for the 2010s. This result indicates that there is growing variance in political positions over time and suggests that there may be growing political polarization based on positions, despite the fact that society as a whole has trended toward the left in its political positions.

The analysis of the means and variances of political identification and positions by decade is a good start toward understanding whether American society is becoming more politically polarized, but it raises numerous subsequent questions. For example, within the index of political positions, have economic and cultural positions both become more liberal over time? Is there a growing correlation between the two types of positions? Within the index for political identification, have the terms "liberal" and "conservative" become increasingly or decreasingly related to the terms "Democrat" and "Republican?" Although the mean for identification has trended rightward and then leftward, while the mean for positions has trended steadily leftward, has the relationship between identification and positions strengthened or weakened? Is the fact that the variance in both identification and positions seems to have grown over time due to an increasing spread of a unimodal distribution, or it is because what was a unimodal distribution is separating into two distinct distributions, thus providing evidence for polarization?

Answering these questions requires more sophisticated models than the univariate normal distribution with two parameters can address. The added modeling complexity, in turn, necessitates the use of more sophisticated methods in order to produce summaries of posterior distributions. As we will see in the next chapter, however, these methods are reasonably easy and fast to implement with contemporary computers and software, and they open up a large array of possibilities for more realistic modeling of data, more informative summaries, and more thorough assessments of model fit and comparison than classical methods provide.

CHAPTER 4. MARKOV CHAIN MONTE CARLO (MCMC) SAMPLING METHODS

In the last chapter, I showed some simple models that are typical in presentations of the Bayesian approach. The models were simplistic compared to those used in modern social science research but were discussed in part because Bayesian statistics involves mathematical manipulation of distributions, which is unfamiliar to many social scientists without a background in mathematical statistics. But, I also started with simpler examples because deriving posterior distributions and computing posterior quantities in simpler models is relatively easy in models with one or two parameters.

While the mathematics of Bayesian analysis has likely been an impediment to the widespread adoption of the approach in social science, computation perhaps has been a more limiting factor. The development of sampling methods to conduct Bayesian analyses in the 1990s, and the incorporation of these sampling methods into mainstream social science data analysis packages over the past several years, has made the Bayesian approach more feasible and attractive to social scientists.

This chapter will discuss, in detail, contemporary Bayesian computation using MCMC methods. First, I will show that summaries of distributions can be made by sampling from them and computing summary statistics using the samples. These summary measures are typically integrals of a probability distribution, and sampling methods can substitute for analytic integration. The rejection sampler will then be introduced as a steppingstone toward more flexible approaches to sampling from complex distributions. Next, we will discuss key ideas about Markov processes and chains and then describe the general Metropolis algorithm. The Metropolis algorithm will then be generalized with the incorporation of the Hastings ratio in a description of the independence sampler—a basic Metropolis–Hastings algorithm. The Gibbs sampler will be developed and illustrated as a special case of the Metropolis–Hastings algorithm. Finally, the slice sampler will be introduced as a general sampling approach. Although most of the subsequent examples in this volume will involve Gibbs sampling, it is important to discuss these other sampling strategies, because (1) not all problems lend themselves to Gibbs sampling, and (2) all of these approaches, in theory, can be used to achieve the same goal: producing samples of parameters from their joint posterior distributions.

In this chapter, we will also discuss the importance of, and methods for, evaluating algorithm performance. This is a feature of Bayesian statistics that necessarily and substantially differentiates Bayesian and classical analyses. Contemporary statistical software packages commonly used by social scientists have built-in procedures to provide parameter and standard error estimates for the most common models used in our research. Statisticians and programmers have derived generic likelihood functions for the most common models used, performed the differential calculus necessary to obtain estimates from them, and programmed algorithms to find them. Most of these algorithms ("procedures") have built-in checks to monitor convergence (e.g., "tolerance limits"), methods to compensate for errors in numerical procedures (e.g., "exception handling"), and ways to report when estimates cannot be obtained (e.g., "crashing" and printing "does not converge"). Until recently, there were few canned procedures to conduct Bayesian analyses, and even the early such packages required extensive user input. Even with the development of Bayesian procedures in contemporary software packages, more effort is required to conduct Bayesian analyses, because integration using sampling methods requires that algorithms converge to a *distribution* rather than a *point*, as we will discuss.

Logic of Sampling to Summarize Distributions

Classical statistical analyses involving maximum likelihood estimation produce estimates of parameters and uncertainty in them using a combination of differential calculus applied to the likelihood function and asymptotic theory and assumptions about sampling distributions. In contrast, the Bayesian approach requires a fair amount of integral calculus to produce summaries of posterior distributions. Table 4.1 lists some of the most common posterior summary measures for a generic parameter, θ. For example, the posterior mean is a common summary measure of θ, and it is an integral over the posterior distribution. As the table shows, the posterior variance is also an integral, as are various quantiles, such as the median and bounds on interval estimates. We used each of these summary measures in the previous chapter.

Further, whereas the classical approach requires *partial differentiation* of the likelihood function to obtain estimates in multiparameter models, many summaries in the Bayesian approach require *multiple integration* of the posterior distribution over (possibly nuisance) parameters. For example, suppose our posterior distribution is $f(\theta_1, \theta_2, \theta_3 | y)$, but we are only interested in summaries for θ_1. In that case, the marginal posterior distribution for θ_1 would be obtained as $f(\theta_1 | y) = \int_{\theta_2} \int_{\theta_3} f(\theta_1, \theta_2, \theta_3 | y) d\theta_3 d\theta_2$.

Analytic integration is often difficult and sometimes impossible, especially in high dimensions. For example, even the univariate normal density

Summary	Integral
Posterior mean	$\mu(\theta) = \int_\theta \theta f(\theta\|y)d\theta$
Posterior variance	$V(\theta) = \int_\theta (\theta - \mu_\theta)^2 f(\theta\|y)d\theta$
Median	$M = x : \int_{-\infty}^x f(\theta\|y)d\theta = .5$
2.5th percentile	$Q(.025) = x : \int_{-\infty}^x f(\theta\|y)d\theta = .025$
97.5th percentile	$Q(.975) = x : \int_{-\infty}^x f(\theta\|y)d\theta = .975$
General quantile	$Q(p) = x : \int_{-\infty}^x f(\theta\|y)d\theta = p$

Table 4.1 Common summary measures of posterior distributions used in Bayesian analyses.

has no simple, direct analytic integral over x. Fortunately, by the same token that sample statistics can be used to estimate population parameters, we can use samples from a posterior distribution to approximate the integrals that are of interest for summarizing it. For example, suppose we are interested in summarizing our knowledge of θ from a posterior distribution $f(\theta|y)$ using the posterior mean $\mu(\theta)$. If we can sample a sequence of values for θ (say $\theta_1 \ldots \theta_n$) from the distribution and compute $\bar{\theta}$, we can use $\bar{\theta}$ as an estimate of $\mu(\theta)$, using the usual sample computation $\bar{\theta} = \sum \theta/n$. As the classical central limit theorem tells us, $\bar{\theta}$ can be made arbitrarily close to $\mu(\theta)$ by simply taking a larger sample from $f(\theta|y)$.

In some cases, sampling from posterior distributions is simple. In our die-rolling example from the previous chapter, for example, we can directly sim-

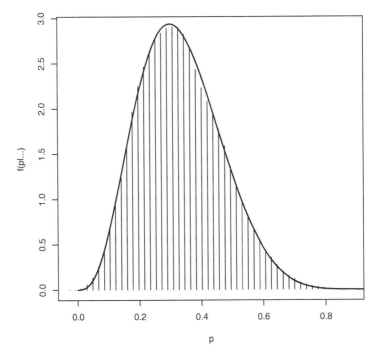

Figure 4.1 Samples from the Beta(4, 8) distribution (bars) versus true density function (dark line).

ulate from the Beta(A, B) posterior distribution using preprogrammed, basic commands in software such as R or Stata. For example, in R, we could use the rbeta(n,a,b) function to produce n draws from the posterior distribution. Figure 4.1 shows a comparison of a histogram of 10,000 draws from the Beta(4, 8) distribution with the true density superimposed. As the figure shows, the sample mirrors the density function closely. Table 4.2 shows a comparison of true and sample-based summaries of interest from this beta distribution. As the table indicates, the mean, median, variance, and central interval estimates are nearly identical. Further, the probability that the die is weighted to favor 6—the real question of interest in the example—is almost exactly the same when computed using the proportion of sampled values for p that exceed 1/6 as when computed directly from the beta distribution using pbeta((1/6),4,8,lower.tail=F) in R.

Quantity	True Value	Computed Value From Sample
Mean	.33$\overline{3}$	.333
Median	.324	.324
Variance	.017	.017
95% central interval	[.109, .610]	[.109, .614]
$pr(p > 1/6)$	.904	.907

Table 4.2 True versus sample-based summaries of the Beta(4, 8) distribution.

A Simple Method for When Direct Simulation Is Impossible

In the beta distribution example, direct simulation was straightforward. In many if not most cases, however, it is difficult or impossible to sample directly from a distribution. For example, the correlation parameter, ρ, in a bivariate normal distribution has no known distribution. Thus, we cannot directly simulate from it. Instead, other methods must be employed. We will discuss rejection sampling as one such method before turning to more sophisticated strategies, some of which include elements of rejection sampling in their approach.

Rejection sampling is a two-step method in which a *candidate* value is proposed as having come from the density of interest (the "target distribution") and then it is evaluated for acceptance/rejection. First, the candidate, c, is generated from a distribution, $g(x)$, that is easy to simulate from and can be made to envelop the target density, $f(x)$. That is, the envelope density can be multiplied by a constant, k, so that its height is greater than that of the target density at all points (i.e., $k \times g(x) > f(x), \forall x$). Because all that is required is that the envelope fully cover the target density, it does not matter whether $f(x)$ is normalized: It simply affects the value of k required for $k \times g(x)$ to cover $f(x)$. Second, c is evaluated to determine whether it should be accepted or rejected as a draw from the target distribution, based on a random uniform draw, u, on the interval between 0 and $k \times g(c)$. If $u < f(c)$, then c is accepted as coming from $f(x)$; if $u > f(c)$, c is rejected. This two-step process is repeated until one has obtained a desired number of samples from the distribution.

To illustrate the rejection sampler, consider Figure 4.2. The contrived target density shown in the figure is bimodal, and its domain is restricted to the [0,1] interval. We can envelop this density with a $U(0,1)$ density that is scaled to be twice as tall as usual ($k = 2$); this envelope is shown as a dashed horizontal line in the figure. In the first step of the rejection sampler, we select a draw $c \sim U(0,1)$. This process is illustrated with the bolded line labeled "draw 1" at the bottom of the figure. For this illustration, say that value is $c = .75$, as labeled in the figure. In the second step, we sample a uniform draw, u, along the bolded vertical segment labeled "draw 2" from 0 to $k \times g(c)$ (i.e., between 0 and 2). The figure shows two such sam-

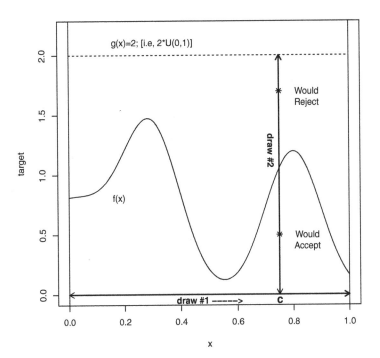

Figure 4.2 Rejection sampling illustration. The arbitrary curve represents the distribution from which we wish to sample. It is bounded on the [0,1] interval. The dashed line toward the top represents the envelope function. Draw #1 (the value c) is a draw from the envelope function; draw #2 is a vertical draw between 0 and the height of the envelope function. Two possible values are noted by asterisks.

pled points (marked with asterisks). If the u that was generated in Step 2 were the higher (larger) value, c would be rejected as coming from $f(x)$; if it were the lower (smaller) value, c would be accepted. We would repeat this propose-accept/reject process until we have obtained as many sampled values as desired.

The rejection sampler is fairly intuitive. One can imagine throwing darts at a dartboard the size of the area bounded by the domain and range of the envelope, $g(x)$ (here, 0 and 1 on the x axis and 0 and $k \times g(x) = 2$ on the y axis), and simply retaining the darts that land under $f(x)$. Despite the intuitive appeal, the rejection sampler is often presented in a less intuitive fashion. For example, the step evaluating whether $u < f(c)$ is often presented as evaluating whether $\frac{f(c)}{k \times g(c)} > u \sim U(0,1)$, but this is the same as asking whether a random uniform draw on $[0, k \times g(c)]$ is less than $f(x)$, as can be seen by multiplying the denominator on the left across the inequality. We will see this similar evaluation step in which a ratio is compared to a uniform draw in other samplers below.

The rejection sampler is easy to understand and use, but it has significant limitations for use as a general method for sampling from posterior distributions without significant modifications. First, it can be difficult to find an envelope for many target distributions. In the example in Figure 4.2, it was easy to find an envelope because the domain of the target density was bounded. Most distributions are not bounded, making finding an envelope that is guaranteed to cover the tails of the target distribution potentially difficult. Second, rejection sampling can be very inefficient. Since both $f(x)$ and $g(x)$ are scalable to be true densities, the area under both of these curves is proportional to 1 by definition. Thus, the constant k, which ensures $g(x)$ is a true envelope of $f(x)$, determines the rejection rate. If k is large, so as to ensure the $g(x)$ envelops $f(x)$ at all points, the rejection rate may be very high, making the rejection sampler incredibly inefficient. Both of these problems with rejection sampling are exacerbated when the target distribution is high dimensional, as is the case for most posterior distributions of interest in social science research. To be fair, the rejection sampler can be adapted to become increasingly efficient (Gilks & Wild, 1992), but adaptive methods are still often more complicated and less efficient than alternative sampling methods.

Markov Processes and Chains

Fortunately, we are not limited to rejection sampling for obtaining samples from posterior distributions. In 1990, Gelfand and Smith published a seminal paper that described some basic methods for sampling from posterior distributions. Since then, the use of these methods— Markov chain Monte Carlo (MCMC) methods—has driven the explosion in the use of the Bayesian approach to statistics.

MCMC methods are general algorithms (systematic, iterative rules) for sampling from potentially high-dimensional distributions. The name "MCMC" derives from the use of Markov process theory in developing random sampling ("Monte Carlo") schemes that produce Markov chains with stationary distributions that are equal to a target distribution. There are numerous MCMC methods; indeed, many of the advances in Bayesian statistics over the past few decades have been in the development of increasingly efficient MCMC methods for an ever-expanding array of models to which they can be applied.

Although a complete discussion of Markov theory is not possible here, some background information about Markov processes is warranted for an understanding of how MCMC methods work. Here, I will illustrate the basic concepts of MCMC using a finite-space discrete-time Markov process. Suppose there are three "states" (or positions) a unit or object may occupy at different points in time ($s = 1, 2, 3; t = 1, t = 2, \ldots, t = T$) and a collection of probabilities that govern the rate of transitions between the states. A transition probability, p_{ij}, is the probability that, if the unit is in state i at time $t - 1$, it is in state j at time t: Thus, the unit transitions from state i to state j over the time interval with some probability. In general, this process of transitioning can be called a stochastic process. Figure 4.3 depicts this simple, three-state state space with possible transitions. The states are represented with boxes, while the arrows represent the possible transitions.

The collection of all transition probabilities in a state space can be represented in a "(right) stochastic matrix," P. The rows in the matrix reflect the state occupied at time $t - 1$, and the columns represent the state occupied at time t. Thus, the ijth element in the matrix represents the probability of transitioning from state i to state j, and each row of the matrix therefore sums to 1. In this example:

$$P = \begin{bmatrix} p_{11} & p_{12} & p_{13} \\ p_{21} & p_{22} & p_{23} \\ p_{31} & p_{32} & p_{33} \end{bmatrix}. \tag{4.1}$$

What makes a stochastic process such as this one Markovian is that the probability of transitioning from one state to another at a given time depends only on the current state occupied: $p(x_t | x_{t-1}, x_{t-2}, \ldots, x_{t=1}) = p(x_t | x_{t-1})$. Define the initial state of the process as x_1. x_1 could be represented as a

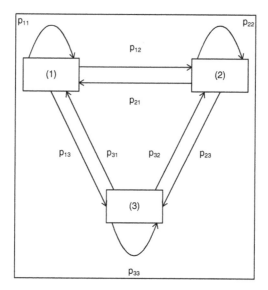

Figure 4.3   A three-state space showing possible transitions over a time interval. Curved arrows reflect staying in a state (retentions).

vector of indicators—for example, $x_1 = [1\,0\,0]$—or it could simply indicate the state (e.g., $x_1 = 1$). The next state of the process is randomly determined based on the relevant transition probabilities. Thus, if $x_1 = 1$, then the chain moves to State 2 with probability p_{12} (i.e., so $x_2 = 2$) and to State 3 with probability p_{13}. The collection of states $x_1 \ldots x_T$ visited over time is called a Markov chain.

If the matrix P does not change over time, the process is said to be "time homogeneous," and the expected state of the chain at any time $t + 1$ can be computed by postmultiplying the vector x_1 by the tth power of P:

$$x_{t+1} = x_1 P^t. \tag{4.2}$$

For each power of t, this multiplication process will yield a vector of probabilities reflecting the probability the unit is in each state at each time point. The limiting distribution of x_t as $t \to \infty$ (if it exists) is called the "stationary distribution" of the Markov chain and reflects that, at some point, the chain may stabilize so that $x_{t+1} = x_t$, where x_{t+1} is a vector representing the proportion of times the chain has visited (and will visit) each state. Importantly, under certain conditions, the stationary distribution does not depend on x_1. Indeed, one may simply take P itself to some large power to obtain the stationary distribution: Each row of P^∞ will contain the stationary distribution.

As an alternative to obtaining the stationary distribution by raising P to a sufficiently high power, one familiar with linear algebra may recognize that finding the stationary distribution can be viewed as an eigendecomposition problem. That is, the stationary distribution is a vector that, when multiplied by a matrix, yields the same vector:

$$Px = \lambda x \qquad (4.3)$$

$$x^T P^T = \lambda x^T. \qquad (4.4)$$

Thus, the left eigenvector of P (or right eigenvector of P^T) that corresponds to the value of $\lambda = 1$ is the unnormalized stationary distribution.

These principles of Markov processes and how they are used in MCMC methods will be illustrated below. Importantly, although the state space in this illustration is finite, state spaces need not be finite (e.g., continuous probability distributions are not finite), and in some applications, transition probability matrices may change over time, making them time-inhomogeneous (e.g., as in multistate demographic methods). However, in order to fix ideas, I will focus here on the simpler, finite case.

Basic Markov Chain Monte Carlo Methods

Raising P to a high power or using an eigendecomposition to find the stationary distribution gives the *expected* stationary distribution of the Markov chain. In application, a *specific* instance of a Markov chain is obtained by placing a unit (e.g., a model parameter) in a specific initial state (i.e., a starting state) and randomly simulating actual transitions for it at successive times (iterations). The collection of states visited by the unit over time (iterations), $x_1 \ldots x_t$, will be the observed Markov chain, and it is that collection that is treated as a sample from a distribution.

Thus, MCMC methods are rules for producing transition probabilities so that the stationary distribution of the implied Markov chain based on these probabilities is the target distribution from which one wishes to sample. The Metropolis algorithm is a basic MCMC algorithm, involving four iterative steps for producing a Markov chain, $\theta_1 \ldots \theta_n$, with a desired stationary distribution, $f(\theta)$. For simplicity, I present these steps as if θ is only one random variable, but this general algorithm is easily extendable to vectors (for multiparameter models) as we will discuss:

1. Select a starting state (value), $\theta_{t=1}$.

2. Increment the counter, t, by 1.

3. Propose a "candidate" value of θ (θ^c) from some distribution, $g(\theta)$ (a "proposal" distribution).

4. Compute the ratio $R = min \left(\frac{f(\theta^c)}{f(\theta_{t-1})}, 1 \right)$ and compare to $u \sim U(0,1)$. If $R > u$, set $\theta_t = \theta^c$ (i.e., accept the candidate). If not, set $\theta_t = \theta_{t-1}$ (i.e., reject the candidate and retain the previous value as the new value).

5. Return to Step 2.

In Step 1, we select an initial value for θ. This value may be a maximum likelihood estimate, a guess at a reasonable value for θ, or a random value. Under MCMC theory, if we follow the rules laid out in Steps 3 and 4, the starting value only matters to the extent that selecting a starting value far from the main support of the target distribution (i.e., the area of the density with the greatest mass, usually the center) may imply a much longer time for the Markov chain to converge to the target distribution.

Once a starting value is selected, an iterative process is followed to generate a sequence of draws from the target distribution (i.e., $\theta_1, \theta_2, \theta_3, \ldots, \theta_n$). Thus, a counter, or index, is incremented in Step 2 to reference the sequence of samples (i.e., the Markov chain). As a side note, this counter is sometimes indexed with t but is often indexed with i or j, which are more commonly used as indexes for loops in programming. Further, in some programming languages, the first position in a vector is indexed with 0, rather than 1, and starting values are often indexed with 0. For the sake of simplicity in counting, and to be consistent between equations and programs, I use 1 as the first value in all counters, but I switch between i, j, and t as index variables.

In Step 3, a candidate value is generated from a proposal distribution, $g(\theta)$, to be considered as the next sampled value from the target distribution. This step is reminiscent of the rejection sampler: The proposal distribution differs from the target distribution (i.e., $g(\theta) \neq f(\theta)$). However, in the Metropolis algorithm, the proposal distribution need not be an envelope of the target distribution, $f(\theta)$. It can be any distribution, but (1) it should be easy to simulate from (that's the whole point—we use these methods when we can't directly simulate from $f(\theta)$), and (2) it must be of such a form that the Markov process implied by the proposal meets several criteria (see Bremáud, 1999). First, the Markov chain must be "irreducible" or "ergodic," meaning it must be able to reach all areas of support in $f(\theta)$ eventually. Specifically, it can visit every location in the target distribution, even if it cannot do so in one step. For example, in the state space represented in Figure 4.3, even if we set $p_{12} = 0$, the chain can visit State 2 from State 1 by first transitioning to State 3. Thus, it cannot reach State 2 in one step, but it can in two steps. Second, the chain must be "recurrent," rather than "transient," meaning it is able to revisit every state, regardless of its current location. For example, in the state space in Figure 4.3, if p_{21} and p_{23} were both 0, the process would be transient, because once the chain entered State 2, it would not be able to leave the state (State 2 would be "absorbing"). Similarly, the process would be transient if p_{21} and p_{31} were both 0, because once the chain left State 1, it could never return to that state. Third, the process must be "aperiodic," meaning that there is no state that can only be visited at regular intervals (such as odd or even values of t). These requirements seem intuitive: A Markov process that cannot visit every location in $f(\theta)$ in proportion to its probability—which would be the case if the process could not visit a state at all, could do so only once, or could do so only at restricted intervals—clearly cannot produce a Markov chain that represents the distribution!

The choice for $g(\theta)$ partially determines the (name of the) specific type of Metropolis algorithm. Here, we will limit discussion to two general Metropolis algorithms: the independence sampler and the random walk Metropolis–Hastings algorithm. In the independence sampler, the proposal distribution must be able to reach all regions of the target distribution immediately from any other state, because the proposal distribution is fixed in place (constant). It need not be an envelope of $f(\theta)$, but it must cover the entire domain of $f(\theta)$. In the random walk Metropolis–Hastings algorithm, the proposal need not be able to reach all regions of the target distribution in one transition, because the proposal shifts location over time/across iterations.

In order to develop some intuition about MCMC methods, consider a discrete probability distribution with three possible values (states)—1, 2, and 3—with probabilities of .6, .3, and .1, respectively. Our goal is to construct a Markov process with a transition probability matrix that has a stationary distribution that reflects these probabilities. That is, we need a transition probability matrix that produces a Markov chain that visits each of the three states in proportion to their probability under the distribution. The state space shown in Figure 4.3 seems appropriate, so long as we establish the "right" values for $p_{11}, p_{12}, \ldots p_{32}, p_{33}$.

Although the distribution above is easy to sample from, assume it isn't. For example, suppose we only have the ability to select values 1, 2, and 3 with equal probability using a three-headed coin (call this $g(\theta)$). We will implement an independence sampler to sample from $f(\theta)$ using $g(\theta)$ as the proposal density. The independence sampler involves a stable proposal distribution (i.e., no matter what the current value of the chain is, the same proposal density is used). Thus:

$$g(\theta) = \begin{cases} 1/3 & \text{iff } \theta \in \{1,2,3\} \\ 0 & \text{otherwise} \end{cases} \tag{4.5}$$

In Step 3 at each iteration of the algorithm, we will randomly propose θ^c to be 1, 2, or 3. In Step 4, we will compute the ratio R based on the proposed value and the previous value of θ. For this example, this computation will produce one of nine different values, based on which of the three states was proposed as θ^c and the current state, θ_{t-1}. Table 4.3 shows these nine values. Given these values, we can produce the transition matrix for the Markov chain whose stationary distribution is the target distribution.

In order to produce this transition probability matrix, we must recognize that the probability of making a particular transition depends on (1) the current state (θ_{t-1}), (2) the candidate state (θ^c), and (3) the probability of proposing the candidate state $g(\theta^c)$. That is, the R ratios shown in Table 4.3 are the probabilities of accepting the candidate, *given that it was proposed and given the current state of the chain*. That is a conditional probability, so that the elements in Table 4.3 do not sum to 1. To obtain transition probabilities, we must incorporate the conditioning.

θ_{t-1}	Proposed θ^c		
	1 ($p = .6$)	2 ($p = .3$)	3 ($p = .1$)
1 ($p = .6$)	$R = \frac{.6}{.6} = \boxed{1}$	$R = \frac{.3}{.6} = \boxed{\frac{1}{2}}$	$R = \frac{.1}{.6} = \boxed{\frac{1}{6}}$
2 ($p = .3$)	$R = \frac{.6}{.3} = \boxed{1}$	$R = \frac{.3}{.3} = \boxed{1}$	$R = \frac{.1}{.3} = \boxed{\frac{1}{3}}$
3 ($p = .1$)	$R = \frac{.6}{.1} = \boxed{1}$	$R = \frac{.3}{.1} = \boxed{1}$	$R = \frac{.1}{.1} = \boxed{1}$

Table 4.3 Possible values of R in a three-state example. Numbers in parentheses are the probabilities for each state under the density. Note that when $R > 1$, it takes the value of 1.

Let Ek represent "ends in (or transitions to) state k at time t," let Pk represent "proposes state k at time t," and let Sk represent "starts in state k at time $t-1$. Then, the probabilities in the stochastic transition matrix can be represented as

$$p_{11} = p(E1|P1,S1)p(P1|S1) + p(E1|P2,S1)p(P2|S1) + p(E1|P3,S1)p(P3|S1) \qquad (4.6)$$

$$p_{12} = p(E2|P1,S1)p(P1|S1) + p(E2|P2,S1)p(P2|S1) + p(E2|P3,S1)p(P3|S1) \qquad (4.7)$$

$$p_{13} = p(E3|P1,S1)p(P1|S1) + p(E3|P2,S1)p(P2|S1) + p(E3|P3,S1)p(P3|S1) \qquad (4.8)$$

$$p_{21} = p(E1|P1,S2)p(P1|S2) + p(E1|P2,S2)p(P2|S2) + p(E1|P3,S2)p(P3|S2) \qquad (4.9)$$

$$p_{22} = p(E2|P1,S2)p(P1|S2) + p(E2|P2,S2)p(P2|S2) + p(E2|P3,S2)p(P3|S2) \qquad (4.10)$$

$$p_{23} = p(E3|P1,S2)p(P1|S2) + p(E3|P2,S2)p(P2|S2) + p(E3|P3,S2)p(P3|S2) \qquad (4.11)$$

$$p_{31} = p(E1|P1,S3)p(P1|S3) + p(E1|P2,S3)p(P2|S3) + p(E1|P3,S3)p(P3|S3) \qquad (4.12)$$

$$p_{32} = p(E2|P1,S3)p(P1|S3) + p(E2|P2,S3)p(P2|S3) + p(E2|P3,S3)p(P3|S3) \qquad (4.13)$$

$$p_{33} = p(E3|P1,S3)p(P1|S3) + p(E3|P2,S3)p(P2|S3) + p(E3|P3,S3)p(P3|S3) \qquad (4.14)$$

We will not discuss the computations of all transition probabilities, but consider p_{11}. The probability of transitioning from State 1 to State 1 between $t-1$ and t (i.e., staying in State 1) is the probability that the chain stays in State 1, given that State 1 is proposed ($= 1$) multiplied by the probability State 1 is proposed ($= 1/3$), plus the probability the chain stays in State 1, given that State 2 is proposed ($= 1 - 1/2$) multiplied by the probability that State 2 is proposed ($= 1/3$), plus the probability the chain stays in State 1, given that State 3 is proposed ($= 1 - 1/6$) multiplied by the probability State 3 is proposed ($= 1/3$). Thus, $p_{11} = 7/9$.

In these equations, many of the terms are 0. For example, in the equation for p_{12}, the probability that the chain will transition to State 2 if the chain begins in State 1 and State 1 is proposed is 0. Put simply, the probability of transitioning to a state that is not proposed is 0. Further, many terms are 0 because whenever a state with higher probability is proposed, the transition will occur (the proposal will be accepted): R must be 1 when $f(\theta^c) > f(\theta_{t-1})$. For example, if the chain is in State 3 (which has probability .1 under the target distribution) and State 1 is proposed, the chain will move to State 1, because its probability is .6 under the target distribution. However, when the chain is in a state that has greater probability than the one proposed, the candidate still may be accepted. Thus, p_{11} and p_{22} have more than one nonzero term.

Given the discrete uniform proposal, all terms of the form $p(Pk|Sj)$ are equal to 1/3 and can be factored out. It should be noted that, in each expression in these equations, I did not include the marginal term, $p(Sk)$, to complete the probability chain rule described in Chapter 2, because this value is always 1, given each row implies a specific state of the chain at $t - 1$.

Using the results from Table 4.3 and the proposal distribution described above, the transition probabilities are

$$p_{11} = (1/3)[1 + (1 - 1/2) + (1 - 1/6)] \tag{4.15}$$
$$p_{12} = (1/3)[0 + 1/2 + 0] \tag{4.16}$$
$$p_{13} = (1/3)[0 + 0 + 1/6] \tag{4.17}$$
$$p_{21} = (1/3)[1 + 0 + 0] \tag{4.18}$$
$$p_{22} = (1/3)[0 + 1 + (1 - .1/3)] \tag{4.19}$$
$$p_{23} = (1/3)[0 + 0 + 1/3] \tag{4.20}$$
$$p_{31} = (1/3)[1 + 0 + 0] \tag{4.21}$$
$$p_{32} = (1/3)[0 + 1 + 0] \tag{4.22}$$
$$p_{33} = (1/3)[0 + 0 + 1], \tag{4.23}$$

yielding a transition matrix of

$$P = \begin{bmatrix} (7/9) & (1/6) & (1/18) \\ (1/3) & (5/9) & (1/9) \\ (1/3) & (1/3) & (1/3) \end{bmatrix}. \tag{4.24}$$

As stated earlier, the stationary distribution of the Markov chain implied by this transition matrix can be obtained either by raising the matrix to a sufficiently high power or by performing the eigendecomposition of the transpose of the matrix and examining the eigenvector corresponding to the eigenvalue of 1. Here, that eigenvector is $[.885 .442 .147]$, which, after renormalizing so that the elements in the vector sum to 1, yields $[.60 .30 .10]$—the correct target distribution!

Figure 4.4 shows the evolution of three Markov chains to the stationary distribution under the three different starting states. The figure contains three plots. The upper-left plot shows how the Markov process converges to the stationary distribution when the starting state is State 1 (i.e., $x_1 = [1\ 0\ 0]$). The upper-right and lower-left plots show how the process converges to the stationary distribution when the starting state is States 2 and 3, respectively (i.e., $x_1 = [0\ 1\ 0]$ vs. $x_1 = [0\ 0\ 1]$). In other words, for the upper-left plot, the initial vector, $x_{t=1}$, is $[1\ 0\ 0]$. This vector is multiplied by P to obtain $x_{t=2}$, and the process is repeated 48 more times to obtain $x_{t=3} \ldots x_{t=50}$. As the plots show, regardless of the starting state, the process converges to the desired stationary distribution ($[.6 .3 .1]$) rapidly.

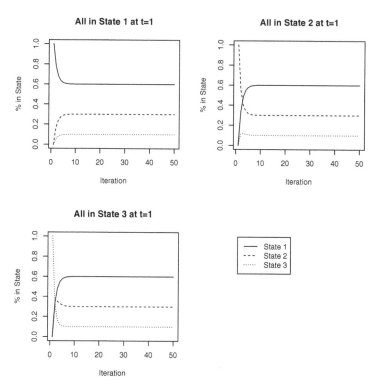

Figure 4.4   Evolution of a Markov process toward its stationary distribution from different starting states.

It is important to note that the process of iteratively multiplying x_t by P to produce an updated x (i.e., x_{t+1}) until time T is equivalent to simply multiplying x_1 by P^{T-1} (P to the power of $T-1$): x_T will be the same either way. Further, the description here simply reveals that following the Metropolis algorithm will produce the *expected* stationary distribution regardless of which state is occupied at $t = 1$—or, equivalently, the probability of being in each state at $t = 1$, such that $x_1 = [1\ 0\ 0]$ means there is probability 1 of being in State 1 at $t = 1$.

To illustrate the algorithm as it would be used in practice to produce a single instance of a Markov chain, I constructed an R program that samples from the three state models as described above (see Item 1 in the Appendix). Table 4.4 shows the results of the first 10 iterations of this programmed algorithm. The second column of the table shows the state of the Markov chain

Iteration (t)	θ_t	θ^c	R	$u \sim U(0,1)$	Decision
1	1 (starting state)	3	.17	.26	Reject
2	1	2	.5	.07	accept
3	2	3	.33	.70	Reject
4	2	1	2(1)	.01	Accept
5	1	2	.5	.27	Accept
6	2	3	.33	.00	Accept
7	3	1	6(1)	.92	Accept
8	1	3	.17	.38	Reject
9	1	3	.17	.46	Reject
10	1	1	1	.41	Accept

Table 4.4 First 10 iterations of a Metropolis algorithm for simple three-state example.

at each iteration of the algorithm (θ_t; I show the state occupied rather than a vector of indicators for states at each point in time). The third column shows the proposed candidate value, based on Step 3 of the general algorithm shown above (θ^c). The fourth column shows the ratio of the target distribution's density function evaluated at the candidate value versus the previous value as defined in Step 4 above. These values correspond to those shown in Table 4.3. If $R > 1$, it is set to 1 as indicated by the parentheses. The fifth column shows the value of the random $U(0,1)$ draw, u, required in Step 4 of the algorithm, and the last column of the table shows the decision to accept or reject θ^c based on the comparison of R to u.

As the table shows, I started the algorithm with the chain in State 1 (i.e., $\theta_1 = 1$). The first proposed candidate was State 3 (i.e., $\theta^c = 3$). The R ratio was .17, and the uniform draw was .26. Since $R < u$, θ^c was rejected, so $\theta_2 = 1$ (the chain stayed in State 1). The second column of the table shows that the chain's values across the first 10 iterations of the algorithm were $[1,1,2,2,1,2,3,1,1,1]$. Although only coincidental, this result shows that the distribution of the first 10 values of the chain was exactly consistent in proportion with what is expected under the stationary distribution: 60% of the time, the chain was in State 1; 30% of the time, the chain was in State 2; and 10% of the time, the chain was in State 3.

I ran the R program for 1,000 iterations. Figure 4.5 shows a time-series plot, or "trace plot," of the sampled values from the algorithm for the first 100 iterations. The horizontal axis of the figure shows the iteration count, while the vertical axis shows the sampled value at each iteration. As the figure shows, the sampled values bounce around the sample space (of $\{1, 2, 3\}$) across iterations. This type of plot is important in evaluating the performance of MCMC algorithms, as we will discuss throughout the remainder of this volume.

At the end of the run of 1,000 iterations, the chain had visited a total of 627 times for State 1, 295 times for State 2, and 78 times for State 3. At one decimal place of rounding, the proportion of sampled values for the three states corresponds directly to the desired target distribution: .6, .3, and .1.

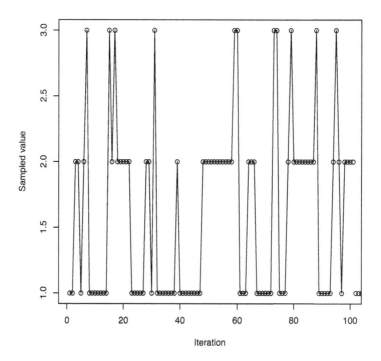

Figure 4.5   First 100 values in Markov chain in the three-state example using discrete uniform proposal.

In the foregoing example, our proposal distribution proposed candidates with equal probability. In real applications, uniform proposals are rare. Given that uniform distributions must be bounded to be proper distributions, uniform proposals are especially rare in independence samplers, because most posterior/target distributions are unbounded, and a bounded uniform distribution would violate the rules above that the proposal must allow the Markov chain to reach all areas of the target distribution. Even in other MCMC algorithms, uniform proposal distributions are rare because they typically do not closely match the shape of target distributions. Indeed, as we will discuss in greater depth later, proposals should be chosen to be as similar in shape to the posterior as possible to improve performance.

When proposal distributions are not uniform, the probability of proposing values may differ depending either on the state occupied at a given time or just in general. Suppose in the previous example that, rather than using a discrete uniform proposal so that each state was proposed with probability 1/3, we used the following proposal:

$$
g(\theta) = \begin{cases} 2/10 & \text{iff } \theta = 1 \\ 3/10 & \text{iff } \theta = 2 \\ 5/10 & \text{iff } \theta = 3 \\ 0 & \text{otherwise.} \end{cases} \tag{4.25}
$$

In that case, the transition probability matrix we derived above would not have produced the correct stationary distribution, because the proposal distribution is not symmetric with respect to proposing candidates, and the "detailed balance" required to achieve the appropriate stationary distribution is lost. In brief, in order to obtain the appropriate stationary distribution, the Markov chain implied by a transition probability matrix must be "reversible." That is, the probability that the chain will move to state θ_i when it is in state θ_j must be proportional to the ratio of probabilities $f(\theta_i)/f(\theta_j)$ (Gamerman & Lopes, 2006). However, if the probabilities of *proposing* states θ_i and θ_j are not equal, the transition probabilities will be wrong, disproportionately favoring movement to some states over others, as suggested by the latter conditional probabilities shown in Equations 4.6 to 4.14.

We can introduce an additional term in the ratio R to regain detailed balance:

$$
R = \left(\frac{f(\theta^c)}{f(\theta_{t-1})} \right) \left(\frac{g(\theta_{t-1}|\theta^c)}{g(\theta^c|\theta_{t-1})} \right). \tag{4.26}
$$

The latter term in the modified R is called the Hastings ratio and is the ratio of the proposal densities evaluated at the candidate and previous values of θ. Specifically, the numerator of the Hastings ratio is the value (height) of the proposal density evaluated at θ_{t-1} when $\theta = \theta^c$, while the denominator is the value of the proposal density evaluated at θ^c when $\theta = \theta_{t-1}$.

In the independence sampler, the proposal distribution does not change: $g(\theta)$ is constant, regardless of the current state of the Markov chain. That is, it is independent of θ_{t-1}. Thus, the Hastings ratio can simply be expressed as $g(\theta_{t-1})/g(\theta^c)$ (which was previously always 1 in the example and could therefore be ignored). This ratio, however, requires the conditioning in other samplers, such as in the random walk Metropolis–Hastings algorithm, as we will discuss, and as in an independence sampler with unequal probabilities for proposing states as described above in Equation 4.25.

For this new example, the general formulas representing the calculation of probabilities shown in Equations 4.6 through 4.14 do not change, but some of the components change to reflect the Hastings ratio and the difference in proposal probabilities. With those adjustments, we have

$$p_{11} = [(6/6)(2/2)](2/10) + [1 - (1/2)(2/3)](3/10) + [1 - (1/6)(2/5)](5/10) \tag{4.27}$$

$$p_{12} = [0](2/10) + [(1/2)(2/3)](3/10) + [0](5/10) \tag{4.28}$$

$$p_{13} = [0](2/10) + [0](3/10) + [(1/6)(2/5)](5/10) \tag{4.29}$$

$$p_{21} = [(6/3)(3/2) = 1](2/10) + [0](3/10) + [0](5/10) \tag{4.30}$$

$$p_{22} = [0](2/10) + [(1)(1)](3/10) + [1 - (1/3)(3/5)](5/10) \tag{4.31}$$

$$p_{23} = [0](2/10) + [0](3/10) + [(1/3)(3/5)](5/10) \tag{4.32}$$

$$p_{31} = [(6/1)(2/5) = 1](2/10) + [0](3/10) + [0](5/10) \tag{4.33}$$

$$p_{32} = [0](2/10) + [(3/1)(5/3) = 1](3/10) + [0](5/10) \tag{4.34}$$

$$p_{33} = [0](2/10) + [0](3/10) + [(1)(1)](5/10) \tag{4.35}$$

In these equations, the terms in brackets include both the ratios of the posterior density and the Hastings ratios. The terms in parentheses to the right of the brackets are the probabilities that each state is proposed (1, 2, 3). In cases in which a term in brackets exceeds 1, the ratio is set to 1 as described in Step 4 of the Metropolis algorithm listed earlier. In these equations, this is indicated with an "= 1" inside the brackets.

Each equation consists of three terms as defined in Equations 4.6 through 4.14. Consider the equation for p_{11}. The first term in the equation is the probability that the chain ends in State 1 given that State 1 was proposed, multiplied by the probability that State 1 is proposed. The ratio of the posterior density evaluated at the candidate and prior state is 6/6, the Hastings ratio is 2/2, and the probability that State 1 is proposed is 2/10. The second term in the equation for p_{11} is the probability that the chain ends in State 1 given that State 2 is proposed multiplied by the probability that State 2 is proposed. The probability that the chain ends in State 1 is the complement that it moves to State 2 from State 1. The ratio of posterior values when State 2 is proposed is 3/6 ($= 1/2$) multiplied by the Hastings ratio of 2/3: $g(\theta_{t-1} = 1 | \theta^c = 2)/g(\theta^c = 2 | \theta_{t-1} = 1) = g(1)/g(2) = .2/.3$. (Again, because we are using an independence sampler, the conditioning within the Hastings ratio is unnecessary.) Thus, the probability of remaining in State 1 when State 2 is proposed is $1 - (1/2)(2/3)$. Finally, the probability that State 2 is proposed is 3/10.

The calculations yield a transition probability matrix of

$$
P = \begin{bmatrix}
(13/15) & (1/10) & (1/30) \\
(2/10) & (7/10) & (1/10) \\
(2/10) & (3/10) & (5/10)
\end{bmatrix}. \tag{4.36}
$$

Although this transition probability matrix is quite different from the one derived when the probabilities of proposing each state were equal, this transition matrix has the same eigendecomposition and therefore has the same stationary distribution of $[.6 \ .3 \ .1]$ as the one obtained under the previous proposal distribution. Importantly, however, the convergence to the stationary distribution is substantially slower, as can be observed by incrementally raising P to successively higher powers. For the case in which proposal probabilities were equal, the chain converged to its stationary distribution at P^{21}. For the case in which the proposal probabilities were unequal, convergence to the stationary distribution occurred at P^{42} (not shown).

The Appendix provides an R program for this independence sampler (see Item 2). To save space, I do not duplicate the previous table showing the first few iterations of the algorithm. However, after running the algorithm, it is clear that it does not provide a sample from the desired stationary distribution in the first 1,000 iterations. After 1,000 iterations, the algorithm visited State 1 for 58% of the time, State 2 for 31% of the time, and State 3 for 11% of the time. Although these proportions are close to the expected values, they are not accurate to two decimal places. If we let the program run for another 1,000 iterations, we find that this latter part of the chain visited State 1 for 61% of the time, State 2 for 30% of the time, and State 3 for 9% of the time, which is close to the desired stationary distribution. This finding illustrates the fact that not all MCMC algorithms are equally efficient, nor can we assume that a program's early samples represent samples from the stationary distribution of the Markov chain. Thus, it is important when using these methods to monitor one's programs for convergence and generally discard early samples prior to convergence—called the "burn-in" samples. We will discuss this issue in greater depth subsequently.

Both of these algorithms were generically Metropolis–Hastings (MH) samplers but are specifically called independence samplers. They are called such because the probability of proposing a particular candidate state to which to move is independent of the current state of the chain. Independence samplers work best when the shape of the proposal distribution closely matches the shape of the target distribution. This is evident here: When the proposal distribution was essentially opposite in shape compared to the target distribution (i.e., $g(\theta) = [.2 \, .3 \, .5]$, while $f(\theta) = [.6 \, .3 \, .1]$), convergence to the stationary distribution took twice as long as convergence for the flat proposal distribution.

The Random Walk Metropolis–Hastings Algorithm

The random walk Metropolis–Hastings (RWMH) algorithm is a common alternative to the independence sampler. Unlike the independence sampler, the proposal density changes location in the RWMH algorithm based on the current state of the chain. Thus, $g(\theta^c | \theta_{t-1}) \neq g(\theta^c)$. A common proposal distribution for the RWMH algorithm is a normal distribution centered over the previous value of the chain: for example, $g(\theta^c | \theta_{t-1}) = N(\theta_{t-1}, \sigma_c^2)$. Here, σ_c^2 is a variance that remains constant across t (to ensure time-homogeneity) and is chosen carefully to encourage efficient convergence of the chain to the target distribution and efficient "mixing" of the chain, meaning that it visits all areas of the target distribution in the right proportions thoroughly and quickly. In general, when σ_c^2 is too small or too large, convergence and mixing tend to be slow. Uniform proposal distributions are also sometimes used, with a width, c, that is chosen to encourage efficient convergence and mixing.

In the RWMH algorithm, the Hastings ratio in Equation 4.26 is 1 when the proposal distribution is symmetric around θ_{t-1}. Figure 4.6 illustrates this point. As the figure shows, the height at θ^c of a normal distribution centered over θ_{t-1} (i.e., $g(\theta^c | \theta_{t-1})$) is the same as the height at θ_{t-1} of a normal distribution centered over θ^c (i.e., $g(\theta_{t-1} | \theta^c)$). Thus, the Hastings ratio will be 1, and we can simply call the algorithm a random walk Metropolis algorithm. In contrast, if (1) the proposal distribution is not symmetric (e.g., it is a gamma or other asymmetric distribution), (2) an alternative value is chosen over which to "center" the proposal (e.g., the 30th percentile of a normal distribution), or (3) the proposal distribution changes, as in the Gibbs sampler discussed below, the Hastings ratio will not be 1 and must be computed.

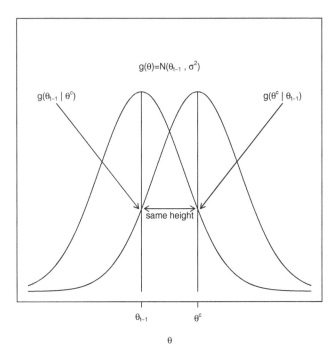

$g(\theta)=N(\theta_{t-1}, \sigma^2)$

$g(\theta_{t-1} \mid \theta^c)$

$g(\theta^c \mid \theta_{t-1})$

same height

θ_{t-1} θ^c

θ

Figure 4.6   Example of symmetry in proposals in RWMH algorithm. Since $g(\theta_{t-1}|\theta^c) = g(\theta^c|\theta_{t-1})$, the Hastings ratio is always 1 and need not be calculated.

To illustrate the RWMH algorithm, consider the posterior distribution for normally distributed data with the reference prior $1/\sigma^2$ in the previous chapter (Equation 3.58):

$$f(\mu,\sigma^2|Y) \propto (\sigma^2)^{-(n/2+1)} \exp\left\{-\frac{n(\mu-\bar{y})^2 + (n-1)s^2}{2\sigma^2}\right\}.$$

This is a bivariate posterior distribution for μ and σ^2, and it cannot be sampled from directly to produce summaries of μ and σ^2. A two-dimensional rejection sampler may be difficult to construct for it, in part because finding an envelope distribution that leads to efficient sampling may be difficult. An RWMH algorithm, however, is fairly easy to develop. The data required for this model are the sample mean, sample variance, and sample size. For the most recent era in our GSS data (2010–2016), these values are $\bar{x} = 5.77$, $s^2 = 8.52$, and $n = 4311$ for the political identification index.

For the sake of illustration, we will use $[\mu_1, \sigma_1^2] = [5, 8]$ as the starting state/values, and we will use a bivariate uniform proposal distribution centered over $[\mu_{t-1}, \sigma_{t-1}^2]$. This distribution is a rectangle on the μ, σ^2 plane (or a rectangular prism, including the density height). Here, I set both the width and the length of the rectangle to $k = .2$, so that the proposal is $\mu^c \sim U(\mu_{t-1} - .1, \mu_{t-1} + .1)$ and $\sigma^{2c} \sim U(\sigma_{t-1}^2 - .1, \sigma_{t-1}^2 + .1)$. Thus, in keeping with the RWMH recipe, at each iteration, candidate values for μ and σ^2 are drawn from this proposal. This is achieved by simply sampling from two, independent uniform distributions.

Next, the R ratio is constructed. In this particular case, because the proposal density is symmetric and centered over the previous value of the parameters, the Hastings ratio need not be computed. Then, the candidate is accepted or rejected based on the comparison of R to a uniform random draw. Item 3 in the Appendix is an R program implementing the algorithm.

In the program, it is important to note that I work with the log of the posterior distribution, rather than the posterior itself, because of "underflow" issues. That is, the posterior is the exponential of a large negative number, given the large n, making its value incredibly small. In social science data sets, n is often large enough that the raw, unnormalized posterior density value is small enough that it exceeds the computational capacity of the computer. Using the log of the posterior usually resolves this problem because it turns products into sums. When using the log scale, only two adjustments are needed to Step 4 of the algorithm: (1) The ratio R becomes a subtraction: $\log(R) = \log(f(\theta^c)) - \log(f(\theta_{t-1}))$, and (2) it must be compared to the log of a uniform random number, rather than the uniform draw, u, itself.

Figures 4.7 and 4.8 show some results of a 5,000-iteration run of the algorithm. The upper-left panel of Figure 4.7 shows a contour plot of the posterior distribution for μ and σ^2 in the upper-right portion of the plot, along with the starting values for the parameters and the rectangular proposal distribution around them in the lower-left portion of the plot. The upper-right panel of the figure shows the results after 10 iterations of the algorithm. A line connects the sequence of sampled values, with the proposal density centered over the parameter values at each iteration. Only five points and rectangles are visible, because only 5 of the first 10 candidates were accepted. That is, $\log(R) < \log(u)$ for half of the proposed candidates. Thus, the algorithm remained in the same location half the time (i.e., half of the first 10 candidates were rejected). The bottom-left panel shows the results after 30 iterations. It is clear from this plot that, although the starting values were far from the center of the target density (the posterior distribution), the algorithm converged toward it fairly rapidly. Further, it is clear from the bottom-right

86

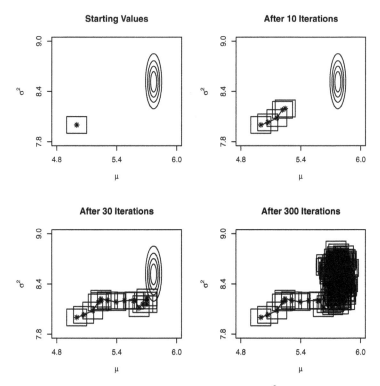

Figure 4.7   Two-dimensional trace plots of μ and σ^2 from run of RWMH algorithm after 1, 10, 30, and 300 iterations. A contour plot of the posterior is shown, along with the history of the Markov chain with the proposal density at each iteration.

panel that, once the algorithm converged to the target density, it wandered around the main support of it pretty quickly and did not appear to stray from it.

The upper-left panel of Figure 4.8 replicates the bottom-right panel of the previous figure but for all 5,000 iterations of the algorithm and without the proposal distributions shown. This plot shows that the algorithm converged to the target distribution pretty quickly and then "mixed" thoroughly around the joint distribution without wandering away from it. Thus, it seems that the Markov chain reached a stationary distribution. The upper-right and lower-left panels show time-series plots for each parameter separately. The plot for μ shows rapid convergence from the starting value of 5 to a region centered around 5.8 and then stable, nontrending mixing around that point. The plot for σ^2 shows a slight increase from the starting value of 8 to around 8.6 and then stable, nontrending mixing.

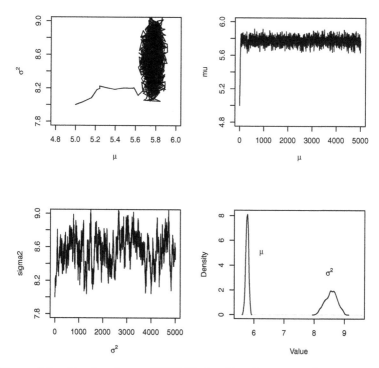

Figure 4.8 Results of run of RWMH algorithm for μ and σ^2. Upper-left panel shows sequence of all 5,000 iterations of algorithm. Upper-right and lower-left panels show trace plots for μ and σ^2, respectively. Bottom-right panel shows histograms of the marginal distributions for μ and σ^2 using last 4,000 sampled values.

These trace plots illustrate that, despite using a poor starting location, the algorithm fairly rapidly converged to the right location, as the MCMC theory discussed above indicated it would. Further, however, it is clear that we cannot treat early samples produced by the algorithm as samples from the target distribution. Instead, we should discard early samples until we see the stable, nontrending behavior that indicates that the Markov chain has reached its stationary distribution. These early, discarded samples are called the "burn-in," as mentioned earlier. We must be sure that, once convergence is obtained (after the burn-in is discarded), we allow the algorithm to run long enough to produce an adequate sample from the posterior distribution so that we can produce reliable summaries of it. The decision of run length depends on how fast the algorithm mixes, as we will discuss in depth in the next section.

The bottom-right panel in the figure presents histograms of the samples for μ and σ^2 after discarding the first 1,000 samples as the burn-in and retaining the remaining 4,000 samples. Thus, although the algorithm sampled from the joint distribution for the parameters, we can treat the samples of each parameter as a sample from the marginal posterior distributions for them. In other words, the algorithm effectively integrates over all parameters so that we can focus on just the parameters that are of interest. Here, that parameter is most likely μ, with σ^2 being a nuisance parameter, although σ^2 may be of interest, as we will discuss as we expand this example in later sections. For μ, the marginal distribution presented in the histogram is a t-distribution. As we discussed in the last chapter, we obtained samples from this marginal t-distribution without directly sampling from it, however.

The Gibbs Sampler

The Gibbs sampler is the most commonly used MCMC method and is often presented first in discussions of MCMC methods. However, although it is an MCMC method, it may not be immediately clear that it is. A Gibbs sampler involves sequentially sampling from conditional distributions for subsets of parameters in a model. As each parameter is sampled (i.e., "updated"), the new value of parameters replaces previous values in subsequent conditional distributions. Thus, a Gibbs sampling routine can be represented generically as

1. Set $t = 1$ and select starting values for relevant values of Θ.

2. Set $t = t + 1$.

3. Simulate $\theta_{1(t)} \sim f\left(\theta_1 | \theta_{2(t-1)}, \theta_{3(t-1)}, \ldots, \theta_{k-1(t-1)}, \theta_{k(t-1)}\right)$.

4. Simulate $\theta_{2(t)} \sim f\left(\theta_2 | \theta_{1(t)}, \theta_{3(t-1)}, \ldots, \theta_{k-1(t-1)}, \theta_{k(t-1)}\right)$.

5. Simulate $\theta_{3(t)} \sim f\left(\theta_3 | \theta_{1(t)}, \theta_{2(t)}, \theta_{4(t-1)}, \ldots, \theta_{k-1(t-1)}, \theta_{k(t-1)}\right)$.

$\vdots$

k+1. Simulate $\theta_{k-1(t)} \sim f\left(\theta_{k-1} | \theta_{1(t)}, \theta_{2(t)}, \theta_{3(t)}, \ldots \theta_{k-2(t)}, \theta_{k(t-1)}\right)$.

k+2. Simulate $\theta_{k(t)} \sim f\left(\theta_k | \theta_{1(t)}, \theta_{2(t)}, \theta_{3(t)}, \ldots \theta_{k-1(t)}\right)$.

k+3. Return to Step 2.

We discussed the derivation of conditional distributions in Chapter 2. In general, it is easy to derive conditional distributions by simply treating all other quantities in the full posterior distribution as constants and discarding them under proportionality where possible. In the normal distribution example from the previous chapter with the reference prior, for example, the posterior distribution was (prior to manipulation as in Equation 3.58):

$$f(\mu, \sigma^2 | y) \propto \frac{1}{\sigma^2} \prod_{i=1}^{n} \frac{1}{\sqrt{2\pi\sigma^2}} \exp\left\{ -\frac{(y_i - \mu)^2}{2\sigma^2} \right\} \tag{4.37}$$

$$\propto (\sigma^2)^{-(n/2+1)} \exp\left\{ -\frac{\sum(y_i - \mu)^2}{2\sigma^2} \right\} \tag{4.38}$$

There are two parameters in this distribution: μ and σ^2. A Gibbs sampler for this problem would consist of deriving the conditional distributions $f(\mu | \sigma^2, y)$ and $f(\sigma^2 | \mu, y)$ and iteratively sampling from them:

1. Set $t = 1$ and set $\sigma_1^2 = 1$.

2. Set $t = t + 1$.

3. Sample $\mu_t \sim f(\mu | \sigma_{t-1}^2, y)$.

4. Sample $\sigma_t^2 \sim f(\sigma^2 | \mu_t, y)$.

5. Return to Step 2.

Deriving the conditional distributions in this problem is straightforward. If we consider μ to be a constant and let $\alpha = n/2$ and $\beta = \sum(y_i - \mu)^2/2$, the conditional distribution for σ^2 is

$$f(\sigma^2 | \mu, y) \propto (\sigma^2)^{-(\alpha+1)} \exp\left\{ -\frac{\beta}{\sigma^2} \right\}, \tag{4.39}$$

which is directly recognizable as proportional to an inverse gamma distribution with parameters α and β. The conditional distribution for μ is slightly more complicated to derive but straightforward. If we treat σ^2 as fixed, then the posterior distribution reduces to

$$f(\mu | \sigma^2, y) \propto \exp\left\{ -\frac{\sum(y_i - \mu)^2}{2\sigma^2} \right\}. \tag{4.40}$$

If we expand the quadratic inside the exponential, rearrange terms, complete the square in μ, and discard constants, we obtain

$$f(\mu | \sigma^2, y) \propto \exp\left\{ -\frac{\sum y_i^2 - 2\mu \sum y_i + n\mu^2}{2\sigma^2} \right\} \tag{4.41}$$

$$\propto \exp\left\{ -\frac{n\mu^2 - 2n\mu\bar{y}}{2\sigma^2} \right\} \tag{4.42}$$

$$\propto \exp\left\{-\frac{\mu - 2\mu\bar{y} + \bar{y}^2 - \bar{y}^2}{2\sigma^2/n}\right\} \tag{4.43}$$

$$\propto \exp\left\{-\frac{(\mu - \bar{y})^2}{2\sigma^2/n}\right\}. \tag{4.44}$$

In the second equation, $\sum y_i^2$ has been removed as a constant (recall that $e^{a+b} = e^a e^b$). In the third equation, the numerator and denominator have been divided by n, and $\bar{y}^2$ has been added and subtracted to complete the square in μ. Finally, in the last equation, $-\bar{y}^2$ has been removed as a constant. In this form, it is clear that the conditional distribution for μ is a normal distribution with a mean of $\bar{y}$ and a variance of σ^2/n. We could also have arrived at this result by recognizing that, in the form shown in Equation 3.58, the latter term in the exponential is a constant.

Thus, a Gibbs sampler for this problem involves sampling first from a normal distribution with a mean of $\bar{y}$ and a variance of σ^2/n, where σ^2 is set to its starting value. Next, we sample a value for σ^2 from an inverse gamma distribution with parameters α (fixed at $n/2$) and β, computed using the just-drawn value of μ. Next, we draw a new value of μ, replacing σ^2 with its just-drawn value. This process is repeated until we obtain enough values of μ and σ^2 to summarize their distributions as desired.

The samples of μ and σ^2 can be considered samples from their joint posterior distribution, even though we sample only from the parameters' conditional distributions, but again, interest generally centers on μ. The samples of μ can be summarized on their own as a sample from the marginal distribution for μ. That distribution is a t-distribution, even though the values of μ were obtained by simulating from normal distributions. In short, the Gibbs sampler enables marginalizing over our uncertainty in σ^2.

Gibbs sampling can be viewed as special case of the Metropolis–Hastings algorithm defined above. Consider the R ratio with the Hastings ratio included for this normal distribution example. When sampling μ, the posterior distribution evaluated at μ^c is $f(\mu^c|\sigma_t^2, \bar{y})$, while it is $f(\mu_{t-1}|\sigma_t^2, \bar{y})$ at the previous value for μ. The proposal distribution for μ when the chain is at μ_{t-1} is $g(\mu^c|\sigma_t^2, \bar{y}, \mu_{t-1})$, and the proposal distribution for μ when the chain is at μ^c is $g(\mu_{t-1}|\sigma_t^2, \bar{y}, \mu^c)$. Thus:

$$R = \left(\frac{f(\mu^c|\sigma_t^2, \bar{y})}{f(\mu_{t-1}|\sigma_t^2, \bar{y})}\right)\left(\frac{g(\mu_{t-1}|\sigma_t^2, \bar{y}, \mu^c)}{g(\mu^c|\sigma_t^2, \bar{y}, \mu_{t-1})}\right) \tag{4.45}$$

$$= \left(\frac{N(\mu^c|\sigma_t^2, \bar{y})}{N(\mu_{t-1}|\sigma_t^2, \bar{y})}\right)\left(\frac{N(\mu_{t-1}|\sigma_t^2, \bar{y}, \mu^c)}{N(\mu^c|\sigma_t^2, \bar{y}, \mu_{t-1})}\right) \tag{4.46}$$

$$= \left(\frac{N(\mu^c|\sigma_t^2,\bar{y})}{N(\mu_{t-1}|\sigma_t^2,\bar{y})} \right) \left(\frac{N(\mu_{t-1}|\sigma_t^2,\bar{y})}{N(\mu^c|\sigma_t^2,\bar{y})} \right) \tag{4.47}$$

$$= 1. \tag{4.48}$$

The second equation shows that the posterior distributions and proposal distributions are all normal distributions. As the third equation shows, the height of the normal distribution depends only on the data mean (here, $\bar{y}$) and the variance (here, σ_t^2 in all cases). μ^c and μ_{t-1} can therefore be removed after the conditional in each of the proposal evaluations, leaving us with cross-products that are equal. Thus, R is 1. This result implies that every proposed value for θ will be accepted. This makes the Gibbs sampler more efficient than other MCMC methods, making it a popular choice for many applications.

At the same time that the Gibbs sampler can be viewed as a special case of the MH algorithm in which the proposal distributions are conditional distributions, the MH algorithm can be viewed as a component of a Gibbs sampler. In an MH algorithm, the parameter vector in a posterior distribution may be split into components, and each component can be updated sequentially, just like in the Gibbs sampler. Then, each MH step in the full algorithm produces an updated value for a component, either by accepting a candidate or by rejecting it and retaining the previous value as the new value. Indeed, a parameter vector can be split into components with some components updated with Gibbs sampling steps (i.e., drawing updates from a full conditional distribution) while other parameter components may be updated with MH steps. Thus, we sometimes hear of "Metropolis-within-Gibbs" and "Gibbs-within-Metropolis" algorithms (Gamerman & Lopes, 2006).

Slice Sampling

In many, if not most, cases, splitting a multivariate posterior into components and sampling from each in turn is a better strategy than attempting to use an MH algorithm with a multivariate proposal as we did in the example above. Yet, even in such cases, the full conditionals may not be of recognizable forms to facilitate Gibbs sampling, and it may be difficult to "tune" a general MH algorithm, as we will discuss subsequently. Slice sampling has emerged as an extremely useful and easy to implement approach to sampling from univariate distributions. It can be extended to multivariate distributions, but importantly, it can be used to sample from multivariate distributions by following a Gibbs-like strategy of breaking the distribution into components and sampling from them sequentially.

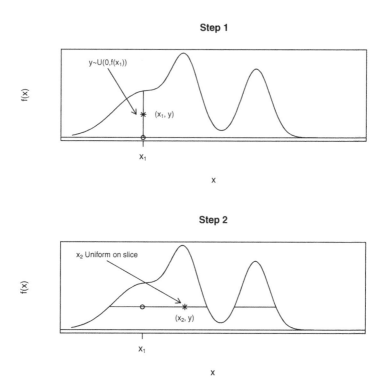

Figure 4.9   Illustration of slice sampling. In Step 1, a vertical draw, y, is selected from the $U(0, f(x_1))$ distribution, where x_1 is an arbitrary starting value. In Step 2, a uniform draw is selected from the horizontal slice at y under the density. The process then repeats, with x_2 replacing x_1.

Slice sampling is reminiscent of rejection sampling, and I use the same distribution as shown in Figure 4.2 to illustrate its implementation. For the rejection sampler, I assumed the bounds on the domain of x were $[0,1]$ in order to facilitate construction of an envelope. In fact, the distribution is a three-component mixture distribution of normal distributions, which has an unbounded domain:

$$f(x) \propto \sum_{i=1}^{3} (\sigma_i^2)^{-1/2} \exp\left\{ -\frac{1}{2\sigma_i^2}(x - \mu_i)^2 \right\} p_i, \qquad (4.49)$$

where $p_1 = .4$, $p_2 = .3$, $p_3 = .3$, $\mu_1 = 0$, $\sigma_1^2 = .2^2$, $\mu_2 = .3$, $\sigma_2^2 = .1^2$, $\mu_3 = .8$, and $\sigma_3^2 = .1^2$.

The lack of bounding on x makes a simple rejection sampler with a uniform envelope difficult to implement: We will not sample from some part of the tails of the distribution, and the further we let the envelope expand into the tails to cover more of the distribution, the greater the rejection rate will be. The slice sampler avoids these problems.

Implementing a slice sampler is straightforward and is illustrated in Figure 4.9. First, we select a value, x_1, as a starting point. Unlike with rejection sampling, in which we sampled across the entire domain of x first, under slice sampling, we may select an arbitrary value for x_1. Next, we sample a vertical value, y, between 0 and $f(x_1)$ from a $U(0, f(x_1))$ distribution (Step 1 in the figure). This value determines the height at which we will take a horizontal "slice" through the density. Next, we sample a new horizontal value, x_2, from a uniform distribution bounded on the left and right where the density function intersects the horizontal slice (Step 2 in the figure). That sampled x then becomes the value from which to sample a new y for choosing the next horizontal slice. We repeat this process until an adequate sample has been drawn from the distribution.

When the distribution of interest is unimodal and it is easy to find the endpoints of a slice—where the horizontal line intersects the density— implementation is straightforward. For example, if the distribution of interest were normal, it is simple to solve for x given a value of $y = f(x)$:

$$y = c \times \exp\left\{ -\frac{(x-\mu)^2}{2\sigma^2} \right\} \quad (4.50)$$

$$2\sigma^2 \ln(y/c) = -(x-\mu)^2 \quad (4.51)$$

$$\mu \pm \sqrt{-2\sigma^2 \ln(y/c)} = x_{bound}, \quad (4.52)$$

where c is the normalizing constant, and y is the vertical value drawn in Step 1 of the sampler. Thus, Step 2 of the sampler is easy to implement: $x_{new} \sim U(x_{(L)bound}, x_{(U)bound})$.

If the distribution of interest is multimodal (as in our mixture distribution) and/or if inverting $f(x)$ to find x_{bound} is difficult, the slice sampler can be modified (Neal, 2003). Once a vertical draw, y, is obtained between 0 and $f(x_i)$, we can expand around x_i to produce a slice at height y. Specifically, we first randomly assign an interval of width w around x_i. We then continue to expand the left and right boundaries of the interval by adding additional intervals of the same width until the interval bounds fall outside the density (i.e., $f(x_{bound}) < y$).

Figure 4.10 provides an illustration. An interval of width w is shown around the point (x_i, y); the interval is off-center from x_i because it is ran-

94

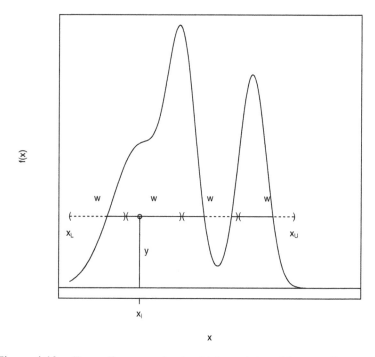

Figure 4.10   Expanding around x_i to obtain an interval for sampling x_{i+1}.
Repeated uniform samples are drawn between x_L and x_U
until a value of x such that $f(x) < y$ is obtained (i.e., any
value of x that is not in the dashed area).

domly assigned. Since the left endpoint of this interval is under the density
(i.e., $f(x_{bound}) > y$), another interval of width w is added. The left end of that
second interval is outside the density, so its left endpoint is the lower bound
for the uniform density from which to draw the next value, x_{i+1}. On the
righthand side, two more intervals of width w are added. Although the interval "skips" over a section in which the density falls below y, the endpoint
of the interval falls under the density. Thus, the right boundary is extended
another interval. The right endpoint of the interval is outside the density, so
it becomes x_U. x_{i+1} is then selected from a $U(x_L, x_U)$ distribution by repeatedly drawing values from this uniform distribution until a value is selected
that falls under the density, that is, it is from the solid segments of the slice
in the figure and not the dashed segments.

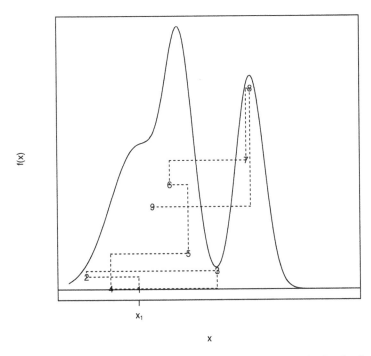

Figure 4.11 First nine samples from mixture distribution obtained using slice sampling. The y coordinates are not needed; the x coordinates of each number 1...9 are the sampled values from the density.

Figure 4.11 shows the first nine iterations of a slice sampler. In the figure, each vertical segment represents an implementation of the first step of the slice sampler (sampling a vertical value between 0 and $f(x)$), and each horizontal segment represents an implementation of the second step (sampling a horizontal value between x_L and x_U). As the figure shows, the first vertical draw is relatively low, and x_2 (labeled "2") is in the left tail of the distribution. The next vertical draw is also relatively low, and x_3 (labeled "3") is between the two modes of the distribution. After nine samples, the sequence of samples has visited both sides of the distribution.

The upper plot in Figure 4.12 shows sampled coordinates after running the slice sampler for 10,000 iterations. The y values in this plot are simply "auxiliary" variables and can be discarded. The lower plot in the figure shows a histogram of the sampled x values.

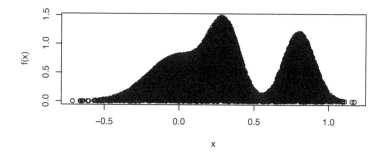

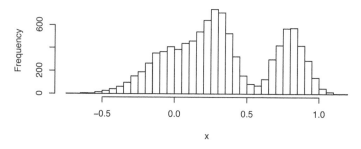

Figure 4.12 Ten thousand samples from mixture distribution obtained using slice sampling (upper plot) and histogram of x values (lower plot) after discarding y values from the slice sampler.

The slice sampler in one dimension is clearly easy to implement. The method can be extended in various ways to sample from multivariate distributions (Neal, 2003), including as a series of steps in a Gibbs sampler.

Evaluating MCMC Algorithm Performance

Before summarizing our knowledge about parameters using samples from posterior distributions obtained via MCMC methods, we must first establish that the algorithm has converged appropriately and mixed thoroughly. When social scientists conduct statistical analyses using classical methods, they usually decide on a particular model, commonly a regression model with the flavor determined by the level of measurement of the outcome variable. They then use a pretested procedure in a favorite software package to obtain their results. The mechanical process of producing parameter estimates is either largely or entirely out of the control of the analyst; parameter estimates and estimates of their standard errors are produced by some unseen process that is often unknown and potentially not understood. The only indication that something is wrong is usually a warning programmed by the team that coded the procedure that the "model failed to converge" or some similar warning.

Using an automated, canned routine approach is generally not possible when conducting Bayesian analyses. Instead, the incorporation of prior distributions, especially nonconjugate priors, can make an analysis unique so that using a set estimation routine is not possible. More important, the use of sampling methods cannot be fully automated (at least not easily), because each data set can possess unique features that require subtle "tweaks" to an MCMC algorithm to produce a sufficient number of usable samples from a posterior distribution. As mentioned earlier, MCMC algorithms must converge to a *distribution* (and sample from it) and not simply to a *point*, as ML routines do. The number of iterations an algorithm needs to be run is based on the speed with which the MCMC routine converges to the stationary distribution of the Markov chain and the rapidity with which the algorithm mixes to produce a large enough sample from the posterior to provide adequate summaries.

To be sure, interest in developing fully automated MCMC routines that determine run length based on on-the-fly calculations of convergence and mixing has existed since the early days of MCMC method development in statistics (see especially Chapter 5 by Raftery and Lewis in Gilks et al., 1996). More recently, a growing number of software packages and procedures in general software packages such as Stata and SAS facilitate Bayesian analyses. These packages often require only the specification of the model. The software derives the conditional distributions for Gibbs sampling or otherwise determines how to sample from the posterior distribution and then implements the sampling routine. However, these procedures are still not fully automatic, because the user must specify the prior and monitor convergence and mixing before summarizing results.

With a few exceptions, the rate of convergence and mixing in a specific problem is not known prior to an analysis, and the analyst must monitor algorithm performance and often revise his or her algorithm and rerun it, perhaps multiple times, before obtaining an adequately sized sample from the posterior for summarization. In the RWMH example above, we constructed trace plots of the parameters to evaluate convergence and mixing. Trace plots are a crucial part of the toolkit for assessing the performance of MCMC algorithms, but they are also problematic. Put succinctly, they are often very useful for showing that an algorithm has *not* converged or mixed well, but they are not definitive for establishing that an algorithm *has* converged and mixed thoroughly.

One problem with trace plots is that they can give a misleading picture regarding how well an algorithm has mixed when an algorithm has been run for an extended period, because the space on the x axis in the plot between iterations becomes more compact with longer runs. A solution to this issue is to plot a limited number of iterations, but we should also record the acceptance rate of candidates in MH algorithms. In the program in the Appendix, the acceptance rate of the RWMH algorithm was computed and retained at every iteration of the algorithm. As the program shows, at each iteration of the algorithm, I create an acceptance indicator (acc); set it to 0, indicating rejection; and then change it to 1 if the candidate is accepted. I then update the acceptance rate by multiplying the previous acceptance rate by $i - 1$, adding the acceptance indicator, and dividing by the current iteration count, i.

An algorithm's acceptance rate should eventually stabilize when convergence is obtained. Of course, the longer an algorithm is run, the less impact any accepted or rejected candidate will have on the overall acceptance rate, but it will be clear that an algorithm has not converged if the acceptance rate trends upward toward 1 or downward toward 0 throughout the run without stabilizing. Thus, the acceptance rate in an MH algorithm should be monitored for stabilization, and the algorithm should be run for many iterations after stabilization. Of course, the acceptance rate of a Gibbs sampler or slice sampler is 1, and so there is no need to monitor it in those algorithms.

Further, the *level* at which the acceptance rate stabilizes is also of concern. Convergence is a necessary condition for observing adequate mixing, but it is not a sufficient condition. An algorithm may converge rapidly but mix very slowly, so that a short run of a program is insufficient for producing enough samples to provide reliable summaries of a posterior distribution. The acceptance rate provides an initial idea about how well an algorithm may have mixed. An algorithm whose acceptance rate stabilizes at 1%, for example, is not mixing well. It is simply not obtaining very many unique samples from the posterior in a short run. Similarly, an algorithm whose acceptance rate stabilizes at 99% may be obtaining many unique samples from the posterior, but it is probably not exploring the entire posterior. Instead, it is most likely stuck in a tail of the distribution and isn't reaching its center if starting values were poor, or it is stuck in the middle of the posterior without reaching both tails if the starting values were good.

Figures 4.13 and 4.14 illustrate these issues. I reran the program in the Appendix using different values for the width of the uniform proposal distributions for μ and σ^2. Recall that that value, k, was .2 for both parameters

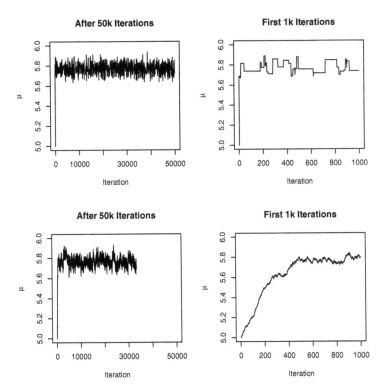

Figure 4.13 Trace plots from RWMH algorithms in the normal distribution problem. The upper plots show the results when the proposal density width is $k = 2$. The lower plots show the results when the proposal density width is $k = .02$.

in the initial run, so that each arm of the uniform proposal extended .1 units to the left/right the current value of each parameter. In the second run of the program, I set $k = 2$, thus making the proposal density much wider in both dimensions. In the third run of the program, I set $k = .02$, making the proposal density much narrower in both dimensions.

I let the program run for 50,000 iterations for each of these new values of k. The lefthand panels of Figure 4.13 show trace plots for μ for all 50,000 iterations in each of these runs. Both plots show apparent convergence and thorough mixing over 50,000 iterations. However, the righthand panels tell a different story for both convergence and mixing. Those panels show only the first 1,000 iterations of their respective runs. The upper-right

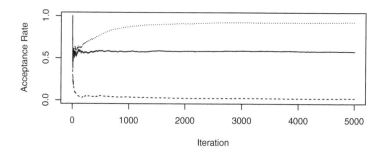

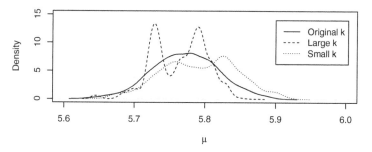

Figure 4.14 Results of RWMH algorithms in the normal distribution problem. Upper plot shows acceptance rates for three algorithms with differing values of k. Lower plot shows histograms of 4,000 samples of μ after discarding the first 1,000 samples as burn-in.

plot shows that the algorithm rarely accepted proposed candidate values for μ. In fact, in the first 1,000 iterations, only 37 proposed values of μ were accepted. Thus, even though the algorithm seemed to converge rapidly, it is clear that it has not sampled thoroughly from the posterior distribution for μ. The bottom-right plot shows that proposed values for μ were frequently accepted. Indeed, in the first 1,000 iterations, 869 proposed values for μ were accepted. However, convergence of the algorithm is not apparent from an examination of the trace plot for the first 1,000 iterations. Did the algorithm converge after 400 iterations? One may think so until he or she sees the "jump" at 800 iterations, where the sampled values increase and then appear to begin to level out again.

The acceptance rate of the algorithm(s) reveal(s) these problems without examining the trace plots. The upper panel of Figure 4.14 shows the acceptance rate at each iteration for the first 5,000 iterations for all three runs of the algorithm (the initial one from above, plus the additional two). The acceptance rate for the original run ($k = .2$) leveled out just above 50% (57%) within the first few hundred iterations. The acceptance rate for the second run when k was large (dotted line), in contrast, rapidly approached 0 early, leveling off at 2.4%. The acceptance rate for the third run, when k was small (dashed line), climbed slowly but eventually leveled off after a few thousand iterations at 95%. The climb was slow, because the starting values were poor so that early proposed values for μ were in the tail of the posterior distribution where the relative likelihood of any value for μ was flat. In contrast, when k was large, proposed values of μ were either *much* closer to the center of the target distribution, making their acceptance significantly more probable, or they were further in the tail, making it relatively easy to reject them. Thus, given the equal probability of proposing candidates toward versus away from the center of the posterior distribution, convergence is rapid. However, once the algorithm has converged toward the center of the posterior distribution, the large k enables the proposal of candidates that are in the tails of the posterior (on either side), reducing the acceptance rate and therefore mixing.

Were we to simply ignore the acceptance rate (and trace plots) of our algorithm, we may obtain very different summaries of the marginal posterior distribution for μ. The bottom panel of Figure 4.14 shows this. The plot presents histograms for μ from all three runs of the algorithm, *after* removing the first 1,000 sampled values as the burn-in. These histograms are quite different in appearance. The histogram for the original run (solid line) is relatively smooth and bell shaped, while the histogram for the run in which k was large (dotted line) is lumpy and bimodal, and the histogram for the run in which k was small (dashed line) is bimodal and very left skewed. These differences in histogram shape may very well produce different numerical summaries. For example, the posterior means are all 5.8, when rounding to one decimal place (5.77, 5.76, and 5.79, respectively, at two decimal places), but the posterior standard deviations for μ vary significantly: .047, .038, and .053, respectively. Although these numbers do not seem to be much different, given their magnitude, the largest is 39.5% larger than the smallest. Importantly, given the lumpiness of the histograms, interval summaries for μ may vary widely, as may posterior probabilities for specific hypotheses. For example, suppose our hypothesis was that $\mu < 5.8$ (to pick an arbitrary value). In that case, the results of the original run would give a posterior probability for that hypothesis of .72. The results of the run with the large

k would give a posterior probability of .84, and the results of the run with the small k would give a posterior probability of .53. Clearly, the substantive conclusions would differ based on these results. With k large, we would almost certainly conclude that $\mu < 5.8$, but with k small, we would be indeterminate.

Of course, as shown in Figure 4.13, we ran the algorithm for 50,000 iterations, so why limit our posterior summaries to the 1,001st to 5,000th samples? In fact, we shouldn't. Early expositions on MCMC methods were written when computing power was sufficient to implement MCMC methods, but those were still early days, and running algorithms for more than a few thousand iterations was often extremely costly, in terms of run times. Computing power today far exceeds that of the 1990s. For this example, generating 50,000 samples took less than a few seconds.

In addition to producing longer runs of an algorithm, it is also useful to run algorithms several times using different starting values to see whether each run converges to the same location and produces similar results. Trace plots are useful for this purpose, but the Gelman–Rubin diagnostic was developed as a formal approach to gauging convergence. Their "potential scale reduction factor," $\hat{R}$, can be intuitively understood using analysis of variance (ANOVA) terminology: It is the square root of the ratio of the total variance in values of θ obtained from multiple MCMC runs to the total within-chain variance. Starting from highly dispersed starting values, this ratio will be much larger than 1 initially, because the starting values will be far apart so that the total variance in θ will contain considerable between-chain variance in addition to the within-chain variance. Assuming the chains converge to the same location (hopefully the target distribution!), the between-chain variance will decrease, and the total variance will be driven entirely by the within-chain variance—the variance of θ in the target distribution.

Formally, for a one-parameter model, let θ_{ij} be the ith sampled value from the jth MCMC run ($i = 1 \ldots n$; $j = 1 \ldots J$), let $\bar{\theta}_j$ represent the mean of the jth chain, and let $\bar{\bar{\theta}}$ be the grand mean of all values. Then, the between-chain variance is $B = (n/(J-1))\sum_{j=1}^{J}(\bar{\theta}_j - \bar{\bar{\theta}})^2$, and the (average) within-chain variance is $W = (1/J(n-1))\sum_{j=1}^{J}\sum_{i=1}^{n}(\theta_{ij} - \bar{\theta}_j)^2$. The total variance of θ is $V = ((n-1)/n)W + (1/n)B$, and $\hat{R} = \sqrt{V/W}$. It is straightforward to see that, if the J chains have converged to the same location (but possibly not the *correct* location!), B should approach 0, so that $\hat{R}$ approaches 1.

Because each chain is started from highly dispersed locations, B cannot reach 0. Gelman and Rubin initially suggested running each chain for $2n$ iterations and computing $\hat{R}$ using only the second half of the chain (i.e., the latter n iterations from each for calculating $\hat{R}$). In that case, B can get close to 0 so that $\hat{R}$ can reach 1. Early on, Gelman and others suggested (see Brooks & Gelman, 1998) that $\hat{R} < 1.1$ was sufficient to indicate convergence, but this has been disputed. In their 1998 paper, Brooks and Gelman presented a revised calculation for $\hat{R}$ that corrected for the fact that the components of $\hat{R}$ are based on sample estimates; offered additional calculations and approaches to computing $\hat{R}$, including interval estimates and estimates based on intervals from separate chains; and extended $\hat{R}$ to multiparameter models. In practice, the correction for using sample estimates of the components of $\hat{R}$ is often trivially small, because n (length of chains) is typically large. Further, in my experience, computing $\hat{R}$ for each parameter separately in multiparameter models and determining that convergence has been obtained based on the last $\hat{R}$ to reach approximately 1 is usually sufficient.

It is important to note again that there is no way to definitively determine that an MCMC algorithm has converged. We can only (possibly) determine that an algorithm has *not* converged. It is always possible, even with highly dispersed starting values, that a given MCMC algorithm will converge to a local mode of a multimodal posterior distribution. Fortunately, many models in social science analyses are well behaved, and we can often compare results to maximum likelihood estimates to provide indication that our MCMC results are reasonable.

Once convergence has been reached (or diagnosed), we must consider how well the algorithm has mixed. MCMC theory assures us that, if we follow the MH recipe, the stationary distribution of the Markov chain of samples produced will be the target distribution. However, there is no guarantee that a finite run of an MCMC algorithm has converged or mixed. The Gelman–Rubin diagnostic is helpful for providing some indication of convergence, but there is no straightforward test to establish adequate mixing. Instead, a common approach is to compare estimates of sample quantities of interest across multiple chains with varying starting values and within chains across intervals. For example, one may compare results obtained from iterations 1,001–2,000 to iterations 2,001–3,000 and 3,001–4,000.

The acceptance rate provides some information regarding rapidity of mixing of an algorithm. Part of the problem of having an acceptance rate that is too high or too low in an MCMC algorithm is that adjacent values of sampled quantities (e.g., μ) will be highly autocorrelated (i.e., nonindependent). Thus, some summary measures, such as the variance and interval estimates, may be underestimated from a short run of an MCMC algorithm. Two solutions to this problem are common: the batch means approach and chain "thinning." Under the batch means approach, collections of sampled values are pooled (into batches), and the mean of each batch is treated as the sampled value. For example, suppose an algorithm run for 50,000 iterations after convergence seems to have been obtained. Then, the mean of each collection of, say, 50 samples is computed and treated as the sample: $\bar{\theta}_{1...1,000}$. The thinning approach simply involves taking every Lth value from the 50,000 samples, where L is chosen to be a lag at which sampled values are no longer autocorrelated. Both of these approaches clearly require lengthy runs from a single chain or multiple, shorter runs to obtain sufficiently large samples for summarization. I prefer the thinning approach, because it is easier to implement and does not require any adjustments to compute the posterior variance of the parameter of interest.

To illustrate these ideas, I reran the RWMH algorithm nine times: three times each from different starting values for μ and σ^2 using the three different proposals discussed above (wide, narrow, and original). The three sets of starting values were $(\mu, \sigma^2) = (0, 12), (5, 6), (12, 1)$. The political identification index has a range from 0 to 12, so the choices for μ include the extremes. The choices for σ^2 include a very low value (1), as well as a value much higher than any observed value for s^2 in any era.

Figure 4.15 presents the original Gelman–Rubin diagnostic, $\hat{R}$, for μ and σ^2 for all three runs of the algorithm based on proposal density widths at different points in the run of the algorithm. Item 4 in the Appendix presents a function that computes $\hat{R}$. The function accepts an $n \times J$ matrix of values, where n is the run length and J is the number of chains ($n = 50,000; J = 3$). The function then computes $\hat{R}$ based on the last half of the samples up to that point. This function was called every 250 iterations so that $\hat{R}$ was computed 200 times for each set of runs, with the last computation (at 200) representing the value obtained from the last 25,000 iterations. The upper plot in the figure shows the values for $\hat{R}$ for μ. As the figure shows, μ appears to have converged rapidly for the runs involving both the wide (solid line) and original (dotted line) proposals for both μ and σ^2. For the wide proposal, $\hat{R}$ was close to 1 after just a few iterations; for the original proposal, $\hat{R}$ began well above 3 but fell to about 1 within a few hundred iterations. In contrast, for the runs involving the narrow proposal, $\hat{R}$ for μ begins far higher than 3 (12; not shown in figure) and does not appear to converge until after 7,000 iterations. Importantly, for σ^2, $\hat{R}$ does not approach 1 until 20,000 iterations and then climbs. An examination of $\hat{R}$ for all 50,000 iterations indicates that σ^2 never falls below 1.04 for this set of runs with the narrowest proposal.

Figure 4.16 shows trace plots for μ (left column plots) and σ^2 (right column plots) for the first 25,000 iterations of all three runs of the RWMH algorithm for each of the three proposal density widths. The trace plots for the runs using the wide proposal (first row of plots) and the original proposal (last row) show that, despite the highly dispersed starting locations for

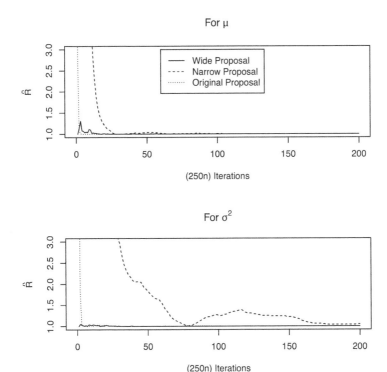

Figure 4.15 Gelman–Rubin $\hat{R}$ for μ and σ^2 based on three sets of starting values for each of three different proposal density widths (narrow, wide, and original) at different points in the RWMH run. The x axis represents the number of iterations ($\times 250$) when $\hat{R}$ was calculated using the latter half of the run up to that point. Thus, the value of $\hat{R}$ where $x = 200$ is based on the last 25,000 samples after 50,000 total iterations.

each chain, samples converged to the same location very rapidly. The plots for the narrow proposal (middle row), in contrast, show very slow convergence. The vertical reference line in each plot shows the point at which $\hat{R}$ suggests convergence has been reached. As the figure shows, σ^2 does not clearly converge in the first 25,000 iterations for the RWMH run involving the narrow proposal. The chains clearly converge to the same general location (about 9), and they appear to do so after about 10,000 iterations,

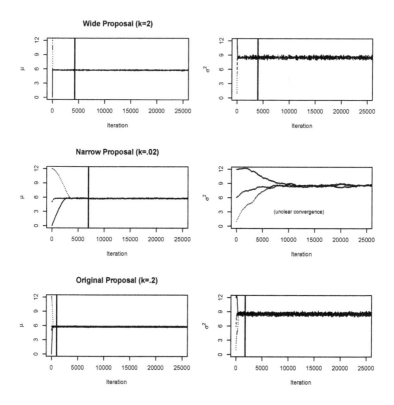

Figure 4.16 Trace plots of μ (left column) and σ^2 (right column) from multiple runs of the RWMH algorithm using different proposal density widths (rows). Each plot shows the evolution of three chains from different starting values to convergence (solid vertical reference line) over the first 25,000 iterations of runs of length 50,000 iterations.

but they appear to diverge again around 18,000 iterations before converging again subsequently. As stated above, $\hat{R}$ never falls below 1.04.

For the wide and original proposal widths, convergence appears to have been reached by 5,000 iterations. Thus, a next step is to consider how well the algorithms mixed after convergence is obtained. For this purpose, I consider the acceptance rates of the algorithms, as well as the extent of autocorrelation, for determining whether we have obtained a sufficient number of samples for summarization. The acceptance rates at the end of each run for the three chains using the wide proposal were 2.5%, 2.7%, and 2.5%. For the three chains using the narrow proposal, the acceptance rates were 93%, 95%, and 92%. Finally, for the three chains using the original proposal, the acceptance rates were all 57%.

As discussed above, the acceptance rate provides some indication of how well (rapidly) an MCMC algorithm mixes. Although MCMC theory guarantees convergence to the target distribution, it does not guarantee rapid convergence, nor does it guarantee thorough and rapid sampling from it once it has converged. Importantly, MCMC theory does not suggest that samples from the target density are independent—in fact, it ensures dependence—and the more *dependent* samples are, the slower an MCMC algorithm is in exploring the target density. Thus, examining the autocorrelation of samples from an MCMC algorithm can be instructive for deciding how long, *after convergence has been assumed*, an algorithm should be run to obtain enough samples to adequately summarize the posterior. A collection of nonindependent samples that is too small will surely produce estimates of posterior uncertainty for a parameter that are also too small.

Figure 4.17 shows autocorrelation function (ACF) plots for the first 100 lags of sampled values of μ and σ^2 from the 5,000th iteration through the 50,000th for the runs of the RWMH algorithm, with starting values close to the middle of the posterior distribution. Because almost all chains converged to these values by 5,000 iterations, the ACF plots should be similar regardless of which chain is used from the subset of three chains with a given proposal density width.

The figure shows that values of μ are highly autocorrelated until at least 60 or lags for both μ and σ^2 when the proposal density is wide (top row of figure). The second row of the figure shows the ACF plots for the samples from the RWMH algorithm with the narrow proposal density. The autocorrelations are extremely large, even at 100 lags, for both μ and σ^2. At 100 lags, the autocorrelation is still above .4 for μ and is still well above .9 for σ^2. The bottom row of the figure shows the ACFs for μ and σ^2 for the run with the original proposal density width. The ACF plot for μ shows that the samples are practically uncorrelated prior to lag 20. For σ^2, the plot shows that the autocorrelation falls rapidly and approaches 0 by 100 lags.

It would be naive to consider using results from the runs of the RWMH algorithm using the narrow or wide proposal distributions to summarize the posterior distribution for μ and σ^2, given what we've seen with the trace plots, the $\hat{R}$ values, and the ACF plots. We, instead, should consider summarizing the results obtained from the run using the original proposal density width, but given the ACF plots, we might consider basing summaries on the batch means or thinning method described above.

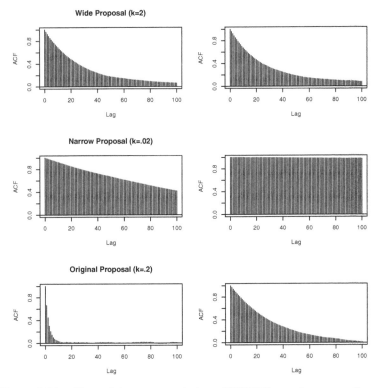

Figure 4.17 Plots of the autocorrelation of RWMH samples across the first 100 lags for μ (left column) and σ^2 (right column) from the algorithm runs with wide (first row), narrow (second row), and original (last row) proposal densities. In each case, plots are for the algorithm with starting states closest to the posterior mean for the political identification index (most recent era, as described in text).

Table 4.5 illustrates some of these ideas. I ran the RWMH algorithm a total of nine times (three sets of starting values and three different proposal density widths). The table shows the results obtained under the best starting values ($\mu = 5$; $\sigma^2 = 6$), with no thinning, thinning to retain every 10th sampled value, and thinning to retain every 40th value. The sample sizes in each case are 40,000, 4,000, and 1,000, respectively, after discarding the first 10,000 iterations of each run as burn-in. As the table shows, the estimates of the posterior mean are the same in all cases to the second decimal

Algorithm	PM(μ)	PSD(μ)	$p(\mu < 5.8)$
RWMH, $k = 2$			
No thinning	5.77	.043	.77
Thin 10	5.77	.043	.77
Thin 40	5.77	.043	.78
RWMh, $k = .02$			
No thinning	5.77	.045	.76
Thin 10	5.77	.045	.76
Thin 40	5.77	.046	.76
RWMH, $k = .2$			
No thinning	5.77	.044	.75
Thin 10	5.77	.045	.75
Thin 40	5.77	.046	.75

Table 4.5 Results of nine runs of the RWMH algorithm with three different proposal density widths, $k = 2, .02, .2$, and with no thinning of the results, thinning to retain every 10th sampled value, and thinning to retain every 40th sampled value. First 10,000 iterations have been dropped as burn-in, with 40,000 iterations retained and then thinned. First column shows the posterior mean for μ; second column shows the posterior standard deviation for μ; third column shows the probability that $\mu < 5.8$.

place and are equal to the sample mean of the original variable. The posterior standard deviations are similar in magnitude, but there is a slight tendency for them to increase as the extent of thinning increases. This reflects the diminishing downward influence on them produced by the autocorrelation of samples: As the thinning increases, the remaining samples are less autocorrelated. The posterior standard deviation, by the central limit theorem, should be σ^2/n. Using the sample estimate of s for σ^2, and dividing by the original sample size of $n = 4,311$ indicates that the "true" posterior standard deviation should be .444 (given the noninformative prior). All estimates in the table are quite close to this value. Finally, the posterior probabilities that μ is less than 5.8 are quite similar, ranging from .75 to .78. Based on a normal approximation, the value should be .75. These results are all quite close to those obtained using a Gibbs sampler (not shown), and the consistency of the results across sampling approaches, starting values, proposal density widths, and degrees of thinning should instill confidence in the results.

It should be clear from the foregoing discussion why it is difficult to fully automate the use of MCMC methods. It is possible to automate *some* parts of MCMC algorithms. For example, in some analyses, I have written algorithms that (1) run multiple chains simultaneously, (2) periodically check acceptance rates and alter proposal density variances/widths until a reasonable acceptance rate is achieved, (3) compute the Gelman–Rubin diagnostic periodically once the proposal density variances/widths are "locked in" (to ensure time-homogeneity), (4) start retaining samples once $\hat{R}$ reaches an acceptable level, and (5) stop once enough samples are obtained for summarization based on several criteria (such as autocorrelation, similarity in summary measures, etc.). Nonetheless, no amount of automation can ultimately substitute for one's own careful investigation of convergence and mixing in any analysis. In the next chapter, we will combine the process of modeling, sampling, and evaluating MCMC performance in several realistic social science examples, as well as illustrate some key advantages to the Bayesian approach in evaluating hypotheses.

CHAPTER 5. IMPLEMENTING THE BAYESIAN APPROACH IN REALISTIC APPLICATIONS

The examples presented in the previous chapter involved either contrived data or real data but overly simple models. In this chapter, I turn to realistic, multiparameter models with real data typical of modern social science applications. Given inherent page constraints, I discuss three specific models: the linear model, the dichotomous probit model, and a basic latent class model. The linear model is the foundation upon which many social science models are built. The strategy of linking an outcome to a linear combination of covariates is used in almost all our modeling techniques involving observational data. Thus, it is an important model to consider from a Bayesian perspective. The dichotomous probit model is perhaps the most basic generalized linear model and, with its sibling the logistic regression model, is likely used more often than the linear model because of the binary measurement of many of our outcomes. It is easily extended to full ordinal data models, and the use of data augmentation—which I illustrate—greatly simplifies sampling regression parameters from their posterior distribution and is useful in many settings beyond generalized linear modeling. For example, it is key in handling missing data in the Bayesian context, as discussed briefly in Chapter 6. Finally, latent class models—or finite mixture models—have a wide array of uses ranging from simply modeling nonnormal outcomes to addressing questions in many fields regarding heterogeneity within populations. In discussing each of these three classes of models, I illustrate some of the advantages of using a Bayesian approach. At the end of the chapter, I discuss Bayesian approaches to evaluating model fit and comparing models using, primarily, posterior predictive simulation.

The Linear Model

Treating an outcome variable as a linear combination of one or more predictors and coefficients plus unobserved factors is a strategy employed in many of the methods most commonly used in social science research. Walking through the Bayesian version of the model is therefore a useful exercise that provides a realistic depiction of some of the complexities involved in Bayesian computation. Given that many other models are direct extensions of the linear model, moving from the Bayesian version of the linear model to the Bayesian version of other types of regression models is not that difficult.

The linear regression model can be specified in several, equivalent ways. In the classical approach, it is common to specify the model as

$$Y = X\beta + e \tag{5.1}$$

$$e \sim N(0, \sigma^2), \tag{5.2}$$

where Y is an $n \times 1$ vector of outcomes for n persons, X is an $n \times k$ "design" matrix of predictors with β a $k \times 1$ vector of coefficients linking the predictors to the outcome, and e is a normally distributed error term (or residual) that has a mean of 0 and a variance of σ^2. This normality assumption is not required for the estimates of β to be unbiased under ordinary least squares (OLS) estimation, but it is required for justifying hypothesis testing on the coefficients under both OLS and ML estimation methods. The key assumptions of the model include that the errors are uncorrelated with X (i.e., $E(X^T e) = 0$; exogeneity) and that the errors have constant variance and are independent of each other (i.e., $E(e^T e) = \sigma^2 I_n$; homoscedasticity and non-autocorrelation).

Classical estimation of the linear model using ML estimation involves a normal distribution likelihood for the errors:

$$L(\beta, \sigma^2 | X, Y) = \prod_{i=1}^{n} \frac{1}{\sqrt{2\pi\sigma^2}} \exp\left\{ -\frac{(e_i - 0)^2}{2\sigma^2} \right\} \tag{5.3}$$

$$= \prod_{i=1}^{n} \frac{1}{\sqrt{2\pi\sigma^2}} \exp\left\{ -\frac{(y_i - \beta^T X_i)^2}{2\sigma^2} \right\} \tag{5.4}$$

$$\propto (\sigma^2)^{-n/2} \exp\left\{ -\frac{\sum_{i=1}^{n}(y_i - \beta^T X_i)^2}{2\sigma^2} \right\} \tag{5.5}$$

$$\propto (\sigma^2)^{-n/2} \exp\left\{ -\frac{1}{2\sigma^2}(Y - X\beta)^T(Y - X\beta) \right\}, \tag{5.6}$$

where the last equation is simply a matrix version of the scalar equation above it. The matrix representation is more useful than the scalar version when β includes more than one intercept and one regression coefficient. I recommend Brown (2014) for in-depth exposition on the linear model using matrix algebra.

The ML estimate for β is obtained by logging the likelihood, differentiating it with respect to the β vector, setting the derivative to 0, and solving for β. The result is identical to that obtained via OLS, because, after taking the log of the likelihood, the interior of the exponential is the same as the quantity obtained under the least squares criterion: It is a quadratic form in β. The only difference is that the expression in the exponential is negative, while the least squares criterion is positive (hence *maximizing* the likelihood is equivalent to *minimizing* the sum of squares). After solving for β:

$$\hat{\beta}_{MLE} = \hat{\beta}_{OLS} = (X^T X)^{-1}(X^T Y). \tag{5.7}$$

For both the ML and OLS estimators, the standard error estimates are obtained by square-rooting the diagonal elements of the covariance matrix $\sigma^2(X^T X)^{-1}$, which can be obtained by following the steps discussed in Chapter 2 involving the second derivative of the log-likelihood function.

The linear model looks the same in the Bayesian paradigm as it does in the classical paradigm, but Bayesians generally specify models using distribution notation, for example, $Y|X \sim N(X\beta, \sigma^2)$. This specification implies the same likelihood function. What remains is specification of a prior distribution. Here, we will discuss two priors. One approach is to assume that β and σ^2 are independent in their priors, give each β an improper uniform prior over the real line, and give σ^2 the reference prior of $1/\sigma^2$ as we did in the normal distribution example in Chapter 3 (Model 3 in Table 3.1). This approach assumes that the β parameters are also independent in their prior, but they generally will not be in their posterior.

Under that prior, the posterior distribution is

$$f(\beta, \sigma^2|X, Y) \propto f(Y|X, \beta, \sigma^2) f(\beta) f(\sigma^2) \tag{5.8}$$

$$\propto c \times \frac{1}{\sigma^2} \times (\sigma^2)^{-n/2} \exp\left\{ -\frac{1}{2\sigma^2}(Y - X\beta)^T(Y - X\beta) \right\} \tag{5.9}$$

$$\propto (\sigma^2)^{-(n/2+1)} \exp\left\{ -\frac{1}{2\sigma^2}(Y - X\beta)^T(Y - X\beta) \right\}, \tag{5.10}$$

where the second equation rearranges terms relative to the first by simply placing the prior for σ^2 upfront. This result looks like the likelihood function but with an extra $(\sigma^2)^{-1}$ term outside the exponential: That is, the exponent for σ^2 is $-(n/2+1)$ rather than $(-n/2)$.

As we have seen in previous examples, the posterior must be manipulated algebraically in order to clarify the distributional form for β and σ^2. Here, the posterior distribution is multivariate, so manipulating it involves a fair amount of matrix algebra. However, the process is similar to that which we followed in Chapter 3 for determining the posterior distribution form for the mean in the normal model: Expand the quadratic, rearrange terms, complete the square, and drop constants. Furthermore, as discussed earlier, manipulating posterior distributions for Gibbs sampling involves deriving the conditional distributions for each parameter (or parameter vector) for iterative sampling. This is easier than it may seem, because, in deriving the conditionals, one simply drops other parameters and data terms as constants whenever they can be extracted as a multiplicative constant.

Determining the form of the conditional for σ^2 in this model is extremely easy. First, recognize that $(Y - X\beta)$ is simply a vector of error terms, e, so that $e^T e$ is simply a sum of squares. This sum of squares is fixed, *given a specific value for β*. Then, the conditional posterior for σ^2 is immediately recognizable as an inverse gamma distribution with parameters $A = n/2$ and $B = (e^T e)/2$.

Deriving the conditional posterior for β requires more effort. First, drop the leading term outside the exponential, because it does not contain β, and expand the quadratic term to obtain

$$f(\beta|\sigma^2,X,Y) \propto \exp\left\{-\frac{1}{2\sigma^2}(Y^T Y - Y^T X\beta - B^T X^T Y + \beta^T X^T X\beta)\right\}.$$
(5.11)

Next, drop $Y^T Y$ as a constant, combine $Y^T X\beta$ and $\beta^T X^T Y$, and rearrange terms. Note that the two central terms can be combined, because they are both 1×1, and the transpose of a scalar is itself. Thus:

$$f(\beta|\sigma^2,X,Y) \propto \exp\left\{-\frac{1}{2\sigma^2}(\beta^T (X^T X)\beta - 2\beta^T X^T Y)\right\},$$
(5.12)

where I have simply grouped $(X^T X)$ between β^T and β using the distributive property of matrix algebra for clarity. The remaining expression in parentheses within the exponential is reminiscent of the expression $n\mu^2 - 2n\mu\bar{y}$ in Equation 4.42 in the last chapter and similar expressions in Chapter 3. In those cases, we then completed the square and dropped remaining constant terms to expose the form for μ. We must do the same thing here to expose the form for β, but in matrix form. Unlike in the scalar case, we cannot simply factor out and divide by constants, such as $(X^T X)$, because there is no commutativity of multiplication in matrix algebra. Instead, we must be somewhat creative in considering how to perform factoring and division. $\beta^T (X^T X)\beta$ is, in fact, a quadratic form, just as $(Y - X\beta)^T (Y - X\beta)$ was. Consider, for example, inserting an $n \times n$ identity matrix between $(Y - X\beta)^T$ and its transpose to obtain $(Y - X\beta)^T I_n (Y - X\beta)$, and the similarity in form is apparent. Thus, in order to complete the square in matrix form here, we need to determine a value, B, to subtract from β so that the product $(\beta - B)^T (X^T X)(\beta - B)$ gives us the terms involving β in the conditional posterior above. It is clear from this expression that the first term in the expansion will be $\beta^T (X^T X)\beta$, which is identical to the first term in the posterior above. The next terms will be $\beta^T(X^TX)B$ and $B^T(X^TX)\beta$, which are simply transposes of one another. Thus, $2\beta^T(X^TX)B$ must equal $2\beta^T(X^TY)$, or, $(X^TX)B = (X^TY)$. It is clear, then, that B must be $(X^TX)^{-1}(X^TY)$. The final term in the expansion is $[(X^TX)^{-1}(X^TY)]^T(X^TX)[(X^TX)^{-1}(X^TY)]$, which could be reduced, but it is not necessary to do so: It is a constant with respect to β and can therefore be extracted and removed under proportionality. After doing so, the conditional posterior for β is

$$f(\beta|\sigma^2,X,Y) \propto \exp\left\{-\frac{1}{2\sigma^2}(\beta - (X^TX)^{-1}(X^TY))^T(X^TX)(\beta - (X^TX)^{-1}(X^TY))\right\}.$$
(5.13)

Although this form may not be immediately recognizable, realize that $(1/2\sigma^2)$ is a scalar and can therefore be inserted anywhere in the matrix expression. If we let $\Sigma^{-1} = (\sigma^2)^{-1}(X^TX)$ (so that $\Sigma = \sigma^2(X^TX)^{-1}$), then the conditional posterior for β is

$$f(\beta|\sigma^2,X,Y) \propto \exp\left\{-\frac{1}{2}(\beta - B)\Sigma^{-1}(\beta - B)\right\},$$
(5.14)

where B is the OLS/ML estimate $((X^TX)^{-1}(X^TY))$. This form is easily recognizable as that of a multivariate normal distribution with a mean vector of $B = (X^TX)^{-1}(X^TY)$ and covariance matrix of $\Sigma = \sigma^2(X^TX)^{-1}$. Thus, we have the conditional distributions necessary for constructing a Gibbs sampler (see Gelman et al. (2013) for derivation of marginal posterior distributions for the parameters, rather than conditional distributions).

The second prior for the linear model we will discuss is a conjugate prior that parallels that for the mean in Chapter 3. Under that prior, we assume the joint prior $f(\beta,\sigma^2) = f(\beta|\sigma^2)f(\sigma^2)$. As before, we establish an inverse gamma prior for σ^2: $\sigma^2 \sim IG(a,b)$. We establish a multivariate normal distribution for β: $f(\beta|\sigma^2) \propto MVN(Q,\Omega)$, where Q is a $k \times 1$ prior mean vector for β and $\Omega = \sigma^2 S$ is a $k \times k$ prior covariance matrix. With these priors, the posterior distribution is

$$f(\beta,\sigma^2|X,Y,Q,S,a,b) \propto \frac{1}{(\sigma^2)^{n/2}}\exp\left\{-\frac{1}{2\sigma^2}(Y - X\beta)^T(Y - X\beta)\right\} \times$$
$$\frac{1}{(\sigma^2)^{1/2}}\exp\left\{-\frac{1}{2\sigma^2}(\beta - Q)^T S^{-1}(\beta - Q)\right\}\frac{1}{(\sigma^2)^{(a+1)}}\exp\left\{-\frac{b}{\sigma^2}\right\}. \quad (5.15)$$

The conditional posterior for σ^2 is straightforward to derive but contains a number of terms:

$$f(\sigma^2|\beta,X,Y,...) \propto \frac{1}{(\sigma^2)^{[n+1+2(a+1)]/2}}\exp\left\{-\frac{Z}{\sigma^2}\right\}, \quad (5.16)$$

where

$$Z = \left(\frac{1}{2}\right) [Y^T Y + \beta^T (X^T X + S^{-1})\beta - 2\beta^T (X^T Y + S^{-1} Q) + Q^T S^{-1} Q + 2b].$$
(5.17)

This term is lengthy but is obtained simply by expanding the quadratic forms in the exponentials and grouping terms. Thus, the conditional posterior for σ^2 is an inverse gamma distribution with parameters $A = [n + 1 + 2a]/2$ and $B = Z$.

The conditional distribution for β is more difficult to derive, despite having fewer terms than the conditional posterior for σ^2. First, the terms outside the exponentials and the exponential term that is part of the inverse gamma prior for σ^2 can be removed: None of these terms involves β and are therefore proportionality constants when considering the conditional distribution for β. What remains, then, is the exponential term from the posterior for σ^2 in Equation 5.16. Second, terms not involving β in Z can be removed, leaving

$$f(\beta|X, Y, \sigma^2, \ldots) \propto \exp\left\{ -\frac{1}{2\sigma^2} [\beta^T (X^T X + S^{-1})\beta - 2\beta^T (X^T Y + S^{-1} Q)] \right\}.$$
(5.18)

As before, β is a quadratic form, and we can complete the square to expose a recognizable form for it. Specifically, we can recognize that β is multivariate normal with a mean of $M = (X^T X + S^{-1})^{-1}(X^T Y + S^{-1} Q)$:

$$f(\beta|X, Y, \sigma^2, \ldots) \propto \exp\left\{ -\frac{1}{2\sigma^2} (\beta - M)^T (X^T X + S^{-1})(\beta - M) \right\}. \quad (5.19)$$

It is straightforward, albeit tedious, to recognize that the central term in this equation, $(X^T X + S^{-1})$, is necessary to "cancel" with its inverse to leave the term $(X^T Y + S^{-1} Q)$:

$$M^T (X^T X + S^{-1}) = [(X^T X + S^{-1})^{-1}(X^T Y + S^{-1} Q)]^T (X^T X + S^{-1}) \quad (5.20)$$

$$= (X^T Y + S^{-1} Q)(X^T X + S^{-1})^{-1}(X^T X + S^{-1}) \quad (5.21)$$

$$= (X^T Y + S^{-1} Q)I \quad (5.22)$$

$$= (X^T Y + S^{-1} Q). \quad (5.23)$$

Thus, the conditional posterior distribution for β is multivariate normal with mean M and variance $\sigma^2 (X^T X + S^{-1})^{-1}$.

It is worth noting that, if we have no prior information regarding β, so that $S^{-1} = 0$ (which is equivalent to saying that $S = \infty$—infinite prior variance for β), the conditional posterior for β reduces immediately to the posterior for β in the case above in which we used the reference prior for σ^2. Similarly, if we also set $a = b = 0$ in the inverse gamma prior for σ^2, the conditional posterior distribution for σ^2 reduces to the posterior in the case above. Further, it is worth noting that other, equivalent approaches to deriving the conditional posterior distributions are possible and sometimes shown in the literature.

Example

Earlier, we found that political positions have trended toward the liberal end of the spectrum over time, while political identification trended toward the conservative end of the spectrum from the 1970s until sometime in the 1990s, when it began to trend the other direction. Those findings were based only on means of the political positions and identification indexes by decade, without controlling on any compositional change in the population (or sample) that may account for the trends. For example, growth in the nonwhite population over time could affect trends in political positions/identification without any change occurring *within* racial subpopulations. One may therefore wish to control on compositional change, if the hypothesis under consideration involves subpopulation change rather than gross, macro-level change. Even if one is interested purely in macro-level change, controlling on composition is warranted to compensate for any change in the GSS sampling strategy over time. At a minimum, controlling on covariates increases the precision with which trends can be estimated.

Further, our previous strategy of examining means by decade is not particularly useful for determining exactly when the trend in identification reversed course if that is of interest. We might ask, When did this trend begin to reverse itself? Was it during the Clinton presidency? Answering this question requires that we specify a regression model with a linear and quadratic term for year, along with other covariates, to capture the inflection point:

$$\text{Identification}_i = \beta_0 + \beta_1 \text{year}_i + \beta_2 \text{year}_i^2 + \gamma^T X_i + e_i, \qquad (5.24)$$

where $\gamma^T X_i$ is a linear combination of relevant covariates and their effects. The year at which the peak of the trend toward more conservative identification occurred can be found using a little differential calculus applied to the regression equation:

$$\frac{\partial y}{\partial x} = \frac{\partial\ Identification}{\partial\ year} = \beta_1 + 2\beta_2 year. \qquad (5.25)$$

Setting this equation to 0 and solving for year yields

$$\text{year at maximum/minimum} = \frac{-\beta_1}{2\beta_2}. \qquad (5.26)$$

This quantity is an unknown parameter of direct interest, but it is not itself directly represented in the model; we may call it a secondary parameter. If we are interested in evaluating hypotheses regarding it—such as whether the peak followed the 1994 Republican takeover of Congress, for example— we can obtain a sample from its distribution by computing this quantity from the output of a Gibbs sampler for the original regression parameters, as I will illustrate.

Assume we have no prior information, so we opt to use the reference prior $f(\beta, \sigma^2) \propto 1/\sigma^2$. A Gibbs sampler can be implemented by iteratively sampling from the conditional posterior distributions derived above:

1. $\beta | X, Y, \sigma^2 \sim MVN((X^TX)^{-1}(X^TY), \sigma^2(X^TX)^{-1})$ and

2. $\sigma^2 | X, Y, \beta \sim IG(n/2, e^Te/2)$.

Item 5 in the Appendix is a Gibbs sampler, written in R, for the linear regression model with this reference prior. The function requires a matrix, X, of covariates; an outcome vector Y; and a number of iterations to run the sampler. The starting values for all regression coefficients are set to 0, and the starting value for the error variance parameter, σ^2, is arbitrarily set to 1. The function first samples β from its conditional multivariate normal distribution using the previously sampled value for σ^2 (1 at the start) and then samples σ^2 from its inverse gamma distribution using the sum of the squared error terms computed using the newly updated value of β (i.e., $SSE = e^Te = (Y - X\beta)^T(Y - X\beta)$).

I ran this Gibbs sampler for 5,000 iterations, with age, sex (male), race (nonwhite), educational attainment (years), and region (South) as control variables. Figure 5.1 shows time series/trace plots of some of the sampled parameters from the model. The top-left plot shows the sampled intercept values. The top-right and bottom-left plots show the sampled values for the year and year^2 coefficients. The bottom-right plot shows the bivariate samples of these latter two coefficients. These plots show that the algorithm converged quickly from starting values of 0 and mixed quickly as well. The bottom-right plot shows that the year and year-squared coefficients are highly correlated with one another—a well-known issue with polynomial terms for uncentered variables—but our interest lies in a function of these two parameters and not these parameters themselves.

Table 5.1 summarizes the Gibbs sampler results and provides ML/OLS estimates for comparison. The first column in the table presents the posterior means and standard deviations obtained from 1,000 samples. Although the Gibbs sampler was run for 5,000 iterations, I dropped the first 1,000 samples as the burn-in and "thinned" the remaining samples by retaining every

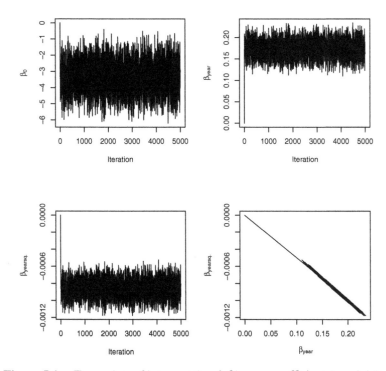

Figure 5.1   Trace plots of intercept (top left), year coefficient (top right), year^2 coefficient (bottom left), and both (bivariate) year and year^2 coefficients from Gibbs sampler for linear regression model.

fourth sampled value. Although trace plots suggested the burn-in period was shorter than 1,000 iterations, and ACF plots indicated no serious autocorrelation even at lag 1, the cost of running the algorithm for 5,000 iterations and discarding most of the samples is minimal. And 1,000 samples is sufficient to summarize this posterior: Additional analyses using longer runs yielded the same results.

The second column of the table presents the ML/OLS estimates and their estimated standard errors. As the table shows, the Bayesian and classical estimates are very similar, even identical to two or three decimal places in most cases. This result is not surprising: With noninformative priors, Bayesian and classical estimates often coincide, differing primarily in interpretation. Indeed, with no prior, the posterior mode will be equal to the MLE, and the posterior standard deviation will generally equal the estimated stan-

Variable	Posterior Mean (*SD*)	OLS/MLE (*SE*)
Intercept	−3.33 (.900)	−3.32 (.923)
Year	.173 (.019)	.173 (.020)
Year-squared	−.00086 (.0001)	−.00086 (.0001)
Age	.0063 (.001)	.0062 (.001)
Male	.211 (.032)	.210 (.032)
Nonwhite	−1.66 (.045)	−1.66 (.044)
Education	.032 (.005)	.032 (.005)
South	.280 (.034)	.281 (.033)
σ^2	7.00 (.060)	7.00
R^2	.0617 (.003)	.06147

Table 5.1 Results of linear regression model predicting political identification (GSS 1974–2016; $n = 28,273$). First column contains posterior means and standard deviations obtained from Gibbs sampling. Second column contains OLS/ML estimated coefficients and standard errors. All coefficients in the second column are statistically significant at the $p < .05$ level (two-tailed).

dard error. As may be expected, older persons, males, and southerners tend to claim to be more conservative than younger persons, females, and those from other regions. Education also increases conservative identification slightly, which may seem surprising, except that income is not included in the model. The bottom of the table presents the posterior mean for the error variance term, along with its standard deviation. Finally, the table presents the model R-squared. In the Bayesian setting, we can easily compute a standard deviation for the R-squared by computing a value for R-squared using each of the drawn values of β and computing the standard deviation of this distribution of values (see Gelman et al., 2019).

Our parameters of key concern—for year and year^2—are positive and negative, respectively, indicating an inverted parabolic pattern in the mean of

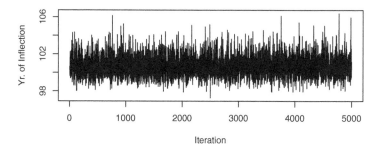

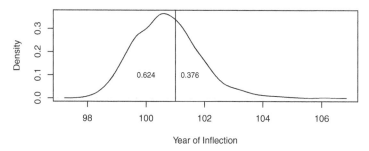

Figure 5.2   Trace plot of the unestimated (secondary) parameter, $-\beta_{year}/(2\beta_{year^2})$ and density plot of 1,000 samples after deleting the first 1,000 samples as burn-in and thinning to every fourth sampled value.

political identification over time, which is consistent with our mean results obtained in Chapter 3. Figure 5.2 presents a trace plot of the secondary parameter representing the inflection point of the curve: $-\beta_{year}/(2\beta_{year^2})$. This parameter also appears to have converged and mixed well over the course of the Gibbs sampling run. The bottom plot in the figure is a density plot of the 1,000 sampled values of this parameter computed from the retained sampled values for the year and year^2 parameters. This density has a mean of 100.72 ($SD = 1.13$) and is skewed to the right. In total, 62.4% of the mass of the density is to the left of 101 (the year 2001), indicating that the inflection in political identification most likely occurred prior to the end of the Clinton presidency, perhaps following the conclusion of his impeachment trial in 1999.

A next question is whether there is a similar such inflection point for the political positions index. Furthermore, given that both the identification and positions indexes are composed of two items or subindexes, we may wish to examine each of the four items separately. Thus, I implemented the Gibbs sampler five more times and constructed a "peak" parameter for each. Results from those analyses can be found in Table 5.2. All six items evidence a quadratic shape that is "statistically significant" from a classical perspective, despite the fact that the $year^2$ parameter is quite small in each case. Further, all but one item was found to have a peak (or minimum) within the survey period. As mentioned above, the identification index reached a peak just prior to 2001. Its constituent measures peaked in 1997 (conservatism) and 2002 (Republican). Conservatism in positions peaked prior to the beginning of the GSS, in 1970. Its constituent measures have opposite patterns. Economic conservatism was declining until 1999 but has increased since then, while cultural conservatism peaked in 1984/1985 and has declined since then. Finally, a composite measure of the identification and positions indexes shows that conservatism broadly peaked just prior to 1991 and has declined since. In general, the GSS data suggest that cultural conservatism has been declining since the Reagan/Bush Sr. era, and although claims of economic conservatism have been increasing since the latter years of the Clinton era, claims of conservatism and Republicanism have been declining since the latter years of the Clinton era or early years of the Bush Jr.

Variable	β_{year}	β_{year^2}	Year of Peak*
Identification	.173 (.02)	−.00086 (.0001)	100.72 (1.13)
Conservative	.049 (.01)	−.00026 (.00005)	96.99 (1.55)
Republican	.123 (.01)	−.00060 (.00007)	102.34 (1.32)
Position	.061 (.01)	−.00043 (.00006)	70.36 (3.64)
Economic cons.*	−.080 (.006)	.00041 (.00003)	98.95 (.60)
Cultural cons.	.142 (.009)	−.00084 (.00005)	84.55 (.63)
Ident. + position	.234 (.027)	−.00130 (.00014)	90.68 (.77)

Table 5.2 Coefficients for year and $year^2$ and the year in which political identification and positions reach a peak (*or minimum) from linear models (GSS 1974–2016; $n = 28,273$).

administration. In short, one making claims regarding growing or declining conservatism in American society must, at a minimum, clarify what is meant by these terms.

These trends suggest that the relationship between identification and positions at the individual level is probably complex and suggests additional questions. For example, assuming that individuals' positions determine how they identify themselves, do economic positions or cultural views play a larger role in affecting self-definitions? Has the process of self-definition based on positions changed over time? In the next section, we will examine the extent to which individuals' political positions are related to their self-definitions, an important step for thinking about polarization.

The Dichotomous Probit Model

More often than not, outcomes in social science research are dichotomous, ordinal, or count variables, rather than continuous ones. Although the linear model can be applied in each of these cases, it is well known that, at a minimum, standard errors of parameter estimates are biased. Equally problematic is that the linear model can predict values outside of the range of the observed variables, probably reflecting a misspecification of the relationship between covariates, X, and the outcome. Generalized linear models (GLMs) help resolve these issues. GLMs provide a general approach for linking a linear combination of covariates to the outcome that restricts predicted values to an appropriate metric and range, given the limited nature of the outcome variable. Johnson & Albert (1999) provides an exhaustive exposition on ordinal data models in a Bayesian setting. Long (1997) provides a broader treatment of GLMs, but in a classical framework.

In this volume, we will focus on one particular GLM: the probit model for dichotomous outcomes. The probit model models the probability of a response of "1" on a dichotomous outcome by linking the linear combination of covariates to the cumulative distribution function (CDF) for the normal distribution, $\Phi(.)$. Thus: $p(y_i = 1) = \Phi(X_i\beta)$, where X_i is the ith row of the design matrix. While $X_i\beta$ can take any real value, $\Phi(X_i\beta)$ is restricted to the $[0,1]$ range. Thus, this and other CDFs are reasonable link functions for modeling probabilities. In social sciences, the logit model is the more common alternative to the probit; in the logit model, the cumulative logistic distribution function is used as the link function so that $p(y_i = 1) = e^{X_i\beta}/(1+e^{X_i\beta}) = 1/(1+e^{-X_i\beta})$. In Bayesian statistics, the probit model is more commonly used, because the probit link is easy to work with.

With a collection of binary responses, Y, an appropriate likelihood function is a product of Bernoulli distributions for each person:

$$L(Y|P) \propto \prod_{i=1}^{n} p_i^{y_i} (1 - p_i)^{1-y_i}. \tag{5.27}$$

Each p_i *could* be represented as a linear combination of covariates and coefficients, β, as $p_i = X\beta$, but this linear link function lets p_i take values below 0 and above 1. Substituting $\Phi(X_i\beta)$ in for p_i, we obtain

$$L(Y|X, \beta) = \prod_{i=1}^{n} \Phi(X_i\beta)^{I(y_i=1)} (1 - \Phi(X_i\beta))^{I(y_i=0)}. \tag{5.28}$$

Because of the nonlinear function $\Phi(.)$, this likelihood function cannot be simplified to obtain a closed-form solution for β. Thus, iterative algorithms must be used to maximize the function and obtain parameter estimates and standard error estimates in a classical (ML) setting.

The Bayesian version of this model requires the incorporation of a prior for β to obtain a posterior, and samples of parameters from the posterior distribution for β can then be obtained using MCMC methods. It is straightforward to implement an MH sampler for the problem (S. M. Lynch, 2007), but a Gibbs sampler is more efficient. Unfortunately, there is no way to implement a Gibbs sampler directly, even with uniform priors for the regression parameters.

In 1993, Albert and Chib, building on Tanner & Wong (1987), presented a method that uses an alternative approach to specifying the model that incorporates "augmented data" to facilitate Gibbs sampling. Their approach uses the latent variable formulation for GLMs (see also Long, 1997). From that perspective, our observed outcome, y, is simply a crudely measured representation of an underlying, or latent, continuous variable, z, that is linearly related to X as in the linear model:

$$Z = X\beta + e. \tag{5.29}$$

The observed y are related to the latent z as

$$y_i = \begin{cases} 1 & \text{iff } z_i > \tau \\ 0 & \text{iff } z_i \leq \tau \end{cases}, \tag{5.30}$$

where τ is a threshold parameter that divides the latent normal distribution into bins representing the dichotomous response. The latent variable, z, has no inherent location or scale, necessitating the imposition of some constraints to identify the regression parameters. That is, β depends on the location and scale of z such that different values of β can produce the same likelihood value if the location and scale of z are changed. The two most common identification constraints that are imposed include (1) $e \sim N(0, 1)$ and (2) $\tau = 0$. The former constraint sets the scale of β, and the latter constraint sets its location so that β_0 (the regression intercept) can be uniquely estimated.

We can rewrite the model with the latent variables as

$$f(\beta, Z | X, Y) \propto f(Y | X, \beta, Z) f(\beta), \qquad (5.31)$$

where $f(\beta)$ is the prior for β. The likelihood function is modified to include the latent data as follows:

$$f(Y | X, Z, \beta) \propto \prod_{i=1}^{n} \{ I(z_i > \tau) I(y_i = 1) + I(z_i \le \tau) I(y_i = 0) \} \exp \left\{ -\frac{(z_i - \beta^T X_i)^2}{2\sigma^2} \right\},$$
$$(5.32)$$

where, again, $\tau = 0$ and $\sigma^2 = 1$ as identifying constraints (note that this is largely the original notation of Albert & Chib 1993). The latter portion of the likelihood function is simply a normal density, representing that, if we know Z, we have a typical linear model as shown in Equation 5.29 above. The first part of the likelihood function requires some explanation. It is the sum of two products of indicators. If $y_i = 1$, then we know that the contribution of individual i to the likelihood is an indicator that $z_i > \tau$ multiplied by a normal density term. If $y_1 = 0$, then the contribution of individual i is an indicator that $z_i \le \tau$ multiplied by a normal density term. This collection of indicators expresses the relationship between the latent and observed data as shown in Equation 5.30.

A Gibbs sampler can be developed in a straightforward fashion. First, if we know Z, then we have a linear model, so the conditional posterior for β is the same as that we derived in the previous section for the linear regression model. Under uniform priors for β, and given that σ^2 is fixed at 1, $\beta | Z, X \sim MVN((X^T X)^{-1}(X^T Z), (X^T X)^{-1})$. If we have a normal distribution prior for β, the posterior for β is the same as what we derived in the previous section for the linear model with a normal prior for β, only several terms are simplified by the constraint that $\sigma^2 = 1$, so that we have no prior for it and no terms in the conditional for β that involve σ^2.

If β is known, then, given Y, we know that Z comes from a normal distribution and is to the left of $\tau = 0$ for cases in which $y = 0$ and to the right of $\tau = 0$ for cases in which $y = 1$. Thus, $Z | \beta, X, Y \sim TN(X\beta, 1, \tau)$, where TN is the truncated normal distribution with truncation point τ. After establishing starting values for the parameters, β, we can implement a Gibbs sampler by iteratively sampling from truncated normal distributions and multivariate normal distributions:

1. $Z \sim TN(X\beta, 1, \tau = 0)$.

2. $\beta \sim MVN((X^TX)^{-1}(X^TZ), (X^TX)^{-1})$.

Drawing values from truncated normal distributions can be done in (at least) two ways: naively or directly. To sample naively, one simply repeatedly draws values from a normal distribution until one is obtained that falls in the appropriate region, based on the value of y_i. This approach can be extremely inefficient when starting values for β are poor or the relationships between the covariates and the outcome are weak. Direct simulation is a better strategy and is relatively easy. This can be done by computing the cumulative area, p_i, under a normal distribution with mean equal to β^TX_i and variance of 1 between $-\infty$ and 0. If $y_i = 0$, one then draws a uniform random number on the interval $[0, p]$ and uses an inverse normal distribution function to obtain z_i. If $y_i = 1$, one draws a uniform random number on the interval $[p, 1]$ and inverts to obtain z_i.

Item 6 in the Appendix presents a function that implements the Gibbs sampler for the probit model. As with the linear model, the function requires a design matrix, X; an outcome vector Y; and a number of iterations for which to run the sampler. This function looks quite similar to that for the linear model with only two significant changes. First, there is no σ^2 parameter to simulate, given that this parameter is fixed at one. Second, there is a block of code that simulates Z from its truncated normal distribution. In R, many functions are "vectorized" so that they can be applied to an entire vector at once. I make use of that feature in several places. First, I compute the areas under the curve below the threshold of 0 for all cases using

```
p=pnorm(0, xb, 1).
```

xb is the $n \times 1$ vector of linear combinations of the covariates and previously sampled values of β. Second, I simulate appropriate uniform random numbers (probabilities) for all cases using

```
u=runif(n,(y*p),p^(y==0)).
```

In this line, n is the number of cases (and thus the number of uniform values to simulate), y is the observed dichotomous response, and p is described immediately above. As stated earlier, for $y_i = 0$, the value must be drawn between 0 and p_i, while for $y_i = 1$, the value must be drawn between p_i

and 1. The expression y*p ensures that the lower bound is 0 for all cases in which $y = 0$ but is p for all cases in which $y = 1$. The expression p^(y==0) ensures that the upper bound is p_i for cases in which $y_i = 0$ (i.e., y==0 evaluates to "True" and hence "1") and that the upper bound is 1 for cases in which $y_i = 1$ (i.e., y==0 evaluates to "False" and hence "0," and $p_i^0 = 1$ regardless of the value of p_i).

Third, I apply the inverse normal distribution function to the vector u to obtain the truncated normal draw using

```
z=qnorm(u,xb,1).
```

Here, both u and xb are vectors, and R simply "knows" to repeat the standard deviation argument "1" for all cases.

Example

To illustrate the Gibbs sampler for the probit model, I examine how economic and cultural positions influence responses to the "Republican" and "conservative" identification items and how the relationship between positions and identification has changed over time. Recall that both of these items are measured on a 7-point scale ranging from "strong Democrat" to "strong Republican" and "extremely liberal" to "extremely conservative," respectively. Thus, they each have a midpoint. For the purposes of this example, I dichotomized both variables so that values at the midpoint or below are coded as 0, while values above the midpoint are coded as 1. Thus, the outcomes are whether the respondent indicated that he or she was a Republican or conservative. I include the same covariates as in previous examples (age, sex, race, region, and educational attainment), and I include year, year^2, and interactions between these variables and the cultural and economic positions variables. I estimate two models: one for the "Republican" item and one for the "conservative" item.

The top of Figure 5.3 shows time series/trace plots of the intercept parameter from each model. As these plots show, the Gibbs sampler appears to have converged and mixed rapidly. Trace plots of the other parameters indicate so as well (not shown). The bottom plots in the figure show sampled values for the latent values, z, in both models for Person 28,000 (arbitrarily selected from the $n = 28,273$ respondents). This respondent indicated he or she was a conservative Republican; thus, his or her latent values are drawn from above 0 in both models.

Figure 5.4 presents density plots of latent z values for four additional, arbitrarily selected persons in the sample. As in the linear model, I dropped the first 1,000 sampled values of all parameters, including the latent scores, and

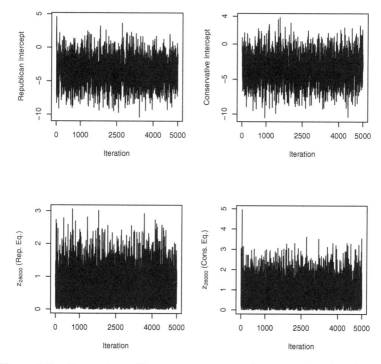

Figure 5.3   Trace plots of intercept parameters from probit models for "Republican" response (upper left) and "conservative" response (upper right), as well as for sampled latent values for Person 28,000's values of "Republican" (lower left) and "conservative" (lower right). Person 28,000 was arbitrarily selected from the sample of $n = 28{,}273$ respondents.

retained every fourth value. Thus, these density plots show 1,000 sampled values of these four individuals' latent scores. The first person (upper-left plot) claimed not to be Republican but did claim to be conservative, based on his or her distribution of scores (negative and positive for the two models, respectively). The 1,000th person (upper-right plot) claimed not to be Republican or conservative. His or her latent scores have almost the same distributional shape across the two models. The 10,000th person (lower-left plot) claimed to be a Republican but not to be conservative. Finally, the 20,000th person was much like the 1,000th, but his or her distribution of latent scores is less dispersed, suggesting that his or her covariate values

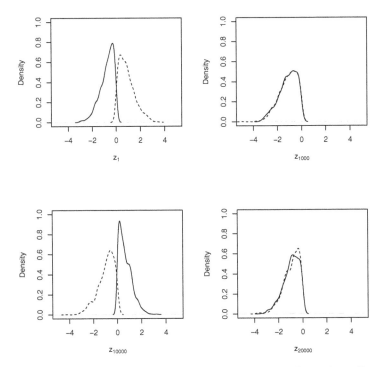

Figure 5.4 Density plots of sampled latent z values for four arbitrarily selected sample members in the probit model. Solid lines are for the model with "Republican" as the outcome; dashed lines are for the model with "conservative" as the outcome.

are more discriminating in pinpointing his or her lack of support for conservatism and Republicanism. This result suggests that we may be able to use distributions of latent scores to evaluate model fit. Indeed, we can, and we will discuss this in the last section in the chapter.

Table 5.3 presents posterior means and standard deviations for the parameters in the probit models. Many of the coefficients are rather small, largely because there is considerable multicollinearity due to the quadratic form for year and interactions with the economic and cultural positions variables. Most effects would not be considered statistically significant from a classical standpoint. The posterior mean for the effect of age, for example, is hardly larger than its posterior standard deviation in both models. From a classical perspective, we would find that the effect of sex (male) on identification as a Republican is not significant but is positively related to identification as

Variable	Republican or Not	Conservative or Not
Intercept	-3.59 (1.99)	-3.48 (1.99)
Economic	-1.13 (.62)	.94 (.63)
Year*Econ	.024 (.013)	-.018 (.014)
Year^2*Econ	-.000086 (.00007)	.00011 (.00007)
Cultural	.45 (.42)	-.32 (.404)
Year*Cult	-.012 (.009)	.007 (.009)
Year^2*Cult	.000091 (.000048)	-.000009 (.00005)
Year	.055 (.043)	.038 (.043)
Year^2	-.00048 (.00023)	-.00033 (.0002)
Age	.00066 (.00053)	.0007 (.0005)
Male	.009 (.02)	.09 (.02)
Nonwhite	-.67 (.03)	-.07 (.023)
South	-.009 (.02)	.09 (.02)
Education	.06 (.003)	.047 (.003)

Table 5.3 Results of probit model predicting "Republican" and "conservative" identification with economic and cultural positions as predictors.

a conservative. Nonwhites are less likely to consider themselves Republicans or conservatives. There is no regional difference in identification as a Republican, but southerners are more likely to call themselves conservative. Finally, education has a positive relationship with identifying as a Republican and a conservative. These variables are not of primary interest, however. The key question is whether the associations between economic and cultural positions and the two measures of identification have strengthened, weakened, or stayed the same over time. Because of collinearity—which would only be partially remedied by centering year—answering this question with the coefficients is difficult.

As we did in the previous example, we can compute functions of the parameters that help with answering this question. The effect of cultural positions on Republican identification can be determined by factoring the variable "Cultural" (C) from its main effect and interaction effects with Year (Y) and Year^2 (Y^2) in the model:

$$\Phi^{-1}(p(y=1)) = b_0 + b_1 C + b_2 YC + b_3 Y^2 C + \dots \tag{5.33}$$

$$= (b_1 + b_2 Y + b_3 Y^2)C + \dots. \tag{5.34}$$

We can generate a posterior distribution for the effect of cultural position on the probability one considers oneself a Republican in each year by applying this function to a sequence of values for years for each value of the relevant parameters obtained from the Gibbs sampler. We can repeat this process for the effect of economic position, and we can repeat it for the model with the conservatism outcome as well. What we obtain is a sample from the distribution for the effect of each x on each y in each year, net of all other variables in the model. The coefficient will be in the probit (i.e., standard normal) metric.

Figure 5.5 consists of two plots, one for the Republicanism outcome (top) and one for the conservatism outcome (bottom). In both plots, the darker lines reflect the effect of economic positions on self-definitions, while the lighter lines reflect the effect of cultural positions. The solid lines are the posterior means for the effects in each year; the dashed lines are 95% bounds, meaning there is probability .95 that the true effect falls in that interval in a given year. These were obtained by sorting the 1,000 computed sample values in each year and using the 25th and 975th values as the lower and upper bounds, respectively.

The associations between economic and cultural views and Republican identification have increased over time. It also appears that economic views are more strongly related to Republicanism than are cultural views, although this conclusion requires some caution, given that the effects are not standardized. In contrast, both economic and cultural views seem relatively equally predictive of conservative identification, and although there appears to be an upward trend in the association, it is not clear that the trend is particularly strong. We can assess the probability that the association between economic positions and conservative identification is stronger in 2016 than in 1974 in two ways. Since we have 1,000 samples from the posterior distribution for the effect of positions on identification in each year, we can simply randomly draw a value from each sample and compare them. The proportion of draws in which $\theta_a > \theta_b$ is an estimate of the probability that $\theta_a > \theta_b$. Alternatively, given that the sampled parameter values are from the same model, we can simply compare the jth value for the computed effect of x in a given year to the jth value computed in the base year.

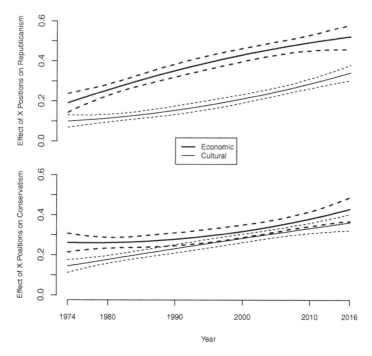

Figure 5.5   Effects of economic (dark lines) and cultural (lighter lines) positions on Republican (top plot) and conservative (bottom plot) self-identification from 1974 to 2016. Dashed lines are 95% bounds on estimates. Solid lines are posterior means.

This calculation is unnecessary for the upper plot in the figure: It is clear that the effect of cultural and economic positions on Republican identification has increased over time. The bottom plot is less clear, but the probability that the effect of both has increased from 1974 to 2016 is estimated to be 1. Indeed, there is almost no overlap in the posterior samples. For example, the largest sampled value for the effect of economic positions on conservative identification in 1974 was .35007, while this is slightly smaller than the fifth smallest sampled value in 2016. Thus, only 4/1,000 sampled values for 1974 are larger than the smallest values for 2016.

In sum, the results indicate that both economic and cultural positions have become increasingly aligned over time with identification as a Republican. This pattern is also true, but somewhat weaker, for identification as a conservative. This result may not be surprising, based on what a cursory look at what the past few decades has shown in media: The political parties in the United States have come to be identified with several key issues, such as abortion and gun control. Thus, it is relatively easy for even a relatively uninformed potential voter to recognize which party identification he or she *should* claim, given his or her particular views on these key issues. In contrast, the terms "conservative" and "liberal" are much less precise and more fluid over time. For example, to be opposed to abortion and gun control have been hallmarks of Republicanism for the entire GSS period. In contrast, support for interracial marriage in the 1970s and gay marriage in the 2000s have traditionally been "liberal" views, so that opposition would be "conservative." However, supporting these positions now would probably be considered mainstream.

The examples thus far have shown that political positions and political identification have experienced very different trends over the past half century. The analyses of means by decades showed that overall positions have trended steadily toward the more liberal end of the spectrum, while identification trended toward the conservative end of the spectrum until the late 1990s, when it began to trend in the other direction. However, we found that cultural and economic political positions have not uniformly trended toward the liberal end of the spectrum. Instead, while cultural conservatism increased and then declined starting in the mid-1980s, economic conservatism declined and then began increasing in the late 1990s. In the next example, we will explore whether these trends are universal in the population or whether the distribution of identification and positions has bifurcated over time, suggesting polarization.

A Latent Class (Finite Mixture) Model

In Chapter 3, we examined trends in political positions and political identification by estimating means of these indexes across decades. The implicit assumption in estimating these means was that the population was homogeneous, with a single mean and variance in each decade. Although we can estimate a single mean and variance, as well as possibly consider an increase in the variance or kurtosis of the distribution over time as an indication of growing polarization (e.g., DiMaggio et al., 1996), a more natural model may be one that explicitly assumes that the data are generated by more than one population and allows us to estimate the separate parameters for the underlying subpopulations. Mixture modeling constitutes such an approach.

In a finite mixture model, an observed sample of data is assumed to comprise members coming from two or more distinct subpopulations characterized by their own parameters. Usually, the subpopulation distributions are assumed to be of the same form (e.g., normal), and some parameters may differ across subpopulations (e.g., often the mean) while others may be invariant across subpopulations (e.g., sometimes the variance). As an example, consider the distribution of body weight in the population. We may estimate a single mean and variance for the overall population, but the population is really more reasonably viewed as a mixture of male and female body weights, with males being heavier and most likely having greater variation than females. Thus, were we interested in modeling body weight, we would probably estimate separate models by sex or, in a regression framework, include a dummy variable to capture the difference in means and—net of other covariates—assume residual variation to be equal across sexes (i.e., homoscedastic errors).

Importantly, with body weight, the grouping characteristic—sex—is known and observed. Finite mixture models are generally used in social science research when the grouping characteristic is not known or observed. Thus, the use of finite mixture models in social science is often called latent class analysis (LCA; see Lynch & Taylor, 2016). There are two questions that are generally addressed in LCA: (1) How many latent classes exist in the population and what do we call them?, and (2) to what class do individuals belong and what predicts membership in a class? Answering the first question typically requires estimating multiple models, each with different numbers of latent classes, and comparing their relative fit, taking the number of parameters estimated into account (i.e., considering and preferring parsimony). For example, a two-class model necessarily requires estimation of more parameters than a one-class model, so does using a two-class model provide enough better fit to the data than a one-class model so as to justify the larger number of parameters? This determination is often made using the Bayesian information criterion (BIC) discussed below.

There are different strategies for answering the second question, and these strategies remain an open area of investigation. One strategy treats the estimation of latent classes as separate from predicting membership in classes. Under that strategy, one estimates the latent class structure, then assigns individuals to latent classes based on their "posterior probabilities of class membership," and then estimates a multinomial logit model predicting membership in classes as a function of observed covariates. This is sometimes called a "two-step" or "three-step" method, depending on how class membership is assigned. Another strategy combines the estimation of the latent class structure with membership prediction (a "one-step" method). This approach tends to lead to estimation of fewer latent classes, because part of what may appear as distinctions between latent subpopulations may in fact be differences that are accounted for by observed covariates that predict differences in means *within* classes (see Bakk et al., 2013; Bakk & Kuha, 2018; Nylund-Gibson et al., 2019).

Here, we will not address these more complicated questions but rather restrict discussion to a relatively simple set of latent class models so as to illustrate a few key issues in Bayesian statistics. First, as we will see, the data augmentation approach we used in the probit model will be used here and will greatly simplify construction of a Gibbs sampler for obtaining samples from the posterior for the parameters of the model, reinforcing a strength of using a Bayesian approach. Second, as the discussion regarding the implications for the number of latent classes found using the one-step versus two/three-step methods suggests, latent class modeling can be very sensitive to a variety of modeling choices. This includes, especially, the choice of priors one specifies in the Bayesian context.

Mixture models can be represented using a variety of notations, in part reflecting differences in the complexity and specification of a particular model. Latent class models can be used for multivariate outcomes, such as repeated measures across time or multiple measures on one occasion (e.g., see Congdon, 2003, for some definitions that are slightly different from those used in social science applications, including here). Further, probabilities that an individual belongs to a specific latent class may be general, representing the overall proportion of the population in each class, or they may be specific and predicted by individual-level covariates. For our purposes, I will keep the notation fairly general here but become more specific in the example. Assume that there are J latent classes, $c_1 \ldots c_J$, in the population, and let c_{ij} represent membership in class j for individual i. For each individual, c can be thought of as a vector of length J with a value of 1 for the class to which the individual belongs and values of 0 for the other classes. To keep notation as simple as possible, instead of writing $p(y_i \in c_j)$ to represent the probability that the individual's response y belongs in class c, I will simply use $p(c_{ij})$, p_{ij}, or just p_j. Further, I will use θ_j to represent the parameters associated with class j. Differences in θ_j are what distinguish latent classes from one another, so I will use a semicolon whenever both c and θ appear together, simply to indicate that they are not separable. Finally, I will omit subscripts when referring to values of p, c, and θ across all classes.

Assume membership in latent classes is unknown (as stated above, this is the typical assumption). By the law of total probability (see Chapter 2), an individual's probability density—and hence his or her contribution to a likelihood function—is

$$f(y_i) = \sum_{j=1}^{J} p(c_{ij}) f(y_i | c_{ij}). \tag{5.35}$$

A likelihood function for the collection of Y can be constructed as usual by assuming independence of observations and taking the product across the sample:

$$f(c; \theta | Y) = \prod_{i=1}^{n} \left(\sum_{j=1}^{J} p(c_{ij}) f(y_i | c_{ij}; \theta_j) \right), \qquad (5.36)$$

where Y is the vector of all n responses on y, and I have explicitly included θ to remind us that these are the parameters of interest in the model.

To complete a Bayesian specification, we must specify the distributions for $p(c)$ and $f(y|c; \theta)$ and incorporate priors for their parameters. The distribution for $p(c)$ is called the "mixing distribution" and is finite and discrete: That is, there are J distinct classes. The distributions $f(y|c; \theta)$ are the "component" distributions. Although I have written $p(c)$ in the likelihood in terms of c_{ij}, the simplest approach is to assume that probability of class membership does not vary across individuals. Thus, we could write $p(c_j)$, indicating the general probability of membership in class j for all individuals; put another way, this is simply the proportion of the population that is in class j. As discussed before, an appropriate distribution for proportions is the Dirichlet distribution if $J > 2$. Thus, a prior for p may be written as

$$f(p|\alpha) \propto \prod_{j=1}^{J} p_j^{\alpha_j - 1}, \qquad (5.37)$$

with $\sum_{j=1}^{J} p_j = 1$, and α_j can be considered prior counts of members in class j. Recall that, if $j = 2$, the Dirichlet distribution reduces to a beta distribution:

$$f(p|\alpha, \beta) \propto p^{\alpha - 1}(1 - p)^{\beta - 1}, \qquad (5.38)$$

with p representing the probability of being in the first class and $1 - p$ representing the probability of being in the second class. Here, we will concentrate on a two-class model, so I will sometimes simply refer to this distribution as a beta distribution rather than a Dirichlet distribution.

Let's assume that the component distributions are normal so $\theta_j = [\mu_j \quad \sigma_j^2]$. These distributions are assumed to be independent across classes, so we may write a joint prior for the parameters μ_j and σ_j^2 as a product of priors across classes:

$$f(\mu, \sigma^2) \propto \prod_{j=1}^{J} f(\mu_j, \sigma_j^2). \qquad (5.39)$$

We discussed several possible priors for the parameters of the normal distribution in Chapter 3. Here, we will use the prior $f(\mu, \sigma^2) = f(\mu|\sigma^2) f(\sigma^2)$, where $f(\mu|\sigma^2)$ is a normal distribution with a mean of M and a variance of

σ^2/n_0, and $f(\sigma^2)$ is an inverse gamma distribution with parameters a and b. Each of these distributions is subscripted with j in the full specification, because each component distribution has its own parameters and therefore priors. The full posterior, then, is

$$f(\mu,\sigma^2,p|Y) \propto \left(\prod_{i=1}^{n}\sum_{j=1}^{J} p_j f(y|\mu_j,\sigma_j^2)\right) f(p|\alpha)\prod_{j=1}^{J} f(\mu_j|M_j,\sigma_j^2,n_{0j}))f(\sigma_j^2|a_j,b_j),$$
(5.40)

where μ, σ^2, and p to the left of the proportionality symbol are vectors, p and α on the righthand side are also vectors, and I have omitted the collection of hyperparameters α, M, n_0, a, and b in the conditional expression for the posterior simply to save space.

A Gibbs sampler can be developed to obtain posterior samples of the parameters, but the sum in the likelihood makes deriving the conditional posteriors for μ, σ^2, and p difficult, much as the nonlinear normal distribution function made deriving the conditional distributions difficult in the probit model. As in the probit model, we can use a data augmentation strategy to facilitate the derivation of and sampling from the conditionals.

Suppose we knew to which latent class each individual belonged. Then, $p(c_{ij}) = 1$ if $y_i \in c_j$ and 0 otherwise. One way to view this result is that the sum in the likelihood function for each individual would only consist of one term, because other terms for which $p(c_{ij})$ were 0 would drop from the sum. Alternatively, if the c_{ij} were known, we could view the likelihood function as multinomial. For an individual:

$$f(c_i|p) \propto \prod_{j=1}^{J} p_j^{c_{ij}}.$$
(5.41)

For the entire sample:

$$f(c|p) \propto \prod_{i=1}^{n}\left(\prod_{j=1}^{J} p_j^{c_{ij}}\right)$$
(5.42)

$$\propto \prod_{j=1}^{J} p_j^{\sum c_{ij}}$$
(5.43)

$$\propto \prod_{j=1}^{J} p_j^{n_j},$$
(5.44)

where n_j is simply the number of persons in the sample who are in class j.

With the incorporation of the latent data (known class memberships), the conditional posterior distributions of all other parameters are straightforward to derive from the full posterior density using derivations we have seen in Chapter 3. Specifically, given the latent data, the only terms in the posterior distribution that contain p are the multinomial distribution containing the latent data and the Dirichlet prior for p. The $f(y|\mu_j, \sigma_j^2)$ terms can be factored out and dropped as proportionality constants. Thus, the conditional distribution for p is

$$f(p|\alpha, \ldots) \propto \prod_{i=1}^{J} p_j^{\alpha_j + n_j - 1}. \tag{5.45}$$

This is a Dirichlet distribution with parameters $\alpha_j + n_j$ ($\forall j$). Again, if there are only two latent classes, this conditional posterior reduces to a beta distribution.

If the latent data are known, so that the sum in the likelihood function contains only one term per person (or we think of each person as contributing a term to the multinomial likelihood), then the conditional posterior distribution for each μ involves only the likelihood terms for members of the corresponding class. Thus, the posterior for each μ is the same as shown in Chapter 3:

$$f(\mu_j|\sigma_j^2, y) \propto \exp\left\{ -\frac{2b_j + n_{0j}(\mu_j - M_j)^2 + \sum_{y_i \in c_j}(y_i - \mu_j)^2}{2\sigma_j^2} \right\}, \tag{5.46}$$

where the sum is taken over only those for whom y_i belongs in class c_j. As shown in Chapter 3, after rearranging terms, simplifying, and completing the square, we find that

$$(\mu_j|\sigma_j^2, y, \ldots) \sim N\left(\frac{n_{0j}M_j + n_j \bar{y}_j}{n_{0j} + n_j}, \frac{\sigma_j^2}{n_{0j} + n_j} \right), \tag{5.47}$$

where $\bar{y}_j$ is the mean of y among those in the class.

Next, if we know the latent data, the distribution of each σ_j^2 is very easy to derive and is also as shown in Chapter 3. The only term of importance missing from the equation for μ is the leading term outside the exponential, which is

$$\frac{1}{(\sigma_j^2)^{a_j + 3/2 + n_j/2}}. \tag{5.48}$$

Thus, the conditional distribution for each σ_j^2 is an inverse gamma distribution:

$$(\sigma_j^2|\mu_j, \ldots) \propto IG\left(a_j + \frac{1 + n_j}{2}, \frac{2b_j + n_{0j}(\mu_j - M_j)^2 + \sum_{y_i \in c_j}(y_i - \mu_j)^2}{2} \right). \tag{5.49}$$

Thus, if we have the latent data—that is, we know the class to which each individual belongs—the conditional distributions for all unknowns are straightforward. What remains is to understand how to obtain the latent data so as to facilitate sampling. That is, how do we assign individuals to latent classes?

If we know the parameters μ_j and σ_j^2, $\forall j$, as well as all the p_j, then the probability a given individual is in class j can be computed using Bayes' theorem:

$$p(c_{ij}|y_i) = \frac{p(c_{ij})f(y_i|c_{ij})}{\sum_{j=1}^{j} p(c_{ij})f(y_i|c_{ij})}. \tag{5.50}$$

In the latent class modeling literature, this computation is often called the "posterior probability of class membership," precisely because it is a Bayesian calculation that reverses the conditional $f(y_i|c_{ij})$. If we know a person's probability of being in each class, it is easy to recognize that we could simulate his or her class membership vector (c_i) from a multinomial distribution with parameters $n = 1$ and $p(c_{ij})$, $\forall j$.

Since the conditional distributions for all parameters can be derived and are known distributional forms, it is straightforward to construct a Gibbs sampler. Specifically, after assigning starting values for the parameters, we simply iterate through the following steps:

1. Simulate c from multinomial distributions, for all sample members, conditional on values of the parameters and hyperparameters.

2. Simulate p from a Dirichlet distribution, conditional on the newly sampled latent class values and other relevant quantities.

3. Simulate each member of μ from the appropriate normal distribution, conditional on other relevant quantities.

4. Simulate each member of σ^2 from the appropriate inverse gamma distribution, conditional on other relevant quantities.

Before implementing the Gibbs sampler, we need to establish values of the hyperparameters α_j, a_j, b_j, M_j, and n_{0j}, $\forall j$. Latent class models are sensitive to distributional assumptions, and they can also be sensitive to choices for priors. For example, if we assume that y in each class comes from a t-distribution, rather than a normal distribution, we may find fewer classes, because the t-distribution has heavier tails than the normal distribution, and extra spread in the distribution for y may be viewed as stemming from one, broader class rather than reflecting the existence of two narrower classes with lighter tails (see Bauer & Curran, 2003). Indeed, the t-distribution itself is a *continuous* (rather than finite or discrete) mixture of normal distributions, where the mixing distribution is inverse gamma for σ^2. This is not to suggest that the normal distribution assumption is necessarily a bad one; it is simply to suggest that one should think carefully about at least the assignment of values to hyperparameters. Although priors in other models are often relatively inconsequential, poor choices for these quantities may have a large impact on results in a mixture model.

Suppose, for example, we assume there are two latent classes underlying our observed y, but there is really only one class. Further, suppose we assigned values of $n_{0j} = 0$ as our prior values for each class, thinking these values represent weak priors. The data will push n_j toward 0 for the nonexistent class, which will, in turn, make the variance in the conditional posterior for the corresponding μ_j infinite (see Equation 5.47). Without adequate "exception handling," a Gibbs sampler will "crash" when it attempts to sample μ_j from a normal distribution with infinite variance. At a minimum, convergence and mixing will be problematic.

Next, suppose we also set each a_j and b_j in the priors for σ^2 to a very small number or 0, again, under the assumption that this prior indicates prior ignorance. If there is only one class, then, as n_j moves toward 0, the scale parameter in the inverse gamma posterior distribution for the nonexistent class will tend toward 0. Again, this will cause a Gibbs sampler to crash, because the variance of σ^2 will collapse to 0 (see Equation 5.48). This is a problem that may be handled in a software package that estimates latent class models via a classical framework by the imposition of unseen constraints, but if one is writing one's own code to implement a Gibbs/MCMC sampler, the issue must be addressed by adopting priors that prevent the problem from arising (which is, in fact, essentially what the imposition of constraints is: highly informative priors).

A final consideration is that the hyperprior values one chooses should arguably represent a coherent set of beliefs. If, for example, we have sufficient reason to believe a priori that there are two or more classes in the population, so that we set $n_{0j} > 0$ for all classes, then it would make no sense to set all α_j to 0, since the priors for α establish the proportion of persons in the population we think are in each class. Setting all the α_j to 0 implies that we have no belief about the proportion of the population in each class. This suggests that we believe—with equal probability—that there could really be only one class (i.e., one class has 0%) or two classes with equal numbers of individuals in each class.

This does not mean that there should be one-to-one correspondence between α_j and n_{0j}. One can be more confident about the proportion of persons in each latent class than in the mean of responses on y, which is what n_{0j} reflects. But it is seemingly unreasonable to be confident in latent class means, μ_j, so that n_{0j} is large, while simultaneously being completely uncertain about the proportion of the population in such a well-defined class. These issues are also relevant in the maximum likelihood framework, but most software packages have built-in exception handling procedures to prevent undefined or impossible solutions that may arise from (in the ML context) having no priors. The Bayesian analyst engaged in his or her own programming, however, must be aware of these issues.

Example

The concept of political polarization suggests that there are two latent classes that underlie our observed data or, if polarization is viewed as a process, that two latent classes have emerged and separated over time. Here, we will estimate a series of latent class models—one for each decade—for the political identification and political positions variables. My prior belief is that polarization is largely a myth: that, although there may be two subpopulations within the larger population—a more conservative one and a more liberal one—these populations overlap considerably and have not experienced any substantial increase in separation over time in their political positions. However, to the extent that politicians use increasingly inflammatory language, there may be some recent separation in how people define themselves. This view is consistent with McCarty's (2019) summary of the literature, which he says has demonstrated clear polarization of elites (politicians) but is mixed with regard to polarization among the public.

To reflect these prior beliefs, I use the following priors. For the means, I set $M_1 = 5$ and $M_2 = 7$. These values are on either side of the midpoints of the identification and positions indexes. I assume that approximately half of the population is in each class but that there could reasonably be an 70/30 split. Thus, I set α_1 and α_2 to 10 each. Given that there are only two classes, the distribution for p is a beta distribution. Assigning α_1 and α_2 to the same value yields a prior mean for p of .5. Setting them both to 10 yields a prior standard deviation for p of .11, for a 95% interval that roughly covers the range from .30 to .70. I also set n_{01} and n_{02} each to 10 as well.

Finally, I set a_1 and b_1 to values that reflect my prior belief that there is considerable overlap between "liberal" and "conservative" subpopulations. The mean of the inverse gamma distribution is $b/(a-1)$, and the variance of the inverse gamma distribution is $b^2/(a-1)(a-2)$. Values for a and b can be induced by establishing a prior mean for σ^2 and variation in it to reflect the belief that the two distributions overlap. Since I set the prior means for the latent classes two units apart, I opt for a mean of 4 for σ^2 and a prior variance of .25. Thus, the prior mean of the standard deviation for the normal distribution is 2, itself with a standard deviation of .5 units. This means that σ is expected to be 2 but may reasonably range roughly from 1 to 3. The values of a and b that yield this prior for σ^2 are $a_1 = a_2 = 18$ and $b_1 = b_2 = 34$.

Item 7 in the Appendix is a Gibbs sampler for a two-class latent class model with these priors. The program is substantially longer than the previous ones, but it is not fundamentally more complicated. It is simply longer because there are more parameters. The program first samples latent class memberships for each person from the appropriate multinomial (binomial here) distribution, given each person's posterior probabilities of class membership. Then, the latent class probabilities are simulated from their Dirichlet (beta) distribution. Finally, the mean and variance of each latent class is sampled.

One issue that we have not discussed is that of "label switching" (see Gelman et al., 2013). Latent classes are defined by their parameters. There is nothing inherently "real" about them otherwise, so they should not be reified—a reason that a key part of latent class analysis is naming the latent classes. It is quite possible, for example, for two latent classes to "switch" places in a Gibbs sampler, such that the mean of the first latent class climbs to exceed that of the second latent class. In that case, individuals' memberships in classes will also switch, and the result is simply the same as switching the names of the latent classes. In the program in the Appendix, I prevent switching by constraining the mean of the first latent class to be smaller than that of the second class. This is accomplished by simply not accepting Gibbs samples for either mean that are below/above that of the other. This constraint is of little consequence if (1) the data suggest strong separation of the means or (2) the priors are strong enough to keep the means apart.

I ran the Gibbs sampler for 20,000 iterations and saved every 10th value. After determining that the Gibbs samplers had converged and mixed well, I retained the last 1,000 sampled values for summarization. Table 5.4 shows the posterior means and standard deviations from 10 latent class models: one for each decade for both the political identification and political positions indexes. The first column of the table shows the posterior means for the mean of the first class, while the third column shows the means for the second, more conservative, class. The mean identification for Class 1 was 4.08 in the 1970s and increased and leveled off across the survey period. The mean for the second class also increased, but more substantially, across the period from 8.16 in the 1970s to 9.19 in the 2010s. Thus, both classes became more conservative in their identification over the period, but the more conservative class increased in its conservatism to a greater degree than the more liberal

	Class 1 (Liberal)		Class 2 (Conservative)		
	μ_1	σ_1^2	μ_2	σ_2^2	p_1
Identification					
1970s	4.08 (.07)	2.51 (.12)	8.16 (.12)	2.61 (.20)	.64 (.02)
1980s	4.20 (.07)	2.76 (.12)	8.42 (.10)	2.61 (.17)	.63 (.02)
1990s	4.41 (.09)	3.53 (.18)	8.87 (.12)	2.58 (.20)	.64 (.02)
2000s	4.45 (.09)	4.03 (.21)	9.10 (.13)	2.52 (.21)	.69 (.02)
2010s	4.43 (.10)	4.43 (.25)	9.19 (.16)	2.49 (.25)	.72 (.02)
Positions					
1970s	5.07 (.29)	2.45 (.28)	7.09 (.08)	1.74 (.09)	.31 (.07)
1980s	5.40 (.22)	2.19 (.20)	7.05 (.09)	1.73 (.09)	.38 (.07)
1990s	5.39 (.23)	2.28 (.23)	6.65 (.17)	2.13 (.16)	.45 (.10)
2000s	5.28 (.21)	2.48 (.21)	6.33 (.25)	2.53 (.28)	.55 (.10)
2010s	4.85 (.16)	2.49 (.17)	6.54 (.27)	3.04 (.33)	.55 (.09)

Table 5.4 Results of latent class analysis with two latent classes. Posterior means (and posterior standard deviations) shown for parameters representing each class, as well as the proportion in Class 1.

class. The first class saw its variance steadily grow over the time period—from 2.51 to 4.43—while the more conservative class saw its variance shrink slightly. In general, the proportion of the population in each class remained fairly stable, with just under two thirds belonging to the more liberal class in the 1970s and just over two thirds belonging to it in the 2010s.

Figure 5.6 shows these posterior means with 1 *SD* intervals around them. The figure shows that the first class experienced very little change across time, while the more conservative class became more conservative. This increasing separation between the classes is consistent with a story about polarization, but it is not a particularly dramatic one.

144

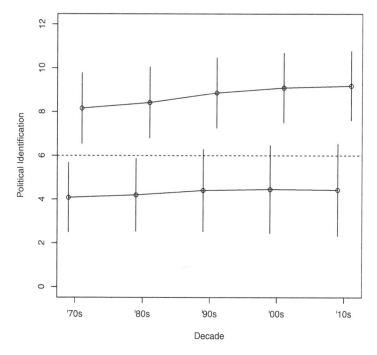

Figure 5.6 Posterior means of latent class means of political identification by decade. Vertical segments are 1 *SD* intervals constructed from the square roots of the posterior means for the class variances. Horizontal dashed line is the midpoint of the range of the measure.

The bottom half of Table 5.4 shows the posterior means for the class means and standard deviations for the political positions variable. The first column shows that the mean for the more liberal class was just over 5 in the 1970s, increased in the 1980s, but then declined from the 1990s onward. The more conservative class experienced a different pattern, becoming less conservative over the period but in a less consistent fashion, increasing slightly in the 2010s but remaining less conservative than in every decade but the 2000s. Further, while the variance for the first class remained relatively constant over the period, the variance for the more conservative class increased across the period. Finally, the population became more evenly split over time, with less than one third in the more liberal class in the 1970s but just over half in the class in the 2010s.

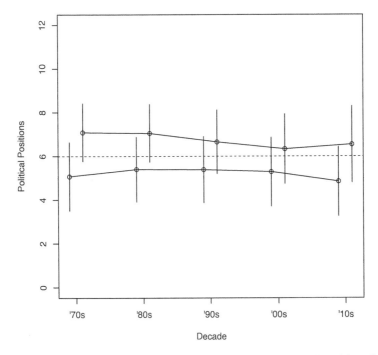

Figure 5.7   Posterior means of latent class means of political positions by
decade. Vertical segments are 1 *SD* intervals constructed from
the square roots of the posterior means for the class variances.
Horizontal dashed line is the midpoint of the range of the
measure.

Figure 5.7 shows very clearly that, although political positions were fairly
stable over time for both classes, both classes have trended leftward in their
positions over the past several decades, and the classes are relatively close
together, as evidenced by the substantial overlap between the 1 *SD* intervals
around both classes. To be sure, the classes were at their closest in the 2000s,
but they were still closer together in the 2010s than they were in the 1970s
and 1980s. Thus, in terms of political positions, it seems that the story is not
one of increasing polarization.

Figure 5.8 presents differences in the class means, computed as $\Delta = \mu_2 -
\mu_1$, for each model. This value is computed for each sampled posterior value,
so we have a distribution of 1,000 values of Δ. The figure shows even more
clearly that the gap between the classes for political identification widened

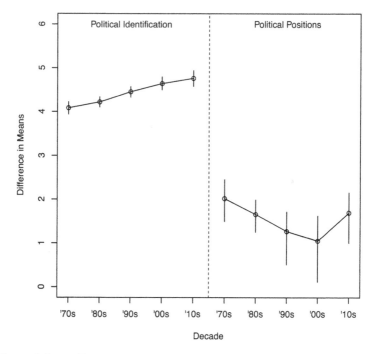

Figure 5.8 Differences in latent class means for political identification (left half) and political positions (right half) by decade. Vertical segments are 95% empirical credible intervals.

over the past five decades, while the gap between the classes for political positions declined until the 2010s before increasing. However, the gap in positions in the 2010s was still less than it was in the 1970s. The vertical line segments in the figure are 95% empirical credible intervals derived as discussed earlier by taking the 2.5th and 97.5th percentile values of the posterior samples. The intervals appear to overlap in some decades, but we can be more precise than simply eyeballing the intervals. Specifically, we can compute the probability that the gap is shrinking or increasing as discussed before, by sampling from each posterior distribution and calculating the proportion of samples from one decade that are greater (or less) than that of another.

For the political identification index, the probability that the gap between the latent class means is greater in the 1980s than in the 1970s is .93. The probability that the gap is greater in each subsequent decade is 1. Thus, there is strong evidence that American society has become more polarized in terms of political labels. As we noted above, both subpopulations have become more conservative, but the more conservative subpopulation has increased its claimed conservatism at a faster pace than the less conservative subpopulations. For the political positions index, the interval widths are substantially larger. Still, the gap between the means for the two latent classes declined from the 1970s through the 2000s. The probability that the gap was smaller in the 1980s than in the 1970s was .90. The probability that the gap was still smaller in the 1990s and the 2000s than in the 1970s was .99 for both decades. Although the gap increased in the 2010s, the probability that it was still smaller than in the 1970s was .82. All in all, it is pretty clear that polarization in political identification has increased over the past half century, but also that American society in general is less polarized now than it was throughout most of the rest of the past half century. These findings are consistent with the confused findings in the literature on the topic (McCarty, 2019).

These results were obtained using a somewhat informative prior. An important part of the process of conducting Bayesian analyses is to evaluate the sensitivity of results to choices for priors. As I said above, we need to have priors (in models like this one) that prevent "crashing" of our samplers, but we also don't want to have priors that are so strong as to overly influence substantive conclusions, especially those obtained from large data sets. Here, I considered two additional sets of priors. The first is rather noninformative. As with the original prior, I set the prior class means to 5 and 7, but I set the prior sample sizes to 2 in each class. Further, I set the priors for both α parameters for the proportion of the population in each class also to 2, indicating the proportion in each class is expected to be .5 but may reasonably range from .1 to .9. I set the a_0 and b_0 parameters in the inverse gamma prior for the class variances to 3 and 4, respectively. These latter values imply a prior mean for the class variances of 2 but with a variance (of the variance parameter) of 4. This suggests the true variance may fall reasonably between .5 and 6.5, a pretty wide range.

The second alternative prior is more informative than the first but reflects a prior belief that, although there are two classes in the population, 80% of the population belongs to a moderate class, while 20% belong to an extremely conservative class. Thus, I set $M_1 = 6$, $M_2 = 10$, $n_{01} = \alpha_1 = 8$, and $n_{02} = \alpha_2 = 2$. Further, I assume the same hyperparameters for the first class variance as in the original prior—$a_1 = 18$ and $b_1 = 34$—but I assume $a_2 = 6$ and $b_2 = 5$ for the second class. These parameters imply a prior mean for σ_2^2 of 1 and a prior variance of .25. This suggests that the variance in the

148

second, more conservative class is relatively small, so that that class is rather homogeneous.

Figure 5.9 provides a visual comparison of the key results of analyses using all three priors. The upper-left portion of the plot shows the class means for the political identification index. All three priors produce similar patterns for both classes. The lower-left portion of the plot shows the proportions in the first class under all three priors. These results are also consistent across priors. The results for the political positions index appear to be somewhat more volatile. All three priors show similar patterns for the first class mean, but the mean under the second prior is more variable than under the original prior, and the mean under the third prior is substantially greater than it is under the first two priors. All three priors show a very similar pattern and level for the second class mean, but the mean "jumps" considerably under the third prior. The proportions of the population in the first class are similar under the original and second prior, but again, there is

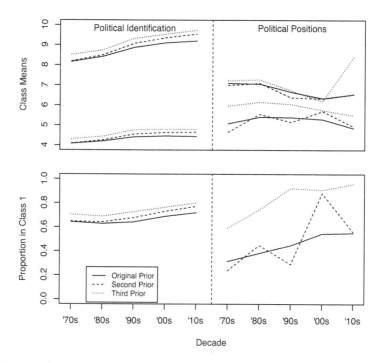

Figure 5.9 Class means and proportions for political identification (left) and political positions (right) by decade for all three priors.

more volatility in the proportion across decades for the second prior than the first. Further, although all three priors show the proportion in the first class to be generally increasing across decades, the proportion in the first class is much larger under the third prior. Indeed, by the 2010s, more than 90% of the population is estimated to be in the first class.

Overall, the results obtained under the three different priors tell a consistent story. However, it is clear that the least informative prior (the second) provided much more volatile results across decades, and the third prior appears to paint a different story in the most recent decade. That story is more consistent with the prior than with the story revealed by the other priors. This result may suggest that the evidence (data) for two distinct classes is relatively weak—that our prior, although relatively weak, is strong enough to suggest a one-class model in the absence of strong data to suggest the existence of a second class.

Taken together, the results of the analyses under the different priors also reveal that the use of priors can help smooth out group-specific—or, in this case, era-specific—idiosyncrasies in data that may otherwise obscure patterns. This is an advantage of priors that is exploited in both hierarchical models and so-called empirical Bayes methods (see Carlin & Louis, 2009; Gelman & Hill, 2007).

As a final note on this example, the latent class models estimated here were relatively simple. I did not incorporate covariates that may predict the probability of membership in particular classes or influence class means or variances. The GSS is pretty close to being a random sample, so it is not clear that "controlling" on demographic characteristics would produce substantially different results than those presented here. It is also not immediately clear that incorporating covariates would yield results that are "truer" in terms of representing population quantities in particular decades. The U.S. population is aging, so controlling on age can yield a distorted view regarding trends in political identity and positions, if the goal is simply to understand larger trends. Similarly, racial composition of the American population has also changed considerably over the past 50 years. Thus, controlling on racial composition would also influence estimated trends in political identification and positions. Thus, whether to control on demographic and related characteristics is a decision that should be guided by the substantive question of interest. As McCarty (2019) notes, many trends in political views, especially among those who call themselves Democrats, are a result of changes in the composition of that party over time and not in change in positions among those identifying with the party over time. Thus, again, whether to include covariates (and which to include) depends on the specific question being addressed.

If one is interested in incorporating covariates into the latent class analyses conducted above, extending a Gibbs sampler is straightforward. First, instead of assuming that the probability of belonging to a particular latent class is a single, population quantity, one can incorporate covariates in a probit regression model to predict class membership probabilities. Similarly, instead of assuming that class means are single population quantities, one can incorporate covariates to predict class means using a linear regression model for each class. Further, as mentioned earlier, one may wish to consider a latent class model in which latent classes are differentiated by a multivariate outcome, rather than a univariate one. Here, I estimated separate models for the identification and positions indexes. Perhaps latent classes, however, should be defined by joint responses on both indexes simultaneously. Such an approach would be more typical of contemporary latent class models (see Congdon, 2003), but it certainly complicates the model. Specifically, latent classes in that case involve not only means and variances for each measure but also covariances between them. Still, extending the model in these ways—including covariates that predict class membership and class means and variances, as well as including multiple outcomes that are used to define classes—is not inherently difficult in the Bayesian setting. I provide some examples in supplemental materials on the webpage for this volume.

Comparing Models and Evaluating Model Fit

In social science, if not more broadly, comparing models is often of interest. The classical approach to statistics offers at least one common way of comparing models, so long as one model is a special case of the other (i.e., one model is nested in the other): likelihood ratio testing. The Bayesian approach offers a more general approach to comparing models that does not require models to be nested. In this section, I first discuss the Bayes factor as an alternative to the likelihood ratio test that does not require nested models. I then spend more time discussing and illustrating posterior predictive simulation, which provides a flexible approach for both comparing models and evaluating model fit. I believe that it is a better approach for comparing models because of its flexibility in enabling the assessment of how well models fit a variety of particular features of data.

Bayes Factors

Consider two models, M_1 and M_0. The posterior distribution for M_k is

$$p(M_k|D) = \frac{p(D|M_k)p(M_k)}{P(D)}, \tag{5.51}$$

so that the posterior odds of M_1 versus M_0 is

$$\frac{p(M_1|D)}{p(M_0|D)} = \left(\frac{p(D|M_1)}{p(D|M_0)}\right)\left(\frac{p(M_1)}{p(M_0)}\right). \tag{5.52}$$

The latter term on the righthand side is the prior odds for Model 1 against Model 0. We often assume that neither model is preferred at the outset so that this term is 1 and can be ignored. The former term is called the Bayes factor and is the ratio of likelihoods integrated over the parameters associated with each model (Raftery, 1995a):

$$p(D|M_k) = \int_{\theta_k} f(D|M_k, \theta_k) f(\theta_k|M_k) d\theta_k. \tag{5.53}$$

For a given model, the conditioning on M_k is implicit and can be ignored, making this expression familiar: It is the normalizing constant in the denominator of the Bayesian calculation for the posterior distribution discussed in Chapter 3.

If (1) M_1 and M_0 are a nested pair, so that one is a subset of the other, and (2) we select a single value for θ_k such as the MLE, the former ratio in Equation 5.52 is simply a likelihood ratio as used in likelihood ratio testing. If these two conditions are not met, we must perform the integration in Equation 5.53. As we discussed previously, computation of this normalizing constant is difficult, but it is fortunately not necessary (as we've seen) for MCMC sampling. However, it must be computed—or approximated—in order to compute Bayes factors. This is one reason Bayes factors have not been used much in sociological research to date (but see other criticisms and responses in Gelman & Rubin, 1995; Hauser, 1995; Raftery, 1995b).

A related quantity—the BIC—however, has received much greater use, especially in latent class analyses. The BIC is an approximation to the integral shown in Equation 5.53. In short, the integral can be approximated by using a Taylor series expansion around the ML estimate and then integrating θ out (see Raftery, 1995a). The resulting statistic is

$$BIC = -2\ln(L) + d\ln(n), \tag{5.54}$$

where $\ln(L)$ is the log-likelihood evaluated at the MLE, d is the number of parameters in the model, and n is the sample size. The input required to compute the BIC is included as standard output of most classical software packages and/or is not terribly difficult to calculate from the output of an MCMC sampler. In comparing two models, the model with the smaller BIC is preferred. Thus, the latter term in the BIC calculation can be viewed as a penalty for overparameterization: The more parameters that are estimated, the larger $d\ln(n)$ is, so the larger BIC is.

The BIC is frequently used in latent class analysis to determine the number of latent classes that exist in a population (S. Lynch & Taylor, 2016). Unfortunately, the BIC often does not "bottom out." Instead, it often continues to decline as more and more classes are added, requiring that other criteria be used to decide how many latent classes exist, such as whether the classes are substantively meaningful, contain a significant proportion of the population, or meet other substantive considerations. For these reasons, as well as other critiques concerning the BIC, such as sensitivity to priors (see Gelman & Rubin, 1999; Raftery, 1999; Weakliem, 1999), I think using posterior predictive simulation provides a better strategy for comparing models.

Posterior Predictive Distributions

The likelihood function used in classical modeling (the sampling distribution for the data in a Bayesian analysis) specifies the distribution from which data are expected to arise under a given model, conditional on the parameters of that model—$f(y|\theta)$. Presumably, future data would arise from the same model. After we have observed data to obtain a posterior distribution for the parameters, however, our uncertainty about θ is reduced relative to the prior, $f(\theta)$, so that uncertainty about future y—y^{new}—is reduced relative to the original sampling distribution/likelihood in which all we knew was the prior for θ and not its posterior. The distribution of such future data—called the posterior predictive distribution (PPD)—can be represented as

$$f(y^{new}|y) = \int f(y^{new}|\theta, y)f(y|\theta)f(\theta)d\theta. \qquad (5.55)$$

The first term under the integral is the distribution of the data, conditional on both the unknown parameter and the observed data. The latter two terms prior to the differential are the original likelihood and the prior. Combined, they constitute the posterior distribution. Thus, the PPD is often written as

$$f(y^{new}|y) = \int f(y^{new}|\theta, y)f(\theta|y)d\theta, \qquad (5.56)$$

or even as

$$f(y^{new}|y) = \int f(y^{new}|\theta)f(\theta|y)d\theta, \qquad (5.57)$$

because y^{new} and y are assumed to be conditionally independent, given θ. Regardless of how the PPD is expressed, it can be viewed as the distribution of future data given the observed data after marginalizing over posterior uncertainty in θ.

The integral required to obtain the closed form of the PPD may be difficult to derive analytically. However, it is simple to simulate new data from it using samples of θ obtained via MCMC methods. Suppose we have obtained M samples from the posterior distribution so that we have a collection $\theta_{m=1}, \theta_{m=2}, \ldots, \theta_{m=M}$. Simulating from the PPD then simply requires that we simulate new observations, y^{new}, from the sampling distribution $f(y^{new}|\theta)$ for each sampled θ_m.

PPD simulation is straightforward and provides a flexible method for evaluating model fit, for detecting outliers, and for forecasting or predicting new, out-of-sample observations. Table 5.5 illustrates these ideas generically. The first column of the table shows observed data, $y_i = y_1 \ldots y_n$. Subsequent columns of the table show new data simulated under the sampling distribution for the data, conditional on the values of θ obtained from MCMC sampling. As the equation in the top middle of the table shows, y_i^{new} is often also conditioned on other data such as predictor variables, X, that are specific to each original sample member (i.e., X_i). Thus, $y_i^1 \ldots y_i^m$ can be viewed as repeated samples of the same individual's y under different values of the parameter. The last column in the table shows that these PPD samples for

Observed	PPD Samples from MCMC Samples						
y_i	θ_1	θ_2	θ_3	$\ldots$	θ_M		Individual
	$y_i^m \sim f(y|\theta_m, X_i)$						Outliers?
y_1	y_1^1	y_1^2	y_1^3	$\ldots$	y_1^m	$\rightarrow$	$g(y_1)$
y_2	y_2^1	y_2^2	y_2^3	$\ldots$	y_2^m	$\rightarrow$	$g(y_2)$
y_3	y_3^1	y_3^2	y_3^3	$\ldots$	y_3^m	$\rightarrow$	$g(y_3)$
$\vdots$	$\vdots$	$\vdots$	$\vdots$	$\ddots$	$\vdots$	$\vdots$	$\vdots$
y_n	y_n^1	y_n^2	y_n^3	$\ldots$	y_n^m	$\rightarrow$	$g(y_n)$
$\downarrow$	$\downarrow$	$\downarrow$	$\downarrow$	$\ldots$	$\downarrow$		
$h(y)$	$h(y^1)$	$h(y^2)$	$h(y^3)$	$\ldots$	$h(y^m)$	$\rightarrow$	Sample Statistics

Table 5.5 Illustration of PPD simulation for evaluation of model fit and outlier diagnosis.

the individual can be collected together as a distribution, $g(y_i^{new})$, of potential values for the individual. If the model fits the individual well, then the histogram of $g(y_i^{new})$ should be centered over y_i. If the PPD for case i is not, then the individual is not fit well by the model: The case may be an outlier. Obviously, if no sample member is fit well by the model, the model provides a poor representation of the true data-generating process.

While each row of the table represents repeated sampling of individuals, each column represents a complete new n sample, $y_1^m \ldots y_n^m$, mirroring the original sample, $y_1 \ldots y_n$. As the last row of the table shows, a function (or functional) of the original sample, $h(y)$, can be computed and replicated for each PPD sample, $h(y^1) \ldots h(y^M)$. This function may be a statistic, such as a sample mean (i.e., $h(y) = \sum y/n$), median, variance, quantile, a coefficient of variation, or some other statistic. Under this approach, $h(y)$ is considered a fixed quantity, like a parameter in the classical paradigm, while the values computed for each of the PPD samples can be viewed as values obtained under repeated sampling. Thus, a "Bayesian p-value" can be obtained by computing the proportion of repeated sample statistics that exceed the fixed value of $h(y)$ (D. Rubin, 1984). Formally, $p = \sum_{m=1}^{M} I[h(y^i) > h(y)]/M$, where $I[.]$ is an indicator function. If this p is close to 0 or 1—perhaps using traditional classical criteria such as one-tailed $p < .05$ or $(1 - p) < .05$—the model does not replicate features of the observed data well, implying that the model does not fit well (S. M. Lynch & Western, 2004).

There is no limit to the number or type of functions that can be computed using this approach, but as Gelman et al. (2013) note, the quantity should not be a sample-level quantity that is guaranteed to be reproduced under the model, such as a sufficient statistic. For example, the sample mean is a sufficient statistic for the population mean under a normal model. Thus, the p-value for $h(y) = \bar{y}$ will be close to .5 by design. Instead, one should consider constructing $h(y)$ that capture features of the data that may be suspect. For example, if the data are highly skewed, but the model is not designed to address this feature, one may consider using the skewness coefficient as a statistic to test. Alternatively, one may use the ratio of the mean to the median or some other ad hoc quantity (S. M. Lynch, 2007).

To illustrate the use of posterior predictive simulation, I return to the linear models discussed earlier in this chapter. I consider the models for both the political identification index and the positions index. Item 8 in the Appendix shows the code used to conduct the simulation. The code is very brief. First, the design matrix (consisting of the covariates) is multiplied by the transpose

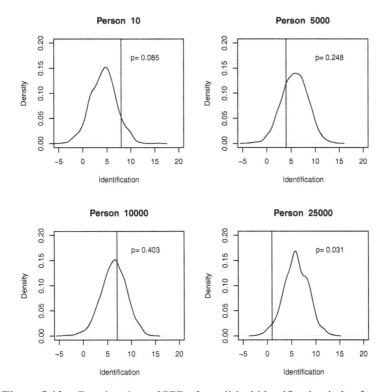

Figure 5.10   Density plots of PPDs for political identification index for four sample members. Vertical reference lines indicate the observed value. Bayesian p-values are displayed for each person and represents the minimum of the area under the density to the right or left of the reference line.

of the entire matrix of retained sample values of the regression coefficients. In this case, $n = 28,273$ and β is $1,000 \times 8$. Thus, this product results in a $28,273 \times 1,000$ matrix following the structure shown in Table 5.5. Next, a random normal value with mean $= 0$ and variance equal to the sampled error variance parameter values, σ_e^2, is added to $\hat{y}$.

The p-values were generated row-wise by computing the minimum of the proportion of individuals' PPD values that were (a) less than or (b) greater than their observed value of y. If the model fits an individual well, his or her p-value should be large. Put another way, those with p-values less than .025 *may* be outliers (.025 because the p-value is computed as two-tailed). I say "may be" because these p-values should probably be adjusted using a Bonferroni or similar correction, because n observations constitute multiple "tests," and so we may expect 5% of cases to be "extreme." For the identification index, 3.6% of respondents had a p-value less than .025; for the positions index, 5.4% had a p-value less than .025. Thus, the model for the identification index appears to fit slightly better by this metric. However, no p-value exceeds a Bonferroni-corrected p-value threshold, suggesting there may not be any real outliers in either model.

Figure 5.10 shows density plots of the PPDs for four arbitrary sample members for the political identification index. Vertical reference lines in the figure correspond to the observed value for the sample member. Person 10's PPD is centered to the left of his or her observed value, but the p-value is well above .025, suggesting he or she is fit reasonably well by the model. Similarly, although Person 5,000's PPD is centered to the right of his or her response, the p-value is .248. Person 10,000's PPD is centered almost directly over his or her response, indicating the model fits him or her quite well. In contrast, Person 25,000's PPD is centered well above his or her response. The p-value for this person is .031, which is still reasonable, but it is clear that this person indicated he or she identifies as being much more liberal than the model predicts.

Figure 5.11 is similar to Figure 5.10 but shows the PPDs for the political positions index for the four sample members. The figure shows that the model fits the first three persons rather well, but Person 25,000 is also more liberal in his or her positions than the model predicts, as indicated by the small p-value. Figure 5.12 reproduces the information shown in the previous plots but does so for both models simultaneously. These models were conducted separately, so the correlation between the PPD values is 0. PPD values for each outcome were simply matched by iteration count of the original Gibbs sampler for each model. The scatterplots show the independence— that is, the clouds of points are round, only distorted in one dimension, reflecting the greater residual variance for the identification index.

This figure shows that Person 5,000 and Pperson 10,000 were both fit quite well by the models. The figure also shows that Person 10 is clearly fit better by the model for political position than by the model for identification and that Person 25,000 is not fit particularly well by either.

As discussed above, although not everyone was fit well by either model, there are no clear outliers in either. Thus, a next step may be to evaluate how

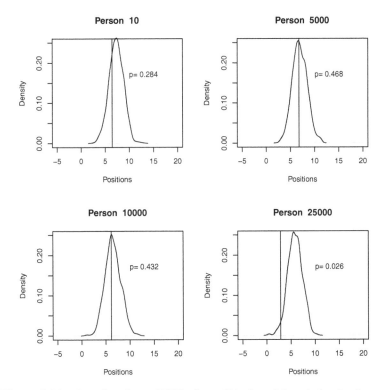

Figure 5.11   Density plots of PPDs for political positions index for four sample members. Vertical reference lines indicate the observed value. Bayesian *p*-values are displayed for each person and represent the minimum of the area under the density to the right or left of the reference line.

well the model fits particular features of the data (i.e., sample-level statistics). We can do so by computing quantities column-wise (i.e., for each PPD sample). Given the bounding at both upper and lower ends of the outcomes in these models, an important sample quantity that might be of interest is the ratio of the sample mean to the sample median for each outcome. The model should predict the mean accurately, but the linear model assumes normality of the error and may not accurately capture any skew that may result from the inability of the model to fit skewness in y. Under the model, the ratio of

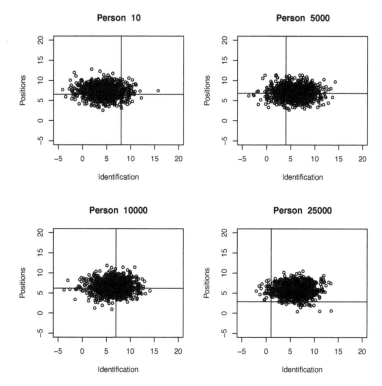

Figure 5.12   Scatterplot of PPDs for identification index and positions index for four persons with observed values indicated by horizontal and vertical reference lines.

the mean to the median should be approximately 1. Thus, the distribution of PPDs should be centered over this value. Figure 5.13 shows the PPD densities for this ratio, with vertical reference lines at the values for the original sample. As the figure shows, both PPDs for this value are centered over 1 (as expected), but the sample values are substantially lower for both observed variables. The p-values in both cases are 0: All PPD values are larger than the ratio in the original data. These results suggest the model does not fit the data particularly well. Indeed, in analyses not shown, this result holds for values at all quantiles, from the 10th percentile to the 90th percentile. All in all, the results suggest that our linear models for these indexes do not fit particularly well, even though we might be pleased with them, given our reasonable R-squared values. Indeed, R-squared is not a measure of model

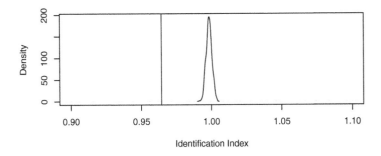

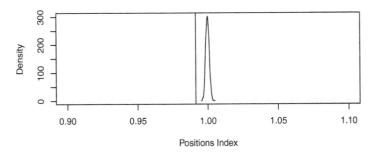

Figure 5.13   Density plots of ratios of the mean to the median of
identification index and positions index. Vertical reference
lines are the values in the sample.

fit, but we often treat it as such in social science research. Our PPD evaluations suggest our models do not fit very well. Here, we could argue that our original linear models were essentially one-class latent class models, and so the lack of fit suggests we may need to move toward a mixture/latent class approach to understand political identification and positions, which we ultimately did in the previous section.

CHAPTER 6. CONCLUSION

This volume has covered the material that is important for understanding the basics of contemporary Bayesian statistics. The second chapter reviewed the probability theory that underlies both Bayesian and classical statistical modeling and reviewed the classical approach to statistics involving maximum likelihood estimation, as well as the classical approach to hypothesis testing. This material is important for persons wishing to conduct Bayesian analyses for two key reasons. First, unlike classical statistical analyses, which can be almost completely automated, Bayesian analyses requires a fair amount of mathematical and programming effort, so having a solid understanding of probability rules and distributions is necessary. Second, having a solid understanding of the mathematics that underlies statistical analyses—classical or Bayesian—can help one understand the advantages of learning about and implementing the Bayesian approach, several of which are discussed below.

The third chapter introduced Bayes' theorem, and then extended its initial form as a recipe for reversing a conditional probability for a single event to its more general form in which data are represented with a likelihood function (or sampling density), and prior information and uncertainty about it are represented with a probability distribution. This chapter showed that prior uncertainty is updated with data to produce a posterior distribution that can be summarized in numerous ways to provide a picture of what we know about a parameter or hypothesis after incorporating new data.

Chapter 4 showed that producing most summaries of posterior distributions involves integral calculus, rather than the differential calculus required to produce classical summaries. Although performing integration analytically is often more difficult than performing differentiation, this chapter showed that integrals of posterior distributions can be approximated to an arbitrary degree of precision by sampling from them and computing basic sample statistics using the samples. The chapter showed some of the key methods that have been developed since the 1990s that have contributed to the explosion in the use of the Bayesian approach.

Finally, Chapter 5 illustrated Bayesian analyses in several familiar models used in social science research, including the linear model, the dichotomous probit model, and basic latent class models. Importantly, the chapter integrated the development of real, multivariate Bayesian posterior distributions with the construction of MCMC algorithms that can be used to sample from them. This chapter also briefly discussed the comparison of models and the evaluation of model fit in a Bayesian context, focusing especially on posterior predictive simulation.

After finishing Chapter 5, readers should be able to begin to conduct their own Bayesian analyses and should certainly be ready to read more advanced texts to learn more about it. However, one may ask, "What's the point?" Or, more generally, what is the advantage to learning about and implementing Bayesian analyses, especially given that we can implement all the models discussed in Chapter 5 using classical methods? In this final chapter, I provide a few answers to these questions and point interested readers to additional literature that provides much greater breadth and depth of coverage than this volume could cover.

Why Take a Bayesian Perspective?

Throughout this volume, I have shown *how* to do Bayesian analyses, but I have spent less time addressing *why* one should. There are several reasons for doing so, some of which have been mentioned in various places in the text but only briefly. These reasons can be grouped into two broad categories: philosophical and practical.

From a philosophical perspective, the Bayesian approach to statistics and probability provides a more direct way of assessing scientific hypotheses than the classical approach. For example, as we saw throughout this volume, the Bayesian view of probability can allow us to answer questions such as, what is the probability that exercise is related to longevity? A Bayesian analysis would involve constructing a posterior distribution that expresses the magnitude of the relationship between exercise and longevity, perhaps a hazard model coefficient, and answer the question by computing the proportion of the mass of the posterior that is above (or below) 0—the same strategy we employed in several examples in the text.

The classical approach, in contrast, would involve assuming that exercise is unrelated to longevity and assessing the probability that we would observe a coefficient like the one we observed in the given sample under that assumption. If that probability—the *p*-value—were small, we would reject the "null" hypothesis that there is no relationship and infer that there is therefore support for the alternative hypothesis that exercise and longevity are related. This strategy seems to be an entirely indirect, even backward way of addressing the question of interest. Although one may argue that this falsificationist approach is the only logically valid way to assess hypotheses, there is a fundamentally inductive step one takes under the classical paradigm when one claims that the rejection of a null hypothesis supports one's pet alternative hypothesis. This reliance on that inductive step seems often to be forgotten by analysts, because it is almost automatic that scholars point to a "statistically significant" result as evidence in favor of their real hypothesis without recognizing that all the analyses did was (potentially—with 5% risk of error) *disprove* the null.

A second, related philosophical advantage of the Bayesian paradigm is its ability to provide a coherent strategy for formally integrating previous knowledge directly into new analyses. As we discussed in Chapter 3, the classical paradigm generally only integrates prior knowledge in the literature review. There are several consequences of this limitation of the classical approach. First, although a classical confidence interval provides us an indication of the range for an effect size, this range is only determined by the current sample. Thus, we may become increasingly certain that an effect exists after multiple studies find a "statistically significant effect," but our precision regarding its magnitude never increases as evidence accumulates. The closest the classical approach comes to accumulating evidence is in meta-analytic studies, which themselves are akin to Bayesian hierarchical models but without the clear, probabilistic interpretation.

A second significant consequence of the classical approach's inability to formally integrate prior knowledge into new studies is the risk of publishing studies with false findings—flukes. As discussed in previous chapters, the critical alpha in classical studies is the p-value at which one is willing to commit a Type I error: that is, to reject a null hypothesis and claim support for an alternative hypothesis even though the null hypothesis is true. The combination of the growth in the number of academics, the pressure to publish in academia, and journals' disinterest in publishing studies with null findings has led us to a point in which social science findings often cannot be replicated. This result is not simply a consequence of research malfeasance, inherent problems with observational (i.e., survey) data, or the inherent difficulty in predicting human behavior. It is a consequence of the lack of understanding among many of what a p-value represents coupled with the fetishism of p-values that has emerged over the past half century (Papineau, 2018; Simmons et al., 2011; Ziliak & McCloskey, 2008).

The Bayesian paradigm avoids this problem because it is not focused on testing null hypotheses and because aberrant findings can be outweighed by formal incorporation of prior information into analyses. For example, if 100 studies involving millions of sample members over multiple decades have established that drinking coffee has no effect on, or possibly a slight benefit for, long-term health, a single *new* study of size $n = 100$ that finds coffee is deadly will likely be published and will receive considerable media attention under the current statistical paradigm. The study will probably not be replicable, and the sudden finding that contradicts prior work will lead the broader population to further question the value of science—especially social science. However, such a study would receive little attention if it had involved a Bayesian analysis with a strong prior based on the 100 previous studies, because the previous studies' findings would swamp the novel one.

Beyond the more philosophical advantages of the Bayesian paradigm, the Bayesian paradigm has practical advantages to offer, as well. One of the key reasons for the increase in publications using a Bayesian approach (see S. M. Lynch & Bartlett, 2019) is the recognition that certain models and quantities of interest are easier to estimate or obtain using the Bayesian approach coupled with MCMC methods than using classical methods. I will briefly discuss two here.

First, the construction and implementation of hierarchical models is straightforward in the Bayesian setting using MCMC methods. A hierarchical model is a model in which unknown quantities (e.g., parameters) and possibly data are nested at two or more "levels" (see Raudenbush & Bryk, 2002). For example, secondary students are nested within classes, classes are nested within schools, and schools are nested in school districts. As another example, repeated measures are nested within individuals in panel studies. In both cases, units within groups might be assumed to be more similar to one another than they are to units in other groups, and it may be of interest to model the similarities and differences at each level (within and between). We may not be interested so much in the extent to which individuals within groups differ from one another, but instead, we may be interested in how groups are differentiated. For example, do students in one class tend to perform better than students in another class? Or, do some people experience change in health across age more rapidly than others?

We can develop a hierarchical model to address these types of questions as follows. First, we might say $y_{ij} \sim g(\alpha_j)$—that the value of some outcome y for individual i in group j follows distribution g with a group-specific parameter α_j. This represents the first level of a hierarchical model. At the second level, we assume the group-specific parameters themselves follow a distribution, h, with a higher-level grouping parameter. Thus, $\alpha_j \sim h(\mu)$.[1] The quantity of greatest interest would probably be the value of μ. We could write the generic posterior distribution as

$$f(\mu, \alpha | y) \propto f(y | \alpha, \mu) f(\alpha | \mu) f(\mu) \tag{6.1}$$

$$\propto f(y | \alpha) f(\alpha | \mu) f(\mu), \tag{6.2}$$

---

[1] Here, I use g and h to represent distributions as opposed to density functions, which I continue to represent with $f()$.

where I have excluded subscripts for the vectors α and y. The posterior distribution is for both the collection of α_j and μ, because both are unknowns. The second equation simply shows that y only depends on μ through α's relationship with μ. We can use the chain rule discussed in Chapter 2 to see that the terms on the right are proportional to the posterior shown on the left. Starting from the right side of the first equation, we can see that $f(\alpha|\mu)f(\mu) = f(\alpha,\mu)$. Then, combining this term with the first term to the right of the proportionality symbol—the likelihood function—yields the posterior distribution to the left of the proportionality symbol.

This specification is generic, but it shows the simplicity with which hierarchical models can be written in probability notation. All that remains is to substitute specific distributions for these generic ones before developing an MCMC algorithm for sampling. A common strategy would be to assume normal distributions for the data, the α_j and μ, and to assume inverse gamma distributions for the variance parameters, σ^2 and τ in the normal distributions. Thus:

$$y_{ij} \sim N(\alpha_i, \sigma^2) \tag{6.3}$$

$$\alpha_i \sim N(\mu, \tau) \tag{6.4}$$

$$\mu \sim N(M, T) \tag{6.5}$$

$$\sigma^2 \sim IG(a, b) \tag{6.6}$$

$$\tau \sim IG(c, d), \tag{6.7}$$

and the full posterior distribution would be

$$f(\mu, \alpha_{j=1\ldots J}|.) \propto \left(\prod_{j=1}^{J} \prod_{i=1}^{n_j} \frac{1}{\sqrt{\sigma^2}} \exp\left\{ -\frac{(y_{ij}-\alpha_j)^2}{2\sigma^2} \right\} \right) \left(\prod_{j=1}^{J} \frac{1}{\sqrt{\tau}} \exp\left\{ -\frac{(\alpha_j-\mu)^2}{2\tau} \right\} \right) \times$$
$$\frac{1}{\sqrt{T}} \exp\left\{ -\frac{(\mu-M)^2}{2T} \right\} (\sigma^2)^{-(a+1)} \exp\left\{ -\frac{b}{\sigma^2} \right\} (\tau^2)^{-(c+1)} \exp\left\{ -\frac{d}{\tau} \right\}. \tag{6.8}$$

Although this posterior distribution may look complicated, it is not fundamentally different from those we developed in the normal distribution problems in Chapter 3, and it is simpler in many ways than those we developed in Chapter 5. Developing a Gibbs sampler for this model is straightforward: The unknowns include $\alpha_{j=1\ldots J}$, μ, σ^2, and τ. We can easily derive conditional posterior distributions for each of these by following the strategies we discussed throughout the volume: simplifying products of exponentials into sums, expanding quadratic expressions, dropping constants, and completing squares. It turns out that, in this particular problem, the conditional posteriors for all of the α and μ are normal distributions, and the conditional posteriors for σ^2 and τ are inverse gamma distributions. Given the efficiency of Gibbs sampling, then, it is easy to produce posterior summaries for the parameters of interest in this basic hierarchical model. Indeed, the conditional posteriors in this problem are well known and can be sampled from easily using some contemporary Bayesian MCMC software packages such as JAGS (Plummer, 2003).

This basic hierarchical model can be easily extended to incorporate more (e.g., higher) levels of observation as well as regression relationships that decompose group parameters (here, α) as functions of variables measured at higher levels rather than a single parameter (here, μ). A full discussion of hierarchical modeling is well beyond the scope of this volume, but Gelman & Hill (2007) provides a thorough treatment from both classical and Bayesian perspectives.

A second area for which the Bayesian approach is well suited is in the handling of missing data. From the Bayesian perspective, missing data are unknown quantities just like parameters. They can generally be thought of as nuisances that must be dealt with in an analysis but usually not of direct interest. The Bayesian approach involves first constructing a posterior distribution for the unknown quantities of interest, generically θ, as well as the unknown missing data, generically z, conditional on the observed data:

$$f(\theta, z|y) \propto f(y|z, \theta)f(z, \theta) \tag{6.9}$$

$$\propto f(y|\theta)f(z, \theta) \tag{6.10}$$

$$\propto f(y|\theta)f(z|\theta)f(\theta) \tag{6.11}$$

$$\propto f(z|\theta)f(y|\theta)f(\theta). \tag{6.12}$$

The first equation shows the posterior for the unknowns, while the latter three equations show different but equivalent ways to represent the terms on the right. The second equation simply shows that z has been removed from the conditional for $y|\theta$. It has been removed, because the missing data are usually assumed to be conditionally independent of the observed data, just as observed data are considered conditionally independent of other observed data when we construct a typical likelihood function. Thus, $f(y|z, \theta) = f(y|\theta)$. The third equation shows that the joint distribution of $f(z, \theta)$ can be decomposed using the rule for nonindependent joint probabilities, and the final equation simply rearranges terms in an order that may look familiar (recall the form for the posterior predictive distribution discussed in Chapter 4).

Ultimately, we probably do not care about z, but only θ, and this posterior —$f(\theta|y)$—can be obtained by integrating z out of the joint posterior for z and θ. As we have discussed throughout the volume, MCMC methods can be used for this task. Here, an MCMC algorithm could easily be constructed in which we alternate sampling from the conditional posterior distributions for z and θ. The last equation shows that, if θ is fixed (conditioned upon), $f(\theta, z|y) = f(z|y, \theta)$, which is simply a draw from the posterior predictive distribution as discussed in Chapter 4. If z is fixed, then $f(\theta, z|y) = f(\theta|z, y)$, which is simply a draw from the posterior as if we had complete (i.e., no missing) data. After a run of the sampler, summaries of θ can be produced using the samples of θ, essentially marginalizing over the uncertainty presented by the missing data (see Little & Rubin, 2002).

This approach to handling missing data may seem somewhat familiar: It is the basis for multiple imputation. Indeed, multiple imputation is fundamentally Bayesian. The key difference between the Bayesian approach using MCMC methods and multiple imputation as it is used in contemporary classical analyses is that, in multiple imputation, samples for the missing values are drawn all at once (from their posterior predictive distribution) before the analytic model is estimated. The analytic model is then estimated on each sample, and the parameter estimates are combined using "Rubin's Rules." The use of Rubin's Rules accomplishes the same task as the MCMC analyses do in terms of addressing the uncertainty in the parameter values introduced by the missing data (see D. B. Rubin, 1987).

The recognition of the problems with the classical approach to statistics using p-values and the ease with which hierarchical models and missing data can be handled in the Bayesian paradigm are key reasons the Bayesian approach is becoming more common in social science research. There are several additional reasons; S. M. Lynch & Bartlett (2019) discuss that Bayesian thinking and methods are becoming increasingly common even though many are unaware they are using Bayesian methods—such as is likely the case when many use multiple imputation. Both S. M. Lynch & Bartlett (2019) and van de Schoot et al. (2017) provide summaries of the use of Bayesian methods in recent years in sociology and psychology, respectively. Unfortunately, further discussion of the advantages and uses of Bayesian methods is beyond the scope of this volume. However, numerous additional texts are available to learn more. I conclude by discussing several.

Some Additional Suggested Readings

There are now a number of books available that provide good introductions to Bayesian statistics. Gelman et al.'s *Bayesian Data Analysis* is now in its third edition and provides one of the most thorough and readable introductions to the topic. The book is written primarily for statisticians, however, and examples often involve non–social science examples involving relatively small data sets (Gelman et al., 2013). In recent years, a handful of books have been written specifically for social scientists, including Gill's *Bayesian Methods: A Social and Behavioral Sciences Approach* (Gill, 2014), Lynch's *Introduction to Applied Bayesian Statistics and Estimation for Social Scientists* (S. M. Lynch, 2007), and Jackman's *Bayesian Analysis for the Social Sciences* (Jackman, 2009). Lynch's book is highly applied and presents R programming code for Gibbs samplers and Metropolis–Hastings algorithms for a number of common models used in social science research. Gill's and Jackman's books are also applied but provide much more detail on prior distributions and Bayesian theory.

Beyond introductory texts, several additional books provide more in-depth discussion of Markov chain Monte Carlo methods, including *Markov Chain Monte Carlo in Practice* (Gilks et al., 1996), *Handbook of Markov Chain Monte Carlo* (Brooks et al., 2011), and *Markov chain Monte Carlo: Stochastic Simulation for Bayesian Inference* (Gamerman & Lopes, 2006). The first book is an edited volume that contains chapters discussing various aspects of MCMC methods, ranging from theory underlying MCMC methods to applications involving very basic and highly specialized MCMC routines, to discussions of evaluating performance of MCMC algorithms. The book is somewhat dated but still a solid addition to a library on Bayesian statistics. The second book is very much like a newer edition of the first book and provides a more up-to-date exposition of the state of contemporary MCMC methods. Finally, Gamerman and Lopes's book is more recent and provides a thorough, detailed presentation of the theory and technical details of MCMC methods.

A number of books available that illustrate the Bayesian approach to specific classes of models are useful for social scientists. Gelman and Hill discuss hierarchical models in both classical and Bayesian frameworks (Gelman & Hill, 2007). Pole, West, and Harrison address time series methods in the Bayesian context (Pole et al., 1994). Congdon discusses generalized linear models, time-series analysis, mixture models, latent variable modeling, hierarchical modeling, and survival methods. His follow-up book, *Applied Bayesian Modelling*, covers much of the same ground with a few additions, including a chapter on causal modeling in the Bayesian context (Congdon, 2001, 2003). Finally, Gelman and Meng have an edited volume that presents a Bayesian approach to causal analyses and missing data handling (Gelman & Meng, 2004).

In addition to books, over the past few decades, a number of articles published in social science journals have used Bayesian methods in substantive problems, as well as developed or extended Bayesian methods for social science applications. Two recent reviews, mentioned above, provide listings of such articles over the past few decades in sociology and psychology (S. M. Lynch & Bartlett, 2019; van de Schoot et al., 2017). All in all, the literature is rich with methodological expositions of the Bayesian paradigm that are geared for social science analyses, and there is a growing body of applications in social science. I hope that this volume will encourage even greater use of the approach.

APPENDIX

This appendix contains R code for some of the programs discussed in the text. More programs and examples can be found on the volume's website.

1. R Program for Simple Three-State Model With Uniform Proposal in Chapter 4

```
set.seed(51265)
f=function(cand,prev){
fcand=.6*(cand==1)+.3*(cand==2)+.1*(cand==3)
fprev=.6*(prev==1)+.3*(prev==2)+.1*(prev==3)
return(fcand/fprev)
}

x=matrix(1,1000)
c=u=r=acc=matrix(1,1000)
for(i in 2:1000){

c[i]=sample(c(1,2,3),1)

r[i]=f(c[i],x[i-1])
x[i]=x[i-1]; acc[i]=0
u[i]=runif(1)
if(r[i]>u[i]){x[i]=c[i]; acc[i]=1}
}
res=cbind(c(1,x[-1000]),c,r,u,acc)[-1,]
```

2. R Program for Simple Three-State Model With Nonuniform Proposal in Chapter 4

```
set.seed(51265)
f=function(cand,prev){
fcand=.6*(cand==1)+.3*(cand==2)+.1*(cand==3)
fprev=.6*(prev==1)+.3*(prev==2)+.1*(prev==3)

hastings=(.2*(prev==1)+.3*(prev==2)+.5*(prev==3))/
(.2*(cand==1)+.3*(cand==2)+.5*(cand==3))

return((fcand/fprev)*hastings)
}

n=5000
x=matrix(1,n)
c=u=r=acc=matrix(1,n)
for(i in 2:n){

c[i]=sample(c(1,2,3),1,p=c(.2,.3,.5))

r[i]=f(c[i],x[i-1])
x[i]=x[i-1]; acc[i]=0
u[i]=runif(1)
if(r[i]>u[i]){x[i]=c[i]; acc[i]=1}
}
```

3. Random Walk Metropolis–Hastings Algorithm

```
set.seed(413)
mu=matrix(5,1000)
sigma2=matrix(8,1000)
accept.rate=matrix(1,1000)

logpost=function(mu,sigma2){
ybar=5.77; s2=8.52; n=4311
logpost=-(n/2+1)*log(sigma2)+(-(n*(mu-ybar)^2 + (n-1)*s2)  /(2*sigma2))
return(logpost)}

c.mu=.1
s.mu=.1

for(i in 2:5000){

mu[i]=mu[i-1]; sigma2[i]=sigma2[i-1]
#propose candidate
mcand=runif(1,mu[i-1]-c.mu,mu[i-1]+c.mu)
s2cand=runif(1,sigma2[i-1]-s.mu,sigma2[i-1]+s.mu)

#accept/reject candidate
accept=0

if(s2cand>0){
r=logpost(mcand,s2cand)-logpost(mu[i-1],sigma2[i-1])
if(r>log(runif(1))){mu[i]=mcand; sigma2[i]=s2cand; accept=1}
}
accept.rate[i]=((i-1)*accept.rate[i-1]+accept) / i
if(i%%100==0){print(i)}
}
```

4. Function for Computing Original Gelman–Rubin Diagnostic

```
gelman=function(x){
lo=round(nrow(x)/2,0)+1
hi=nrow(x)
n=hi-lo+1
J=ncol(x)

dat=x[lo:hi,]
mx=colMeans(dat)
mmx=mean(dat)

B=(n/(J-1))*sum((mx-mmx)^2)
W=0
for(i in 1:J){
W=W+sum((dat[,i]-mx[i])^2)
}
W=W/(J*(n-1))

V=(n-1)/n * W + (1/n)*B
R=sqrt(V/W)
return(round(R,2))
}
```

5. Gibbs Sampler for the Linear Regression Model With Reference Prior

```
gibbs=function(x,y,maxiter){

x=as.matrix(cbind(1,x))
xtxi=solve(t(x)%*%x)
mn=xtxi%*%t(x)%*%y

k=length(mn)
n=length(y)

b=matrix(0,maxiter,k)
s2=matrix(1,maxiter)

for(i in 2:maxiter){
#sample b
b[i,]=t(mn) + t(rnorm(k))%*%chol(s2[i-1]*xtxi)

#sample s2
e=y-x%*%b[i,]

s2[i]=1/rgamma(1,n/2,.5*t(e)%*%e)
if(i%%100==0){print(i)}
}
return(cbind(b,s2))
}
```

6. Gibbs Sampler for the Probit Regression Model With Uniform Priors

```
gibbs_probit=function(x,y,maxiter){
x=as.matrix(cbind(1,x))
xtxi=solve(t(x)%*%x)

k=ncol(x)
n=length(y)

b=matrix(0,maxiter,k)
ystar=matrix(NA,maxiter,5)

for(i in 2:maxiter){

#sample z

xb=x%*%matrix(b[i-1,],k,1)
#print(xb[1:10])

p=pnorm(0,xb,1)
u=runif(n,(y*p),p^(y==0))
z=qnorm(u,xb,1)


ystar[i,]=z[c(1000,1000,10000,20000)]

#sample b
mn=xtxi%*%t(x)%*%z
b[i,]=t(mn) + t(rnorm(k))%*%chol(xtxi)

if(i%%100==0){print(i)}
}
return(cbind(b,ystar))
}
```

7. Gibbs Sampler for Two-Class Latent Class Model With Priors

```
reps=20000

n=length(y)

mu1=mu2=matrix(0,reps)
mu1[1]=min(y); mu2[1]=max(y)
sig1=sig2=matrix(1,reps)
pr=matrix(.5,reps)

#priors
n01=10; m01=5
n02=10; m02=7

alpha=10; beta=10
a1= 18; b1=34
a2= 18; b2=34

for(i in 2:reps){

#simulate latent classes for each person

denom=pr[i-1]*(dnorm(y,mu1[i-1],sqrt(sig1[i-1]))) +
             (1-pr[i-1])*(dnorm(y,mu2[i-1],sqrt(sig2[i-1])))
lprob=pr[i-1]*(dnorm(y,mu1[i-1],sqrt(sig1[i-1])))/denom
lat=rbinom(length(y),1,lprob)

#simulate class probabilities
pr[i]=rbeta(1,sum(lat==1)+alpha,sum(lat==0)+beta)

#simulate mu1
ybar=0
n1=sum(lat==1,na.rm=T)
if(n1>0){ybar=mean(y[lat==1])}

toobig=1
while(toobig==1){
mu1[i]=rnorm(1,mean=(n01*m01 + n1*ybar)/(n01+n1),
                      sd=sqrt(sig1[i-1]/(n01+n1)) )
```

```
if(mu1[i]<mu2[i-1]){toobig=0}
}

#simulate sig1
sh=a1+(1+n1)/2
rt=.5*(2*b1+n01*(mu1[i]-m01)^2+sum((y[lat==1]-mu1[i])^2))
sig1[i]=1/rgamma(1,shape=sh, rate=rt)

#simulate mu2
ybar=0
n2=sum(lat==0,na.rm=T)
if(n2>0){ybar=mean(y[lat==0])}

toosmall=1
while(toosmall==1){
mu2[i]=rnorm(1,mean=(n02*m02 + n2*ybar)/(n02+n2),
                    sd=sqrt(sig2[i-1]/(n02+n2)) )
if(mu2[i]>mu1[i]){toosmall=0}
}

#simulate sig2
sh=a2+(1+n2)/2
rt=.5*(2*b2+n02*(mu2[i]-m02)^2+sum((y[lat==0]-mu2[i])^2))
sig2[i]=1/rgamma(1,shape=sh, rate=rt)

if(i%%100==0){print(c(j,i,mu1[i],mu2[i],sig1[i],sig2[i],pr[i]))]
}
```

8. Posterior Predictive Distribution Simulation (for Linear Model)

```
ppd.claim=x%*%t(b.claim[,1:8])
ppd.posit=x%*%t(b.posit[,1:8])

for(i in 1:1000){
u=rnorm(length(claim),0,sqrt(b.claim[i,9]))
ppd.claim[,i]=ppd.claim[,i]+u

u=rnorm(length(posit),0,sqrt(b.posit[i,9]))
ppd.posit[,i]=ppd.posit[,i]+u
}
```

REFERENCES

Albert, J., & Chib, S. (1993). Bayesian analysis of binary and polychotomous response data. *Journal of the American Statistical Association*, *88*, 669–679.

Allison, P. D. (2002). *Missing data*. Thousand Oaks, CA: Sage.

Bakk, Z., & Kuha, J. (2018). Two-step estimation of models between latent classes and external variables. *Pychometrika*, *83*, 871–892.

Bakk, Z., Tekle, F., & Vermunt, J. (2013). Estimating the association between latent class membership and external variables using bias-adjusted three-step approaches. *Sociological Methodology*, *43*, 272–311.

Bauer, D., & Curran, P. (2003). Distributional assumptions of growth mixture models: implications for overextraction of latent trajectory classes. *Psychological Methods*, *8*, 338–363.

Bremáud, P. (1999). *Markov chains: Gibbs fields, monte carlo simulation, and queues*. New York: Springer-Verlag.

Brooks, S., & Gelman, A. (1998). General methods for monitoring convergence of iterative simulations. *Journal of Computational and Graphical Statistics*, *7*(4), 434–455.

Brooks, S., Gelman, A., Jones, G. L., & Meng, X.-L. (Eds.). (2011). *Handbook of Markov chain Monte Carlo*. Boca Raton, FL: Chapman & Hall.

Brown, J. (2014). *Linear models in matrix form*. Cham, Switzerland: Springer.

Carlin, B., & Louis, T. (2009). *Bayesian methods for data analysis* (3rd ed.). Boca Raton, FL: CRC Press.

Cheng, S., Xi, Y., & Chen, M.-H. (2008). A new mixture model for misclassification with applications for survey data. *Sociological Methods & Research*, *37*(1), 75–104.

Congdon, P. (2001). *Bayesian statistical modelling*. Chichester, UK: Wiley.

Congdon, P. (2003). *Applied bayesian modelling*. Chichester, UK: Wiley.

DeGroot, M. H., & Schervish, M. J. (2011). *Probability and Statistics* (4th ed.). Edinburgh Gate, UK: Pearson Education Limited.

DiMaggio, P., Evans, J., & Bryson, B. (1996). Have Americans' social attitudes become more polarized? *American Journal of Sociology*, *102*, 690–755.

Eliason, S. R. (1993). *Maximum likelihood estimation: Logic and practice* . Newbury Park, CA: Sage.

Freese, J., & Peterson, D. (2017). Replication in social science. *Annual Review of Sociology*, *43*, 147–165.

Gamerman, D., & Lopes, H. (2006). *Markov chain Monte Carlo: Stochastic simulation for Bayesian inference* (2nd ed.). Boca Raton: Chapman and Hall/CRC.

Gelman, A., Carlin, J. B., Stern, H. S., Dunson, D. B., Vehtari, A., & Rubin, D. B. (2013). *Bayesian data analysis* (3rd ed.). Boca Raton, FL: Chapman and Hall/CRC.

Gelman, A., Goodrich, B., Gabry, J., & Vehtari, A. (2019). R-squared for Bayesian regression models. *The American Statistician*, *73*(3), 307–309.

Gelman, A., & Hill, J. (2007). *Data analysis using regression and multilevel/hierarchical models*. Cambridge: Cambridge University Press.

Gelman, A., & Meng, X.-L. (Eds.). (2004). *Applied Bayesian modeling and causal inference from incomplete-data perspectives*. Chichester, UK: Wiley.

Gelman, A., & Rubin, D. (1995). Avoiding model selection in Bayesian social research. *Sociological Methodology*, *25*, 165–173.

Gelman, A., & Rubin, D. B. (1999). Evaluating and using statistical methods in the social sciences: A discussion of "A critique of the Bayesian information criterion for model selection". *Sociological Methods & Research*, *27*(3), 403–410.

Gilks, W., Richardson, S., & Spiegelhalter, D. (Eds.). (1996). *Markov chain Monte Carlo in Practice*. Boca Raton, FL: Chapman & Hall.

Gilks, W., & Wild, P. (1992). Adaptive rejection sampling for Gibbs sampling. *Journal of the Royal Statistical Society. Series C (Applied Statistics)*, *41*(2), 337–348.

Gill, J. (2014). *Bayesian methods: A social and behavioral sciences approach* (3rd ed.). Boca Raton, FL: CRC Press.

Hauser, R. (1995). Better rules for better decisions. *Sociological Methodology*, *25*, 175–183.

Hopkins, D., & Sides, J. (Eds.). (2015). *Political polarization in American politics*. New York: Bloomsbury Academic.

Ioannidis, J. P. (2005). Why most published research findings are false. *PLOS Medicine*, *2*(8), 696–701.

Jackman, S. (2009). *Bayesian analysis for the social sciences*. West Sussex, UK: Wiley.

Johnson, V. E., & Albert, J. (1999). *Ordinal data modeling*. New York, NY: Springer-Verlag.

Little, R. J. A., & Rubin, D. B. (2002). *Statistical analysis with missing data* (2nd ed.). New York, NY: Wiley.

Long, J. (1997). *Regression models for categorical and limited dependent variables*. Thousand Oaks, CA: Sage.

Lynch, S., & Taylor, M. (2016). Trajectory models for aging research. In L. George & K. Ferraro (Eds.), *Handbook of aging and the social sciences* (8th ed., pp. 23–51). London: Elsevier.

Lynch, S. M. (2007). *Introduction to applied Bayesian statistics and estimation for social scientists*. New York, NY: Springer.

Lynch, S. M., & Bartlett, B. (2019). Bayesian statistics in sociology: Past, present, and future. *Annual Review of Sociology*, *45*, 47–68.

Lynch, S. M., & Western, B. (2004). Bayesian posterior predictive checks for complex models. *Sociological Methods & Research*, *32*(3), 301–335.

Massey, D. S. (2005). *Return of the "L" word*. Princeton, NJ: Princeton University Press.

McCarty, N. (2019). *Polarization: What everyone needs to know*. New York, NY: Oxford University Press.

Neal, R. M. (2003). Slice sampling. *The Annals of Statistics*, *31*(3), 705–767.

Nylund-Gibson, K., Grimm, R., & Masyn, K. (2019). Prediction from latent classes: A demonstration of different approaches to include distal outcomes in mixture models. *Structural Equation Modeling: A Multidisciplinary Journal*, *26*, 967–985.

Papineau, D. (2018). *Thomas Bayes and the crisis in science*. https://www.the-tls.co.uk/articles/public/thomas-bayes-science-crisis/.

Plummer, M. (2003, April). JAGS: A program for analysis of Bayesian graphical models using Gibbs sampling. *3rd International Workshop on Distributed Statistical Computing (DSC 2003); Vienna, Austria*, *124*.

Pole, A., West, M., & Harrison, J. (1994). *Applied Bayesian forecasting and time series*. Boca Raton, FL: Chapman & Hall.

Popper, K. (2002). *The logic of scientific inquiry*. London: Routledge.

Raftery, A. (1995a). Bayesian model selection in social research. *Sociological Methodology*, *25*, 111–163.

Raftery, A. (1995b). Rejoinder: Model selection is unavoidable in social research. *Sociological Methodology*, *25*, 185–195.

Raftery, A. (1999). Bayes factors and BIC: Comment on "A critique of the Bayesian Information Criterion for model selection". *Sociological Methods & Research*, *27*(3), 411–427.

Raudenbush, S., & Bryk, A. (2002). *Hierarchical linear models: Applications and data analysis methods* (2nd ed.). Thousand Oaks, CA: Sage.

Ripley, B. D. (1987). *Stochastic simulation*. Hoboken, NJ: John Wiley.

Robert, C. P., Chopin, N., & Rousseau, J. (2009). Harold Jeffreys theory of probability revisited. *Statistical Science*, *24*(2), 141–172.

Rubin, D. (1984). Bayesianly justifiable and relevant frequency calculations for the applied statistician. *Annals of Statistics*, *12*, 1151–1172.

Rubin, D. B. (1987). *Multiple imputation for nonresponse in surveys*. New York, NY: John Wiley.

Simmons, J., Nelson, L., & Simonsohn, U. (2011). False-positive psychology: Undisclosed flexibility in data collection and analysis allows presenting anything as significant. *Psychological Science*, *22*, 1359–1366.

Smith, T. W., Davern, M., Freese, J., & Morgan, S. (2018). *General social surveys, 1972–2016* [machine-readable data file].

Tanner, M., & Wong, W. (1987). The calculation of posterior distributions by data augmentation. *Journal of the American Statistical Association*, *82*, 528–540.

van de Schoot, R., Winter, S. D., Ryan, O., Zondervan-Zwijnenburg, M., & Depaoli, S. (2017). A systematic review of Bayesian articles in psychology: The last 25 years. *Psychological Methods*, *22*(2), 217–239.

Weakliem, D. L. (1999). A critique of the Bayesian information criterion for model selection. *Sociological Methods & Research*, *27*(3), 359–397.

Ziliak, S. T., & McCloskey, D. N. (2008). *The cult of statistical significance*. Ann Arbor: University of Michigan Press.

INDEX